THE CARING CLASSROOM

Using Adventure to Create Community in the Classroom and Beyond

by Laurie S. Frank

Interior Photographs by Susan H. Kaye

Copyright © 2001 by Laurie S. Frank
GOAL Consulting
1337 Jenifer St. • Madison, WI 53703
608/251-2234
ISBN 0-934387-14-1

Challenge by Choice, Full Value Contract are registered service marks of Project Adventure, Inc. and may not be used without the written permission of Project Adventure, Inc.

PERMISSIONS

The author is grateful for permission to use excerpts from:

The preamble to the United Mine Workers constitution.

ITI: *The Model* by Susan Kovalik.

TRIBES, A New Way of Learning and Being Together by Jeanne Gibbs, 2000. Sausalito, CA CenterSource Systems, LLC www.TRIBES.com.

LAY IT ALL DOWN
Words and music by Libby Roderick
© Libby Roderick Music 1996
from the record *Lay it All Down*
Turtle Island Records P.O. Box 203294
Anchorage, AK 99520 (907) 278-6817
libbyr@alaska.net www.alaska.net/~libbyr/

Games Not Names from Playboard located in Belfast, Ireland, and for their work to end sectarianism.

Mid-continent Research for Education and Learning (McRel). © 1997. They can be reached at www.mcrel.com.

Appreciation is given to the Milwaukee Public Schools (MPS) for permission to reprint excerpts of the MPS *Accessible Curriculum Supplement*. Special thanks to the staff members of the MPS accessible curriculum committee for their work in developing the adaptations for students with disabilities.

Books and articles quoted or cited in the text under fair use allowances are acknowledged in the notes and references.

Contents

Introduction vi

Acknowledgements x

Dedication xii

Foreword xiii

Preface xv

Chapter 1: Foundations... 1
      John Dewey: Experience and Education 1
      Kurt Hahn: Outward Bound.................................. 2
      Project Adventure: The Adventure Integrated Model.......... 3
      David Kolb: Experiential Learning Cycle 4
      Howard Gardner: Multiple Intelligences 5
      Daniel Goleman: Emotional Intelligence 6
      Susan Kovalik: Brain Research and Integrated Thematic Instruction 7
      Alfie Kohn: On Compliance and Community 7
      Jeanne Gibbs: The TRIBES Process........................... 8
      Summary 9

Chapter 2: Creating the Conditions for Community................. 11
      Group Development 12
      Sequencing and Flow 17
      Summary.. 19

Chapter 3: Mapping the Journey................................... 21
      A Community-Building Sequence 21
      Community-Building Tools: Creating a Safe Environment 23
      Summary.. 25

Chapter 4: Cooperation: Setting the Stage........................ 27
      Cooperation Issues and Skills.............................. 28
      Cooperation Activities 32
          Ice Breakers/Acquaintance 32
          Deinhibitizer... 45
          Challenge by Choice 56
          Full Value Contract 62
      Summary: When to Move On to Trust 71

Chapter 5: Trust: The Cornerstone of Community 73
      Trust Issues and Skills.................................... 74
      Trust Activities... 76
          Trust 77
          Emotional Self-Awareness: Feelings Literacy.......... 95
          Behavioral Goal Setting............................... 100

   Low Challenge Ropes Course. 104
   Summary: When to Move On to Problem Solving. 107

Chapter 6: Problem Solving: Branching Out. 109
  Problem-Solving Issues and Skills 110
  Problem-Solving Activities 113
   Problem-Solving Initiatives 114
   Low Challenge Ropes Course 133
  Conflict Resolution 139
   Academic Content 146
  Summary: When to Move On to Challenge 149

Chapter 7: Challenge—Stepping Out on One's Own 153
  Challenge Issues and Skills 154
  Challenge Activities. 156
   High Ropes Course. 156
   Outdoor Pursuits 159
   Urban Experience 160
   Public Presentations and Projects 164
  Summary: Where to Go from Here? 164

Chapter 8: Facilitating the Process 165
  Shaping an Adventure Program 165
  Processing. 167
  Debriefing Strategies 172
  Sequence and Flow. 175
  Summary. 178

Chapter 9: Starting an Adventure Program. 179
  Walking the Talk. 180
  Summary. 181

Afterword. 183

Appendices. 185
  Educational Standards and Adventure Education 186
  Want to Go to a Ropes Course? Questions to Ask 193
  Challenge Ropes Course Construction: Some Considerations 195
  Where Do the Activities Come From? 199

Activity Grids. 200

References 208

Adventure/Experiential Education Resources. 210

Activity List 215

Index. 217

Introduction

I'm a late boomer…or is it "bloomer"? Actually, it's both. I was born at the end of the big boom, which means I am firmly planted on the cusp between being a Baby Boomer and a Generation Xer. I came of age during the era of Twinkies™ and Slinkies™, TV and radioactivity, Viet Nam and the American Dream. Rugged independence was the name of the game, which included competing and being number one. We all knew this to be true because we learned it in school and from television every day. We teethed on clichés like, "It's a dog-eat-dog world" and "It's a war zone out there." The casualties? Generosity, affiliation, kindness, community….

Community has gone from the realm of lifestyle and philosophy to the domain of buzzword. Today we struggle to reinvent feelings of connection, sharing, **inter**dependence—in essence, what we had for centuries. Is it really gone? Have we lost our capacities for empathy, respect, kindness, tolerance, and even compassion?

Or are we all just late bloomers?

Although powerful, my lessons in competition never really took hold. The unhealthy mindset of "get ahead at all costs" I wore halfheartedly, wondering if there was another way—yet not knowing there was another way. Don't get me wrong; I struggle every day with our society's teachings about competition. They are ingrained, and I must make a conscious effort to recognize the signs and step back from potentially unhealthy situations. Sometimes I am in the middle of them before I see the symptoms. Other times I can only see it from the vantage point of hindsight.

I carried these lessons with me into the teaching profession. I was certified to teach students with emotional disabilities. My first year was spent "controlling" the students. If there was a problem, I was there in lightspeed, directing traffic, telling kids what to do and how to do it. By the end of the year, the students left the way they had come: no wiser about dealing with their feelings, or treating themselves and others with respect. I had done it all for them, achieving the goal of a quiet room, which looked good from the outside (I had "won"), but accomplished very little for those who mattered most.

As a trained behaviorist, I thought I knew how everyone should act, and I became the ultimate enforcer. Every night I shuffled home with a headache caused by taking on the responsibility of every student's behavior. By the end of the year I reached the startling conclusion that it was no fun playing the role of a goddess.

Year two saw a dramatic shift. I began to draw on my experience as a camp counselor. We played more, interacted more, shared more. Older students tutored the younger, and younger ones tutored the older. We laughed, and even made noise.

We also argued more. When conflicts arose, I did not rush to judgment, but assumed there was a reason for it. We talked it through, came up with solutions, and moved on. By midyear, we had a family feel to the room. We stuck up for each other, cheered each other up, and became friends. My headaches went away…and *A Caring Classroom* was born.

Why Community-Building?

The assembly-line approach to school, work and life in general is a *Titanic* on the sea of a changing social order. Collaboration is the wave that we have tried to ride into the twenty-first century. We live in an information-rich world that is shrinking, almost on a daily basis. As our smaller communities give way to a global society, the number (and kind) of people with whom we come in contact increases. In order to make sense of an increasingly complex society, people specialize, thus causing greater interdependence among us all.

Collaboration is an act of co-creation.[1] It is not a top-down approach, nor is it a jigsaw-puzzle scenario, where everyone does his or her own piece independent of the rest. Collaborative group members must approach a task as equals, willing to take risks that will cause all to sink or swim together. In the world of cooperative learning, this is known as "positive interdependence." This collective stake in an outcome implies a group that thrives on respect, trust and common goals.

Traditionally, our role as educators has been to impart knowledge to our students. This has meant a passive education, where children sit at desks while a teacher pours facts into heads which are attached to bodies that can't wait to get out of there. Today, however, programs such as Expeditionary Learning, Project Adventure and TRIBES are appearing on the scene. Their common themes involve community, integrated curriculum, cooperative and authentic learning. They are based on the foundation that people are whole beings connected to a larger environment and to each other. The benevolent dictator approach to teaching is giving way to participatory democracy. A sense of community is replacing isolationism. Cooperative learning is eroding the notion that we need competition in order to motivate our students.

In order to accomplish this ideal, we must begin with the idea of classroom as community. A community is any group having common interests, where there is joint participation or common ownership. *Creating* community is not so cut-and-dried, however. It is necessary to begin with an environment that values each member, creating a safe place where members can disagree without being torn apart. In *The Different Drum: Community Making and Peace*, M. Scott Peck describes a community in this way:

> In genuine community there are no sides. It is not always easy but by the time they reach community the members have learned how to give up cliques and factions. They have learned how to listen to each other and how not to reject each other. Sometimes consensus in community is reached with miraculous rapidity. But at other times it is arrived at only after lengthy struggle. Just because it is a safe place does not mean community is a place without conflict. It is, however, a place where conflict can be resolved without physical or emotional bloodshed and with wisdom as well as grace. A community is a group that can fight gracefully.[2]

In this scenario, the teacher is an equal member of the community, whose role changes from information provider to facilitator.

Considering that most teachers have grown up in traditional classrooms, and learned traditional teaching techniques from traditional professors in traditional universities, the very idea of relinquishing some control to our students is an exercise in risk taking. The question we must all ask ourselves, however, is: "How can we expect students to learn how to **act** responsibly if they are not given the opportunity to **have** responsibility?" In order to learn how to live in a democratic society, it is necessary to experience democracy. Experiencing true community in the classroom may just breed true community in our society.

We would be laughed out of the teaching profession if we suggested that instead of teaching language arts every day in school, we would substitute a "reading day." This special day would involve learning reading skills and practicing them for just that one day. After that, we would ignore reading unless a problem arose with it. Then the student would be punished for not handling reading very well.

Yet, we do this all the time with skills like cooperation and conflict resolution. We talk about how to cooperate; we drop students into cooperative-learning groups. Then we wonder why they don't cooperate. Many times, conflict resolution is given even less attention. When students "misbehave," "act up," or become "disruptive," they are summarily sent from the room to the "great punisher" known as the principal. This type of disciplinary approach provokes the question, "What are the students learning?" Are we preparing them for life in prison or life with families, work and community?

Imagine, instead, a classroom where students and teachers are partners in learning. Students are not just engaged in the learning process, but excited about it. This is a classroom where it is safe to make mistakes and to *learn* from those mistakes. In this classroom, learning is not seen as smooth and simple. It is regarded as messy, sometimes loud, and often the result of a struggle. Grappling with concepts, theories, algorithms, writer's block, and the fear of giving a speech are ways in which students push the edge of their comfort zones toward knowledge and understanding. In this place, learning is considered an act of risk taking, and the community of learners supports each individual who takes the necessary risks to learn.

> "Community"...is a place in which students feel cared about and are encouraged to care about each other. They experience a sense of being valued and respected; the children matter to one another and to the teacher. They have come to think in the plural: they feel connected to each other; they are part of an "us."—*Alfie Kohn*[3]

Schools are the perfect place to learn collaboration and conflict-resolution skills. They are places that offer constant opportunities to interact. This book provides one process-oriented approach that gives students a chance to learn *and practice* these life skills.

In order to undertake this journey, we must outfit ourselves with the proper tools. The first chapter of this book, Foundations, provides a compass to get our bearings—beginning with a foundational perspective of adventure and experiential education with some of the thinkers who have informed the field. We start with John Dewey and his prescient musings about reconciling the polarized views of concentration on content versus focus on the child; then we move all the way to Howard Gardner and his thoughts on multiple intelligences.

> There is a boy in one of my classes who hasn't said a word all year. Billy is extremely overweight and has a bad complexion. Some of the other kids tease him. This all changed, however, after playing Italian Golf. It turns out that he was the best thrower and catcher. He was the major asset. This surprised me as much as anyone and I was sure to play it up. Ever since that day Billy has joined the group. He has even dared to get into mischief along with the others. This was the best affirmation I had as a teacher.—*Margie, 7th grade teacher*

Along the way we consider Kurt Hahn with the advent of Outward Bound which led to Project Adventure's Integrated Adventure Model. The experiential learning cycle, central to all forms of experiential education, and Susan Kovalik's theories on brain-compatible learning provide structure and rationale, while emotional intelligence and Alfie Kohn's case for building classroom communities give us purpose. Jeanne Gibb's process-oriented approach to actually creating that community (along with the Project Adventure model) offers ways to put these ideas into action. All of these foundations are but the tip of the iceberg when it comes to being a student of experiential education. Yet, without this basic understanding of where we have come from, it is difficult to know where we are now or where we should be heading.

Chapter 2, Creating the Conditions for Community, discusses how group development and sequencing can help us connect our compass with the "big-picture" map of community-building. If we have an understanding of what motivates individuals in groups, we can better prepare a course of action and develop an appropriate sequence of events.

Next, Chapter 3, Mapping the Journey, describes the issues, skills and activities pertinent to any given phase in the process. It also includes suggestions and ideas about how to facilitate the process. This community-building map provides the bridge between theory and practice to guide us on our way.

Chapters 4–7, Cooperation, Trust, Problem Solving and Challenge, provide underlying theory and suggestions for facilitating the process.

The final section addresses how to start a program of your own. It acts as a springboard for developing an action plan to use in your individual situation. The journey itself is up to you.

Any teacher can pick up this book and begin implementing a community-building process in her or his classroom. Each journey begins with one step. Simply using these activities in your classroom signals a change in the status quo for teachers and students alike. With experience, the activities become part of a larger process that creates a foundation of safety, security and trust. This foundation supports the collaboration that propels learning to new heights.

Every journey requires preparation, a little planning, and a bit of expertise. More than anything else, it needs commitment, especially to get through the rough spots. With commitment, a difficulty becomes just one more bump in the trail; struggles are seen as learning opportunities rather than barriers. As you begin your excursion, remember that it will be shared by countless others who will join you in your journey toward the caring classroom.

References
[1] Schrage, Michael. *No More Teams!* New York, NY: Doubleday, 1995. (p. 5)
[2] Schoel, Jim and Mike Stratton, eds. *Gold Nuggets: Readings for Experiential Education.* Hamilton, MA: Project Adventure, 1990. (p. 26)
[3] Kohn, Alfie. *Beyond Discipline: From Compliance to Community.* Alexandria, VA: Association for Supervision and Curriculum Development, 1996. (p. 101)

Acknowledgments

Bert Zipperer is my partner, best friend and biggest encourager. It all begins and ends with him. There is no way this project would have reached fruition without his willingness to hear my ideas, frustrations and periodic whining. Anyone who knows Bert knows that he handled this three-year project with grace and good humor.

The process leading to this book began almost two decades ago, when I was working for the Madison Metropolitan School District in Wisconsin as a special education teacher. Sandy Gunderson offered me an opportunity to go to Project Adventure as part of a grant, because she "knew I'd like it." Was I that transparent? She couldn't have been more correct. I returned from the workshop with renewed spirit, as if I had come home. Pete Albert had been developing the idea of Stress/Challenge for a few years already, and Dee Tull was an administrator willing to take a chance—putting resources into it. Pete and Tom Solyst took me under their wings and taught me the "ropes" about ropes courses. In the early years, before the full-time position was created, I benefited from the unyielding support of my co-teachers: Sara Bringman, Wenda Mincberg and Lynne Behrendt; and Marian Wright, the best educational assistant in the universe, whose organizational skills saved my life on more than one occasion.

I can pinpoint the moment a huge lightbulb went on for me (it felt more like a spotlight). I was working with a class of third-graders who had been struggling. This day they made a breakthrough and really seemed to understand what "trust" was all about. These students (and the others who came before them) made me see that it's not the activities but the *process* that makes the difference, and I started to create the model that is highlighted in this book. I can't thank the teachers enough—especially those who invited me in when Stress/Challenge was a very new concept. These teachers and students are the real pioneers.

The Stress/Challenge program would not continue to exist without the help of Diana Kabat, who took over when I went on leave, and it continues to thrive under the leadership of Carla Hacker and Jim Dunn. Thanks to all the teachers, administrators, social workers, counselors, secretaries, nurses, custodians, educational assistants and parents who have given of their own time to receive training and to work with students on the ropes course. How many school systems can boast of that type of commitment?

The book all but wrote itself. I took two weeks in the northwoods—first in the loving care of Ruth Gudinas and Dorothy Davids. They gave me space, food, encouragement and understanding as I paced around in their bunkroom and talked to my computer. The heart of the book was written there. The next week was spent at Camp Manito-wish YMCA, sequestered in a cabin with a huge supply of firewood and no telephone. The soul of the book was born there.

The final product you see here looks very little like the raw words that tumbled out onto those pages three years ago. This is the work of the people at J. Weston Walch like Lisa French, a fantastic editor whom I've never even met in person. She has an ability to make me sound so smart! Charlie Peers and Rufus Collinson at Project Adventure nurtured this process along. They were able to maintain an equilibrium even in my grumpier days. Dick Prouty articulated the Project Adventure Integrated Model, and Susan Kaye took most of the photos. A professional photographer *and* ropes course facilitator, she was able to see the artistry and process in every classroom.

Then there are the readers. My, how they added to this story! Their insights have provided a texture and richness that I could not accomplish alone. Thanks to:

- Tony Alvarez, Professor at the University of Michigan and School Social Worker in Ypsilanti Public Schools

- Floyd Asonwha, AODA Coordinator and Ropes Course Instructor for Kenosha Unified School District
- Christian Bisson, Professor at Northland College in Ashland, WI
- Dave Braby, Ropes and Challenge Course Coordinator for Milwaukee Public Schools
- Dan Creeley, Professor at Northeastern Illinois University in Chicago
- Carla Hacker, Stress/Challenge Coordinator for Madison Metropolitan School District
- Kathy Hellenbrand, Physical Education Teacher at Marquette Elementary School in Madison Metropolitan School District
- Julie Melton, Classroom Teacher at Lincoln Elementary School in Madison Metropolitan School District
- Jane Panicucci, Director of Training and Consulting, Project Adventure
- Dick Prouty, CEO/Executive Director, Project Adventure
- Mark Schimenz, Middle School Teacher for Milwaukee Public Schools
- Jim Sorenson, Middle School Teacher in Des Plaines, IL
- Nancy Stratton, Academic Strand Manager, Project Adventure

Finally, I must acknowledge four dear friends who probably are unaware of their contribution to this project. Sylvia Dresser, Chris Lupton, Gloree Certoma Rohnke and Nancy Stratton have spent hours chatting with me about Adventure and Experiential Education. Many of my thoughts were clarified through those discussions.

And, of course, it all begins and ends with Bert.

—Laurie Frank
August, 2001

Dedication

To my family:

Delores Hambley
Boris Frank
Karen, Greg, and Dana

Their unconditional love and acceptance is an inspiration.

and to

Deborah J. Smyth

who had a hand in my becoming both a teacher and a writer.

FOREWORD

There is an urgency today in education to take the best we know from brain research to improve the learning for all students. One of the fundamental principles is creating an environment free of threat—a classroom where students can work together toward the common good. Building community to support this fundamental principle is what Laurie Frank, in her new book, *The Caring Classroom,* has done.

In my many years in the education field I have seen thousands of books and materials designed for classroom use. There is no shortage of classroom strategies for teachers to choose. Seldom do I find a book that has a larger purpose in its strategies.

The Caring Classroom is among those materials that understand the necessity of building community and providing opportunities for youngsters to see and experience ways of working together through easy and difficult times. Our society demands that we can work together, play together, and create sustainable communities.

It is clear as you read this book that Laurie Frank has had the practical experience of doing the strategies she suggests. Each strategy is clearly described, includes adaptations for students with disabilities, facilitation guidelines, processing questions and a compilation of educational standards by grade level that will give educators confidence to use them in all educational settings.

Community doesn't just happen because we all occupy a specific space. It demands attention to our individual differences and ways to value each of our talents. This book isn't for students only—the faculty would greatly benefit from doing these activities as they create a school community that has consistency and continuity.

Thank you, Laurie Frank, for assisting all of us as we travel the road of creating communities that have lifelong implications.

—*Susan Kovalik*
Author of ITI: The Model, Integrated, Thematic Instruction

Preface

Her very name, Laurie Frank, like her work and her play, speaks to her life passion of bringing opposites together to create unity. The essence of her career is to bring harmony and unity to people by facilitating the teaching and learning of joyful, yet powerful, strategies that can transform school communities—all the while, making her career look like too much fun! For most of us, finding a career that we are passionate about is not an easy discovery. But it wasn't that way for Laurie. I believe her career path was more about "seizing a moment" and directing her destiny right from the start.

For Laurie it began in 1982 while she was teaching severely emotionally disturbed children in a robust middle school in Madison, Wisconsin. I was working as her district program support teacher at that time. When I told her about the grant I had written to send teachers to a professional development opportunity at Project Adventure in Hamilton, Massachusetts, she jumped at the chance to learn new adventure-based skills to help mend the hearts of wounded children, by teaching social skills and conflict resolution skills using fun strategies and games.

Her bag bursting with new skills, she returned to her stressful classroom, and transformed chaos into peace. She and I were able to witness first hand the magic and power of building a safe and conflict-free classroom. She found her life passion and planned her career right then and there. Serendipity it was not!

Now, almost twenty years later, this distinguished author and worldwide consultant is supporting me in my career, as a principal in a high needs elementary school with a significant level of poverty. This can be a stressful and challenging environment for any adult to work in and it requires a school culture that is supportive, positive, caring and fun. People need to agree on the mission of the school and work together in a conflict-free environment to meet the needs of every child.

As an administrator I wanted Laurie to help me create a school culture that would maximize the potential of each individual. I strongly believe that when we bring out the best in teachers, they will subsequently bring out the best in their students. She did come to our school and first taught the adults the theory and the strategies needed to help us build a positive and supportive school community culture. Then she helped each teacher as they individually worked to build a unifying and peaceful culture within their own classrooms.

The process of improving a school culture using her theories and strategies is very cyclical and takes time and practice. It begins with the principal setting very high expectations and then providing support for building capacity within each person. It then extends to the teachers as they work to improve their collegial working relationships within the school. Next the teachers begin to facilitate the process by implementing the theories and teaching the tools and strategies to the kids. This takes time, practice and support from others. But these skills, once generalized by the students individually and collectively, can transform classrooms into peaceful and joyful rooms for teaching and learning. To fully complete the journey, the circle should also include parents and the greater school community. The cycle of continuous improvement in culture and climate begins again and again, demonstrating small levels of improvement each time.

Building a strong and positive school culture is a continuous improvement process that must be nourished and supported. It is impossible to measure the joy of working in a school climate that is peaceful, supportive and fun. High student achievement is the ultimate reward. I'm sure glad that Laurie Frank "seized her moment" two decades ago. She helped us transform our school and it has been a lot of fun!

—*Sandra J. Gunderson*
Principal, Mendota Elementary School, Madison, WI

Chapter 1

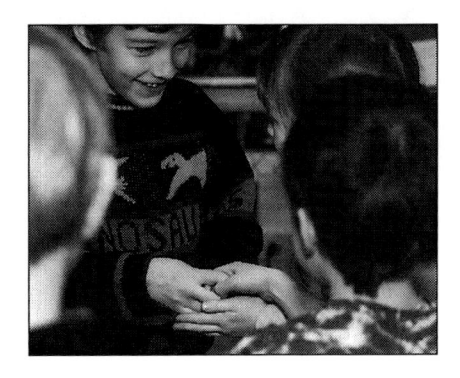

FOUNDATIONS

A casual observer watching a group engaged in an activity of Moonball sees only a game involving hitting a beachball. While it is true that the participants are having fun, it is much more than a game. If the observer sticks around long enough, she might see the group discuss why certain people are "hogging" the ball while others never get to touch it. The "ball hoggers" respond that the others don't seem to want the ball, because all they do is stand back waiting for the ball to come to them. This discussion might turn into a larger metaphor for how the students can be more interdependent when working together on class projects—those who tend to jump in to do the work sharing the load, and those who tend to sit back becoming more assertive about getting involved.

This Moonball scenario is just one brief example of deceptive appearances. There is much more to this type of education than playing games. The broad field of Experiential Education, and the specific field of Adventure Education, are informed by a plethora of thinkers. Some like Dewey, Hahn and Kolb offer philosophical and theoretical bases; others like Gardner, Goleman and Kovalik offer ideas that support the use of experiential and adventure techniques in schools today. Kohn and Gibbs share insights about why creating a classroom community is needed and how to go about it. The combined wisdom of these philosophers, researchers and theorists offer a solid foundation on which to place Experiential and Adventure Education today. The following is a very short introduction to *some* of the theories informing the field of Experiential Education. The bibliography contains more comprehensive resources on these topics.

JOHN DEWEY: EXPERIENCE AND EDUCATION

> The way out of scholastic systems that made the past an end in itself is to make acquaintance with the past as a *means* of understanding the present. Until this problem is worked out, the present clash of educational ideas and practices will continue.[1]

At the turn of the twentieth century, John Dewey was contemplating the role of the child in education. He compared the two opposing views of his time as "...marked by opposition between the idea that education is development from within and that it is formation from without...."[2]

Today we continue to argue about the merits of curriculum-based instruction over a child-centered approach. The current back-to-basics movement calls for standards and an emphasis on test scores, while proponents of affective education call for the teaching of prosocial skills. One of the most visible cases of polarization in educational philosophy today is the phonics versus whole language debate.

Dewey disputed the all-or-nothing approach by calling on both sides to take a slightly different view:

> Abandon the notion of subject-matter as something fixed and ready-made in itself, outside the child's experience; cease thinking of the child's experience as also something hard and

fast; see it as something fluent, embryonic, vital; and we realize that the child and the curriculum are simply two limits which define a single process.... It is continuous reconstruction, moving from the child's present experience out into that represented by the organized bodies of truth that we call studies.[3]

Dewey was no fan of the "assign-study-recite" technique. He considered education a "conscious, purposive, informed activity." He advocated a process-oriented approach that taught students how to solve problems, since "The method of solution...is determined by the problem to be solved. As problems change, modes of solution must also change."[4]

Dewey maintained that education consists of a continuity of developing experiences, where students interact with their environment and gain insight and understanding from those experiences. Experiences are connected, as opposed to interacting with subject matter in isolation. In this way, students can apply present learning to future experiences. In Dewey's view, education must be inherently useful:

> What avail is it to win prescribed amounts of information about geography and history, to win the ability to read and write, if in the process the individual loses his own soul: loses his appreciation of things worth while, of the values to which these things are relative; if he loses desire to apply what he has learned and, above all, loses the ability to extract meaning from his future experiences as they occur?[5]

Almost a century has passed since John Dewey started to ponder the meaning and practice of education, yet his words still ring true today. His writings helped launch a new way of viewing the educative process. Indeed, he helped to show that education *is* a process. Since then, people have taken Dewey's ideas and have continued to forge ahead into an era where Experiential Education meets the needs of a global and information-rich society.

KURT HAHN: OUTWARD BOUND

> I regard it as the foremost task of education to insure the survival of these qualities: an enterprising curiosity, an undefeatable spirit, tenacity in pursuit, readiness for sensible self-denial, and, above all, compassion.—*Kurt Hahn*[6]

A contemporary of Dewey, Kurt Hahn is widely known as the guiding spirit behind the Outward Bound movement. Founded as a way to help sailors survive in difficult times during World War II, it is just one of Hahn's forays into progressive education. His first endeavor was the Salem School in Germany. *Salem*, which means "peace," was a place where students "could learn habits that would protect them against what Hahn saw as the deteriorating values of modern life."[7] This was accomplished by allowing students to experience both success and failure, thus giving them the tools to overcome adversity. Thomas James, in his biography of Kurt Hahn, describes Hahn's experiential approach:

> As an educator, he would always be devising ways to turn his classrooms out of doors, putting students into motion and forcing his teachers to come to grips with the healing powers of direct experience.[8]

One of Hahn's influences came from the Nazi movement in Germany. As headmaster of the Salem School, he saw the Nazis take and twist the progressive teaching methods of the day into destructive and effective tools in which to indoctrinate the Hitler Youth. He recognized that there is a fine line between "compassionate service [and] destructive egotism."[9] After landing in a Nazi jail, Hahn was exiled from his homeland to Britain, where Outward Bound was born in 1934.

Hahn was also profoundly influenced by Plato, as evidenced in the Outward Bound philosophy that personal goals must be compatible with those of the larger community. James describes Hahn's focus on compassion as being placed "above all other values of Outward Bound because it among all emotions is capable of reconciling individual strength with collective need."[10] Service to the community is stressed in Hahn's philosophy. He truly sought to incorporate the human spirit in education.

This spirit lives on today in the many Outward Bound schools around the world. Although Outward Bound was not Hahn's only endeavor, it is the one most widely recognized around the globe. In fact, it has become the parent and grandparent of many other experiential programs. Project Adventure is a child of Outward Bound, as is Expeditionary Learning.

Kurt Hahn had a profound effect upon the Experiential and Adventure Education movements. With his proven methods that teach to the whole person, and his unwavering belief that individuals are members of a larger community, he "believed that education should cultivate a passion for life and that this can be accomplished only through experience, a shared sense of moment in the journey toward an exciting goal."[11]

PROJECT ADVENTURE: THE ADVENTURE INTEGRATED MODEL

The original idea for Project Adventure came from Jerry Pieh, who grew up in the Minnesota Outward Bound School that his father directed. Jerry dreamed of bringing the benefits of Outward Bound to a much larger audience. In 1971, as principal of Hamilton-Wenham High School in Hamilton, MA, Jerry received funding for a grant that proposed to change the school climate and motivate students to achieve through an integrated interdisciplinary program design entitled Project Adventure. After three years of very creative development and implementation, the grant program received an outstanding evaluation from the Department of Education. The Department credited the program with improving the self concept of participants, positively affecting the internal locus of control, and improving school climate for learning.

Now, thirty years later, the methods and techniques that began in that program at Hamilton-Wenham have evolved and spread to many thousands of programs all over the U.S. and abroad. Project Adventure has helped pioneer a whole field of facilities-based Adventure, bringing the team and leadership results of Outward Bound to the masses through an approach of integrated programming at institutions of education, recreation, therapy, and professional development.

Project Adventure has developed three foundational concepts that have affected the field and my work tremendously—Challenge By Choice, Full Value Contract, and Goal Setting.

Challenge By Choice: This concept was coined by Karl Rohnke to describe the method that he, and the physical educators he was working closely with in the first decade of Project Adventure, developed to have students decide on their own, without teacher or peer pressure, to take on a challenge such as deciding to step off of a Zip Wire platform into space 40 feet above the ground (on belay, of course). This method of deepening learning through the leverage of choice, so different from Karl's Outward Bound instructor experience, was calculated to provide more actual learning because the student was in control of the learning. As explained later in this book, this concept has taken on much more meaning, as it has spread over the field worldwide. It is a concept now, that when used with skill, can empower a learner to choose the level of challenge that makes for optimum learning.

Full Value Contract: This concept was first published in *Islands of Healing* (1988) by Schoel, Prouty and Radcliffe. This approach to group process norm development uses the safety of the group, both physical and emotional, as the reason for the contract. The group develops a series of commitments that has the effect of agreeing to find positive value in the efforts of group members. This positive value is expressed in encouragement, goal setting, group dialog, a spirit of forgiveness, and confrontation. The concept makes it possible to develop norms and trust more quickly and effectively in the experiential process.

Goal Setting: Goal setting is a traditional learning method, advocated by many. Kurt Lewin, in 1944, first laid out the importance of goal setting for experiencing psychological success and effectively developing a group. Schoel et al in *Islands of Healing* makes a very practical case that goal setting, both individual and group, should be a key fundamental of an effective group development process for the experiential practitioner. And Mary Henton, in *Adventure in the Classroom* (1996), shows how the classroom teacher can effectively integrate both individual and group goal setting into the classroom experiential process.

These three fundamentals, when used with the widespread activities base of experiential education today (initiatives, games, challenge courses, and project based activities), have allowed Project Adventure to pioneer the way in the development of an Adventure Education model. That model, now widely adopted by many types of institutions and organizations, has fostered a whole field of facilities-based Adventure Education. It is possible for any school to bring the benefits of Adventure to the classroom.

DAVID KOLB: EXPERIENTIAL LEARNING CYCLE

Both Dewey and Hahn were proponents of learning by doing, which is the basis of Experiential Education. The experience itself, though, is not enough. Without taking the time to reflect upon the experience in order to gain insight, and transfer that insight into the rest of one's life, it is learning in isolation. Hahn stressed the need to reflect upon one's experience in order to gain meaning. Dewey stressed the need to connect experiences in order to have an impact upon future learning.

David Kolb articulated this very process in his Experiential Learning Cycle in the mid 1980s.* This model is the cornerstone of Experiential Education, whether used in a classroom academic model, in Adventure Education, during Service Learning, in Outdoor Education, or in any of the myriad incarnations of Experiential Education.

Kolb's four-phase cycle (Figure 1.1) depicts experiences as a related series of educational opportunities rather than isolated activities. When people have experiences, they must take the next step of reflecting upon what has occurred. This reflection time ensures that people

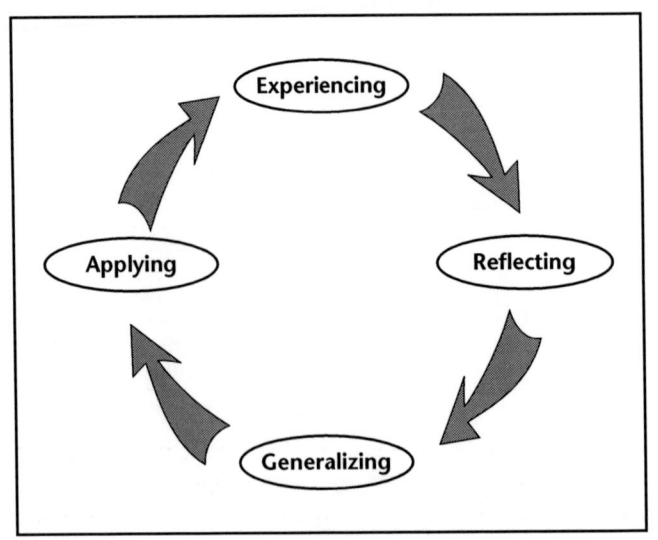

Figure 1.1: Experiential Learning Cycle

---

* The Experiential Learning Cycle will be discussed in greater depth in Chapter 4. It is mentioned here because it is a basic foundation for Experiential Education.

can formulate meaning from these experiences. Generalizing is a time to make connections and look for patterns. Finally, applying the information affords people the opportunity to incorporate the learning into their lives, or into the next experience.

Although two-dimensional in this diagram, the Experiential Learning Cycle is a dynamic and fluid model. It has been described as a spiral, in which people move to higher planes of thinking and understanding.

Kolb and others have also taken the Experiential Learning Cycle into the realm of learning styles. Each phase of the cycle plays to different strengths. Some people naturally reflect upon their experiences; others prefer to make connections through research. Some create and test models, while still others seek out experiences so they can learn by doing. The beauty of the cycle is that it meets a variety of needs, while tapping into learning methods that have been around since the dawn of time. As Aldous Huxley so deftly stated, "Experience is not what happens to you; it is what you do with what happens to you."[12]

HOWARD GARDNER: MULTIPLE INTELLIGENCES

...the purpose of school should be to develop intelligences and to help people reach vocational and avocational goals that are appropriate to their particular spectrum of intelligences. People who are helped to do so, I believe, feel more engaged and competent, and therefore more inclined to serve the society in a constructive way.—*Howard Gardner*[13]

There is a popular story about the animals of the forest starting a school for their offspring. In order to provide a well-rounded education, they design a program for all the animals that includes running, jumping, swimming, and flying. The school administrators decide that running and jumping are the more important skills, because they take place in the areas that make up most of the surrounding habitat.

After the first year, the school counselor sits down with the rabbit to review her grades. He informs her that she is getting excellent grades and should keep up the good work. Later, he calls the turtle into his office. The turtle, it appears, is failing miserably. Although he excels at swimming, he has made absolutely no progress in running and jumping, the core curriculum. Because of this sorry record, the turtle must drop swimming in order to concentrate on the "more important" skills.

At graduation time, the rabbit gives the valedictorian speech, while the turtle has dropped out of school.

This story illustrates a narrow notion of intelligence that has been in vogue since the time of Alfred Binet in the early 1900s. This view is based on the need to quantify intelligence through measuring devices such as the Scholastic Aptitude Test, which is designed to predict future success in school. These tests require the takers to read and write and solve mathematical problems.

Gardner proposes a "...pluralistic view of mind, recognizing many different and discrete facets of cognition, acknowledging that people have different cognitive strengths and contrasting cognitive styles."[14] He posits that intelligence is "the ability to solve problems, or to fashion products, that are valued in one or more cultural or community settings."[15] In his model, there are nine types of intelligence: linguistic, logical-mathematical, spatial, musical, bodily-kinesthetic, interpersonal, intrapersonal, naturalistic and existential.

With the acceptance of this paradigm shift comes a responsibility to change the ways in which students are taught. In Gardner's view, students are seen as whole people rather than just cognitive beings. Students must be given a variety of avenues in which to learn, and other areas of content need to be brought into the curriculum.

The activity focus of Adventure Education, along with the processing techniques used to help students draw meaning from their experiences, bring to the forefront areas of intelligence that have historically been ignored. We ask children to reflect upon their experiences (intrapersonal intelligence), to consider the perspectives of others (interpersonal intelligence), and to move around during games and activities (bodily-kinesthetic intelligence). Many times, we venture out into the natural world for a ropes course experience or other outdoor pursuit (naturalistic intelligence). Through group problem-solving initiatives and school projects, students use a variety of Gardner's intelligences to arrive at mutual academic and behavioral goals.

It is widely accepted that people do not all learn in the same way. Gardner's theory of multiple intelligences gives us a framework, and Experiential Education offers a vehicle in which to educate a variety of people.

Daniel Goleman: Emotional Intelligence

> Educators, long disturbed by schoolchildren's lagging scores in math and reading, are realizing there is a different and more alarming deficiency: emotional illiteracy. And while laudable efforts are being made to raise academic standards, this new and troubling deficiency is not being addressed in the standard school curriculum.—*Daniel Goleman*[16]

Perhaps there is no greater reason to create community in the classroom than because it enhances the emotional literacy of students. Emotional illiteracy manifests itself in depression, aggression, eating disorders, dropping out of school, addiction to drugs or alcohol, and high pregnancy rates. Young people need more than information. They need the emotional skills to deal with difficult issues in their lives. These skills include "self-awareness; identifying, expressing, and managing feelings; impulse control and delaying gratification; and handling stress and anxiety."[17]

Goleman discusses how emotional learning is developed through habit: "...as experiences are repeated over and over, the brain reflects them as strengthened pathways, neural habits to apply in times of duress, frustration, hurt."[18] A classroom community is a place where students can experience and practice emotional skills that will benefit them throughout their lifetimes.

The methods of community-building through Adventure Education are perfectly suited to help students become emotionally literate. Based on Dewey's philosophy whereby students interact with and gain insight from their environment, Adventure activities provide a forum where students can discuss incidents that arise. Instead of sitting around and talking about the abstract possibility that someone might call another person a name, Adventure activities engage learners in real situations. When someone actually calls someone a name during an activity, the class stops to discuss what has happened and how it might be handled. From these experiences, children learn—*and practice*—methods for handling their emotions. In this way, emotions actually become another content area:

> This new departure in bringing emotional literacy into schools makes emotions and social life themselves topics, rather than treating these most compelling facets of a child's day as irrelevant intrusions or, when they lead to eruptions, relegating them to occasional disciplinary trips to the guidance counselor or the principal's office.[19]

Susan Kovalik: Brain Research and Integrated Thematic Instruction

> "How far have we come?" The painful but truthful answer is that we have not changed at all in over a hundred years. The curricular, instructional, and structural features of the American School (high school and elementary) are still virtually identical to the Prussian model brought back from Europe by Horace Mann in 1840, whose instructional traditions stemmed from cadet corps training of a highly regimented military tradition and whose curricular modeling goes back to the catechism of the medieval church (one right answer from a single source, single point of view).—*Susan Kovalik*[20]

Susan Kovalik's Integrated Thematic Instruction (ITI) Model has its foundations in brain research; it offers both a biological and sociological rationale for using experiential techniques in the classroom. Kovalik believes that bringing our educational system up-to-date depends on changing the curriculum to be compatible with how the brain works. She identifies eight brain-compatible elements: absence of threat, meaningful content, choices, adequate time, enriched environment, collaboration, immediate feedback, and mastery (application).[21] By focusing on these elements, students are preparing for life in the real world, as opposed to preparing for the next exam.

Kovalik states that every successful learning experience should contain three or more of these eight components.[22] She also notes that the classroom teacher has much control over these elements, and that schools must work to create an environment that is physically and emotionally safe for all. In Kovalik's words, "The environment—school wide as well as in the classroom—must eliminate all real and perceived threat between teacher and students and among students. Next, the teacher must engineer and nurture trust and trustworthiness."[23]

Unless this basic safety need is met, people cannot learn; their brains won't let them. Information comes through a "gatekeeper" known as the limbic system. If the environment is perceived to be safe, then the limbic system "upshifts" to the cerebral cortex, which is where academic learning occurs. "Consequently, the first step toward brain-compatibility in the classroom is creating an environment with an absence of threat and curriculum that is truly engaging to students."[24]

The ITI model also stresses five lifelong behavior guidelines that are uniquely suited to creating a classroom community: trustworthiness, truthfulness, active listening, no put-downs, personal best.[25] Each of these guidelines is an integral part of any well-functioning community. To strive toward these ideals can only catapult learning to new heights, as students and teacher alike gain a deeper respect for each other and themselves.

Alfie Kohn: On Compliance and Community

> This...is neither a recipe nor a different technique for getting mindless compliance. It requires that we transform the classroom, give up some power, and reconsider the way we define and think about misbehavior.—*Alfie Kohn*[26]

What is wrong with our children? Why don't they just behave?! Alfie Kohn, in his direct manner, confronts us with the notion that it is we adults who must answer this question, not the students. He questions our motives by pointing out that classroom behavior management is designed to control students, sometimes through threats and coercion. When students do not live up to our expectations of "appropriate" behavior, we blame them, and then focus on what they can do to change (read "conform") to meet the required rules and regulations. Kohn asks educators to consider "the possibility that it may be the teacher's request, rather than the child's unwillingness to comply with it, that needs to be addressed."[27]

In many ways, Kohn harkens back to Dewey's questions about purpose: Are we teaching children to mindlessly obey authority, or are we preparing them to live in a pluralistic society? Our teaching techniques have a direct effect on the outcome. The environment that we create in the classroom and school as a whole—how we teach our children—should be a model of what is expected of adults in our society. In other words, if we truly are a participatory democracy, we must teach our children how to live in a democracy by *being* one.

Kohn discusses the need to take on a "community approach [that] goes beyond teacher-student interaction and asks us to consider the broader question of how everyone gets along together. It is a change from the notion of 'doing to' students to 'working with' them."[28] To do so means changing our attitudes about and toward children. Rather than viewing them as empty receptacles needing to be filled, we must see them as partners in the educational process. If we create a classroom community, we can then learn what it means to be members of that community. If we want students to act responsibly, we must *give* them responsibility. This microcosm of "the real world" is at the core of Experiential Education: to learn by doing, and to gain insight from the experience.

JEANNE GIBBS: THE TRIBES PROCESS

> Although massive funds for school improvement, restructuring, and reform have flowed through school districts for more than 20 years, the traditional pattern of interaction between teachers and students has changed very little.—*Jeanne Gibbs*[29]

Jeanne Gibbs and her cohorts are pioneers in the area of rethinking how we teach children. They point us away from a traditional teacher-centered milieu to one that values interdependence and collaboration. The teacher, in this scenario, becomes a partner in the process of learning.

Creating community, though, takes more than an attitudinal shift. It takes perseverance, empathy and commitment. It must be intentional. If a teacher is outfitted with a variety of tools and techniques, it makes the process that much more robust in a world where students have many stresses and preoccupations outside school. In *TRIBES: A New Way of Learning and Being Together*, Jeanne Gibbs offers both a well-articulated rationale and a blueprint for focusing on the *process* of classroom community-building.

Although we may all want a recipe for making our classrooms safe and caring communities, Gibbs reminds us that the process takes time—and it requires making the classroom *student-centered:* "Gradually, as cooperative learning tasks and much of the classroom management are transferred to students themselves, the teacher has time to encourage initiative, give feedback, facilitate student communication, suggest resources, help and praise students."[30] In short, the teacher is no longer the focus of power in the classroom, but is part of a collaborative effort for all to learn.

TRIBES is loaded with tools that help teachers begin and maintain the community-building process. Gibbs talks of the stages of group development (discussed in detail in Chapter 2). She also shares nuts-and-bolts strategies such as convening community circles, creating community agreements, offering appreciations, and the teaching of collaborative skills. Her model has paved the way for educators to rethink their paradigm of what it means to learn in a school setting; it helps us focus on helping *all* students learn in a safe and challenging environment.

Many schools are now combining a TRIBES approach with an Adventure approach to community-building. The Adventure approach, as listed below, was developed and spread widely by Project Adventure. Mary Henton, in *Adventure in the Classroom* (1995), addressed most of the elements in the Creating Community through Adventure graphic listed below. The two processes are similar in philosophy; together they provide strategies to meet the needs of a variety of students (see Figure 1.2).

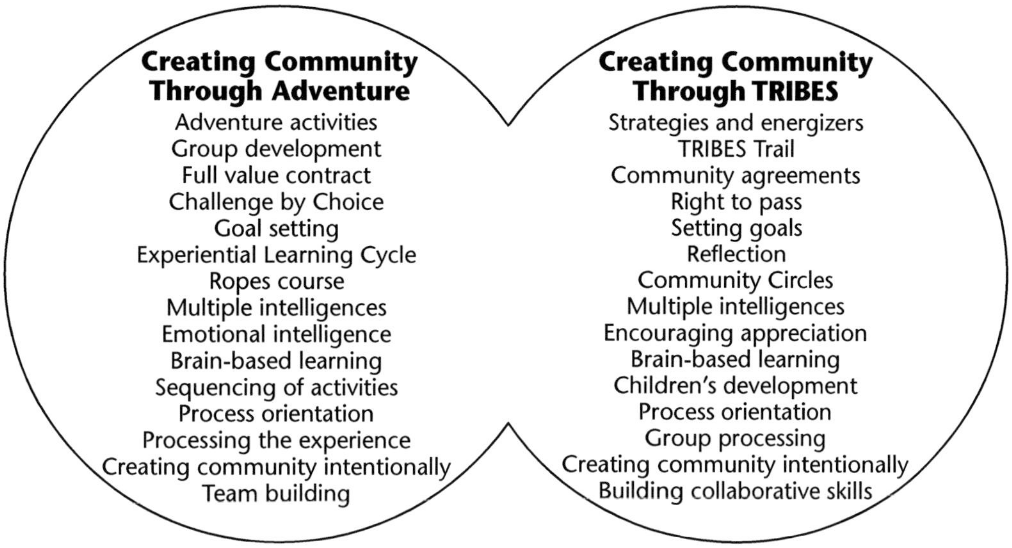

Creating Community Through Adventure
Adventure activities
Group development
Full value contract
Challenge by Choice
Goal setting
Experiential Learning Cycle
Ropes course
Multiple intelligences
Emotional intelligence
Brain-based learning
Sequencing of activities
Process orientation
Processing the experience
Creating community intentionally
Team building

Creating Community Through TRIBES
Strategies and energizers
TRIBES Trail
Community agreements
Right to pass
Setting goals
Reflection
Community Circles
Multiple intelligences
Encouraging appreciation
Brain-based learning
Children's development
Process orientation
Group processing
Creating community intentionally
Building collaborative skills

Figure 1.2: Comparison of TRIBES and Adventure Approaches

Changing the way in which we approach education takes a fair amount of soul-searching, questioning and self-education.

SUMMARY

This chapter presents a collection of theories, philosophies and models that create a foundation for understanding how Experiential and Adventure methodologies can be used to create classroom community—and, ultimately, help all students learn. John Dewey delved into why experiential learning is good learning, while Kurt Hahn showed that progressive education works. David Kolb, then, took the next step by showing how the process works through the Experiential Learning Cycle.

Howard Gardner, Daniel Goleman and Susan Kovalik all present compelling evidence that the classroom must address the whole person, rather than solely focusing on the cognitive being. Multiple intelligences, emotional intelligence, and brain-based learning are essential components of a total classroom experience. Addressing the myriad of student needs can be accomplished through creating a safe environment in which to learn, teaching applicable skills, and offering choices to students.

Finally, Alfie Kohn presents a rationale for creating community in the classroom, and Jeanne Gibbs extends that concept into a vision of how this community can actually be created.

Project Adventure, with the publication of *Islands of Healing* (1988) and *Adventure in the Classroom* (1995), constructed an integrated Adventure approach to work in schools that used strategies from a variety of sources.

As with any paradigm shift, it is necessary to recognize the underlying assumptions in order to put new ideas into action. If we are to make our classrooms inclusive and safe, we must acknowledge the "assumption that interdependence and connection to others is key to human development, learning, and the accomplishment of task."[31] Without accepting this assumption, the methods described in this book are, at best, an interesting exercise. At worst, the tools designed to create community become new weapons in the arsenal of control.

References

[1] Dewey, John. *Experience and Education.* New York, NY: Touchstone, 1938. (p. 78)
[2] Dewey (p. 17)
[3] Dewey. *John Dewey on Education*, 1902. (p. 343)
[4] Archambault, Reginald D., editor. *John Dewey on Education: Selected Writings.* New York, NY: Random House, 1964. (p. xxiv)
[5] Dewey, John. *Experience and Education.* New York, NY: Touchstone, 1938. (p. 49)
[6] Schoel, Jim and Michael Stratton. *Gold Nuggets: Readings for Experiential Education.* Hamilton, MA: Project Adventure, 1990. (p. 128)
[7] Warren, Karen, Mitchell Sakofs, and Jasper S. Hunt, Jr., eds. *The Theory of Experiential Education.* Dubuque, IA: Kendall Hunt, 1995. (p. 35)
[8] Warren, et. al. (p. 37)
[9] Cousins, Emily and Melissa Rodgers, eds. *Fieldwork: An Expeditionary Learning Outward Bound Reader.* Dubuque, IA: Kendall Hunt Publishing. James, 1995. (p. 68)
[10] Cousins and Rodgers (p. 60)
[11] Cousins and Rodgers (p. 63)
[12] Henton, Mary. *Adventure in the Classroom.* Dubuque, IA: Kendall Hunt, 1996. (p. 39)
[13] Gardner, Howard. *Multiple Intelligences: The Theory in Practice.* New York, NY: BasicBooks, 1993. (p. 9)
[14] Henton (p. 6)
[15] Henton (p. 7)
[16] Goleman, Daniel. *Emotional Intelligence: Why it can matter more than IQ.* New York, NY: Bantam Books, 1995. (p. 231)
[17] Goleman (p. 259)
[18] Goleman (p. 263)
[19] Goleman (p. 263)
[20] Kovalik, Susan. *ITI: The Model, Integrated Thematic Instruction.* Kent, WA: Books for Educators, 1997. (p. vii)
[21] Kovalik (p. xxiii)
[22] Kovalik (p. xxiii)
[23] Kovalik (p. xxiii)
[24] Kovalik (p. 19)
[25] Kovalik (p. 25)
[26] Kohn, Alfie. *Beyond Discipline: From Compliance to Community.* Alexandria, VA: ASCD, 1996. (p. 13)
[27] Kohn (p. 13)
[28] Kohn (p.104)
[29] Gibbs, Jeanne. *TRIBES: A new way of learning and being together.* Sausalito, CA: CenterSource Systems, LLC, 1995. (p. 17)
[30] Gibbs (pp. 57–58)
[31] Gibbs (p. 82)

Chapter 2

CREATING THE CONDITIONS FOR COMMUNITY

A few years ago my husband, Bert, and I traveled halfway across the United States by train. It was a 52-hour trip in a car with about 100 other people who represented various slices of life. We shared the space with people of all socioeconomic classes, races and cultural backgrounds. We traveled with children, elders, parents and singles.

At first, we all stayed put, happily reading or looking out the window. Worried that we might disturb others, we rarely raised our voices above a whisper. All of this changed during the trip. By the end of the journey, all the children in the car had become everyone's children. We laughed and shared with the people around us, learning names and even a few life stories. None of us, of course, had taken a shower during the two-plus days, and most of us enjoyed only a few scattered hours of sleep. We said our good-byes as if we were waving to old friends. Somewhere along the tracks a community had formed.

The opposite was true during my college and high-school years. I joined a new high school during my junior year. By the end of the year, I knew a handful of people and considered fewer of them friends. Although my grades were good and I participated in sports, it was an isolated existence in which I focused on listening to my teachers and getting my assignments in on time.

College offered even fewer opportunities to make connections. How is it possible to spend a full semester with dozens of people and not know the name of anyone in the class? Many of us were successful at avoiding eye contact with anyone else for the entire semester. Communities were established in the dorm rooms, not in the classrooms.

If we believe that learning is enhanced by a safe and valuing environment which allows the brain to make connections at a higher cognitive level (highlighted by brain research), it is rational to conclude that some of us learn *in spite of* the conditions in many classrooms across this country. The rest of us are relegated to other situations that rely on labeling: *at-risk, special education,* or *dropout.* Creating a classroom community can be the most important tool at a teacher's fingertips. Once a class of individuals come together to work toward common goals, with everyone valued and respected, the business of learning can take place fully, without reservation.

It is difficult for me to say what made the difference between the train car and the classroom. Certainly the conditions for creating community existed on those western tracks, while those conditions were absent among the rows of desks. It is also my heartfelt belief that, as teachers, we can create the necessary conditions for community in our classrooms *if* we pay attention to the process. Community-building takes work. It is predicated on trust, risk taking and open communication. It is a process that needs constant attention.

The following chapters contain the necessary tools and resources to begin a journey together toward an ideal: a world that values collaboration, cooperation and interdependence. It is a journey undertaken away from the mean-spiritedness that is eating away at the core of our collective being. It is our *journey to create the caring classroom.*

GROUP DEVELOPMENT*

Most classrooms are granted a "honeymoon" period, in which students are quiet, even polite, and arguments are either nonexistent or minimal. Depending upon the personalities and backgrounds of the students, the honeymoon period can last for weeks, hours or minutes. It is a sure bet, however, that the honeymoon will come to an end, and the teacher's classroom management style will be tested. Sometimes every strategy seems futile, with the students locked in eternal conflict with the teacher and each other. At other times, the atmosphere is magic, with students learning to resolve their conflicts and soar. At still other times, the teacher attempts to avoid conflict by clamping down with an ironclad list of rules and punishments.

These observations are not random; they are based on a process that is as consistent as gravity itself: the process of group development. Every group of individuals goes through this process. Some get stuck at certain phases, while others work through the issues and progress to the next phase. A knowledge of group development will help you work with the process, thus enhancing the opportunity to create the conditions for community in the classroom.

Picture a person with whom you have developed a close relationship over a period of time—a partner or a good friend. Remember back to the time when you first met. Hold the memories of those first days and weeks. This was a time when your friend could do no wrong. If something was said or done that did not sit well, you simply ignored it, or felt it did not really matter. This was your new dear friend, after all.

As your relationship progressed, there came a point when those same little things suddenly mattered. Some friction began to develop. The issues were probably not overtly stated; the things that were actually said and done were symptoms of larger issues centering around values, space, power and control. If these themes were not worked through, they did not go away. And if the issues were not dealt with at all, the relationship probably cooled and you grew apart.

If, on the other hand, you worked through the conflict, norms for the relationship began to develop. You learned about your partner's boundaries, and your partner learned yours. This precipitated a time of closeness and affection because you had struggled together, and the relationship had great focus.

After awhile, new conflicts arose. The symptoms may have been different, but the issues were actually the same. It seemed as if you were meeting this person for the first time. In reality, though, you were dealing with the same issues at a deeper level. You worked through them again, and your relationship regained focus—until the next time, as the spiral continues.

Groups of people gathered for a common purpose go through a similar cycle. It is the dynamic nature of relationships that come into play whenever people get together. It is a force that has been documented over and over again, and it is a force to be reckoned with.

This group developmental process is all around us. It is there whether we choose to see it or not. Sometimes conflicts are worked through and we move on; at other times we are stymied, and the group process stagnates or the group disbands. Look around at your family, your church and social groups. The process is there. Look at gangs and political systems. The process is there. It respects no bounds of values, political persuasion or morality.

To recognize this developmental cycle of any group makes it an ally, a companion that can make group work a little less a matter of guesswork. It is common to hear accomplished facilitators say, "Trust the process." They are referring to this group cycle. Especially during times of conflict, when it is necessary to face it rather than run from it, that phrase pops up. Sometimes it feels like a banner in a gale, but it is well worth the effort. If a group

---

* See pp. 76-84 *TRIBES: A new way of learning and being together,* by Jeanne Gibbs, for a concise description of her view of the stages of group development.

of people work through the conflict, there are calmer times ahead—when individuals understand the group norms because they have had a part in establishing them, and when the nature of the group comes into focus. It is a marvelous dynamic to watch in action. I call it magic.

The literature on the stage theory of group development is long and includes treatises comparing the differing models. The terms used vary, but they all describe the same process.

◊ THE LIFE CYCLE OF A GROUP

In this view of group development, a group is seen as an organic entity—one that goes through life stages just as any living being. This view uses human growth and development as a metaphor for group development.

*Forming: Birth and Infancy**

People are brought together for a variety of reasons. They may or may not have a choice about whether to be involved in the group. School is a place where both types of groups are present, since individuals have little choice about who their classmates are, but they gather in social groups of their own choosing during unstructured time. Whether by choice or not, groups are formed for a reason, and the feelings of the individuals joining the groups are similar.

When classes come together for the first time, there is a general feeling of anxiety. Individuals worry about whether or not they will be accepted, if they will like the other students in the class, and if the other students will like them. People are generally polite and unwilling to take risks because they are not clear about what behavior is acceptable in this particular class. This is the "honeymoon" period.

The main issue at this time is one of inclusion. How can we make the environment a safe place where everyone is included? Since norms are not yet established, the students depend on the teacher for leadership. If it is not provided, they will seek other avenues that offer guidance and leadership. Therefore, it is incumbent upon the teacher to provide experiences that help the students get to know each other, allow them to offer their hopes and expectations for the class, and to establish ground rules that protect individuals from physical or emotional bombardments.

Storming†: Adolescence

Once students know each other better, have developed a foundation of trust, and feel it is safe to take some risks, it is inevitable that conflict will arise. As people interact on a more complex level, differences in style, opinion and perspective become evident. Just as in a two-person relationship, the problems that occur in class are symptoms indicating larger issues of power and control. When a class identity has not yet been established, students might alternately turn *toward* the teacher for guidance or turn on the teacher for taking too much control of the class. Individuals struggle with issues of leadership and decision making. **The main concern at this stage is one of influence.**

When signs of conflict arise, the teacher needs to watch her own influence on the class. When students begin to ask for (and sometimes demand) more responsibility, it is essential to give it to them. They are indicating readiness. This does not mean that they are

---

* Forming, Storming, Norming, Performing and Adjourning are stages of group development first identified by Bruce Tuckman and Mary Anne Jensen.

† Denise Mitten, consultant and former director of Woodswoman, prefers the term *sorting* to *storming*, as it changes the negative connotation and honors the positive nature of this stage in the process.

left to their own devices. The role of the teacher simply changes from *leader* to one of *guide*. Time and space must be set aside for students to discuss their issues of conflict. Both scheduled and spontaneous group meetings can be helpful tools for students to either prevent or work through conflicts.

Storming (or Sorting) is a natural part of human interaction, but that does not mean it is easy to deal with. Yet, although difficult, it is usually a time to cheer. Conflicts are indications that the group process is moving along. It is important for teachers to recognize that conflicts are not a direct result of their teaching techniques, but part of a larger process. That realization allows teachers to be most effective; they can provide time for students to discuss conflicts as they arise, and they can choose activities that meet the needs of each class as they practice the developing norms.

Norming: Young Adulthood

As students work through issues around leadership, decision making and group goals, they develop norms for the class. For example, many times during class tasks, one person takes over leadership by doing all of the talking. This can spark complaints from other students about being bossed around or excluded from the activity. Upon discussion, the person in question discloses that since no one else stepped up, he or she was filling a leadership gap—not meaning to be bossy, but in an effort to get the task accomplished. After awhile, the class agrees to apply some structure to class planning time, whereby everyone is asked for an opinion before the class decides on a course of action. They agree to try this scheme for the next task.

At this point, the class has turned the corner from dependence upon the teacher to a growing independence as a cohesive unit. Norms are being developed that are unique to this class. The role of the teacher is now one of process observer and questioner. It is a relationship that is similar to mentoring, where the students have the combined skills to accomplish many tasks, but are still at a point where they are establishing the structure to really strike out on their own.

Denise Mitten, who has decades of facilitation expertise, warns of an uninvited group "member" that may appear at this stage of a group's development. She calls it "Norm" or "Norma." Denise tells about being part of a group that began meeting to plan an expedition. After awhile, they got into the habit of celebrating these meetings with a particular type of cookie. After finishing a difficult task, they would break out the cookies to share. During the actual trek, however, they reached their goal only to find that no one had brought the cookies. There was a tangible feeling of disappointment that their ritual was being broken at so momentous a time. Finally, someone admitted that she did not even like that kind of cookie. In fact, it turned out that nobody did. "Norma" had joined the expedition[1]; a norm had been created without thought. Everyone assumed that everyone else felt the same way about the cookies, and the result was a tradition without real meaning.

Every group's identity is unique. It is formed by individuals working together toward common goals, struggling through conflicts and developing norms. Vigilance must be exercised, however, lest the individuals in the class be superseded by a groupthink mentality. In a classroom, uninvited norms can appear as competition for the best grades, or in the form of scapegoating one particular student or group. In Adventure activities, risk taking can be healthy, or the wielding of peer pressure can cause students to take risks without thinking—for example, doing trust activities when an individual may not be ready to put on the blindfold for a trust walk.

Norms are created whether we think about them or not. Teachers need to help students create norms that are socially enhancing and healthy. The philosophy of Challenge by Choice (discussed in detail later) must always be in place to preserve the rights of individuals, and group members should always question why a particular norm is in place.

Performing: Middle Age

Once students have practiced ways of working together, and have arrived at a mutual understanding of what it means to be part of the class, a remarkable event takes place. The class, sometimes suddenly, begins to act as a cohesive unit. Collaboration is now possible, and people care about each other more deeply than before. People behave less superficially, and are willing to take greater risks without fear of reprisal. Individuals are seen as having unique talents, not just as being part of a class. Each student has had a hand in creating this class. It is not often possible to put a finger on when this happens; it almost seems like magic.

The teacher can now sit back and watch. There is a feeling of needing to be somewhere, but having nowhere to go as your students take steps on their own. There is also a sense of wonder and awe at how efficient and capable a group of individuals can be. They are truly interdependent, and able to take care of needs that arise. When conflicts come up, people understand what is expected because they have been there before. Individuals step up to facilitate the discussion, the students make a decision, and they move on. It is a thing of beauty.

The role of the teacher now is to act as a consultant for the class. Are there safety considerations that are not being discussed? What outside influences need to be brought in? What does the class need in order to accomplish its mission? By asking relevant questions, offering advice when solicited, and helping the students make necessary connections outside their class, the teacher helps them keep focused on their mission.

Transforming: Elderhood and Death

After a group of individuals reaches a level of cohesion and experience, a couple of avenues await. First, it is possible for them to recycle through the phases again. The longer a class stays together, the more times they may recycle through the process. Each time, the students' collective experience and wisdom come into play, allowing the individuals to continue in the spiral at a deeper level of understanding and insight. It is a process that, theoretically, could last forever.

Reality, though, has another agenda. Sooner or later, groups disband, whether because their allotted time is up, the task is complete, or physical age takes its toll. Groups die, and people grieve for what has been. Their group experience may be duplicated by others in the future, but it will never be the same as the experience with this particular group of people.

The teacher's role takes on a temporary level of importance at a time of class transformation. It is important to provide students with the space and the opportunity to "close" this chapter of their lives. If possible, the class should be given an opportunity to decide on its future. Depending on circumstances, they may choose to reconvene for another task, or they may attempt to plan a reunion. It is also necessary to offer time for individuals to celebrate, share memories, and say their good-byes and thank-yous.

◊ STAGES OF GROUP DEVELOPMENT: A COMPARISON

The following chart (Figure 2.1) delineates the similarities among the three schools of thought discussed thus far with regard to their influences on Adventure Education. (The TRIBES program was highlighted in Chapter 1.)

TRIBES (Gibbs)	Life Cycle Metaphor	Tuckman and Jensen
Inclusion	Birth and infancy	Forming
Influence	Adolescence	Storming
Influence/Community	Young adulthood	Norming
Community	Middle age	Performing
Spiral of renewal	Elderhood and death	Transforming (Adjourning)

Figure 2.1

◊ ROLE OF THE TEACHER

Throughout the life cycle of the class, the teacher must pay close attention to his or her role in the process, especially since it keeps changing. At the beginning, it is necessary to take a strong leadership position in order to help the students come together in a safe environment. Then, as the students are ready to take on more leadership responsibility, the teacher must back off and become a guide. Guides offer activities, teach necessary skills and continue to act as safety monitors. Next, during the norming stage, the guide's role changes to one of mentor—asking questions and mediating discussions. As the students become more interdependent, the mentor role then changes to one of consultant. Finally, the teacher must temporarily reassert himself or herself as a leader in order to facilitate the process of closure as a class's life comes to an end.

◊ THE GROUP CYCLE IN ACTION

The artistry with group facilitation, of course, is to assess a particular class's needs and to take on the role that will best suit those needs. Since every group is made up of different individuals, every class is different. Moreover, it is possible to get stuck at any given stage of the cycle. If people do not feel safe or included, they will invariably stay at the forming stage, unwilling to take risks or confront the issues that will allow them to grow as a group. Many times a class stagnates at the storming stage because of unspoken issues that people are unwilling to discuss. Sometimes it takes an enormous amount of patience to wait for these issues to surface. Sometimes they never do, and the class stays put.

It is also possible to regress to earlier stages. When new members join or old members leave, the class as a whole is different. The teacher can arrange both activities to help students get reacquainted, and discussion time to help clarify community standards and norms. As a rule, every time a class meets, a mini re-forming time can be offered to help people ease back into their class.

How a class progresses, however, has as much to do with external pressures as internal group chemistry. If students come together by choice, for example, attitudes about wanting to work together are different than for those who are brought together because of some external requirement in which they have had no voice. The amount of time a class is together is also highly influential when working through group process. The standard 45-minute time period in a high school is not as conducive to developing group dynamics as a block schedule, for example.

Since each class is dealing with a surplus of internal and external variables, it is difficult to predict the pace at which a given class will move through the process. Some classes leap, while others take baby steps. Some classes take two steps forward and one back, while still others take one step forward and two back. This unpredictability makes for an exciting adventure for students and teacher alike.

Although rarely smooth and orderly, the group process *does* move forward. Recognizing the forces that drive groups offers a compass to the teacher for navigating the journey of community-building. As in any journey, it may not be possible to know where we will end up, but we accept that we will know more about who we are when we have traveled the road together.

> **EXPLORING**
> Always in the big woods when you leave familiar ground and step off alone into a new place there will be, along with the feelings of curiosity and excitement, a little nagging of dread. It is the ancient fear of the Unknown, and it is your first bond with the wilderness you are going into. What you are doing is exploring. You are undertaking the first experience of our essential loneliness; for nobody can discover the world for anybody else. It is only after we have discovered it for ourselves that it becomes a common ground and a common bond, and we cease to be alone.—*Wendell Berry*, The One-Inch Journey[2]

SEQUENCING AND FLOW

At a conference a few years ago, Tom Smith, who has been an Adventure/experiential educator longer than I've been alive, made the following statement: "We must remember that sequencing is the most important thing we do. Then we must remember that there is no sequence." After shaking my head to make sure I heard him correctly, and then reflecting upon that statement for three years, it has occurred to me that he was making the distinction between sequencing activities for a class and the flow of the activities when they are used by a class.

There is general agreement in the field of Adventure Education that activities can be sequenced to help facilitate the development of group cohesion. In general, activities are selected to help a group of students progress through four main areas, as shown in Figure 2.2 below.

	Group Formation	Group Challenge	Group Support	Group Achievement
Focus	Cooperation, Trust building	Problem solving	Challenge (individual ropes course elements and projects)	Challenge (outdoor pursuits, urban experiences, small group projects)
Tuckman's Phase of Group Development	Forming	Storming/ Norming	Norming/ Performing	Performing

Figure 2.2: Sequence and Group Development*

A useful approach would be to start out with a sequence of acquaintance activities with a low level of threat, then progress through activities that require more commitment and trust from students. Finally, students will be asked to support—and be supported by—others as they attempt individual challenges.

---

* Adapted from Christian Bisson, unpublished dissertation, 1997 (p.94). Please see Chapter 3 for a detailed description of each level.

One must take into consideration a variety of external and internal group influences when choosing an activity. In the classic book *Islands of Healing,* Schoel, Prouty and Radcliffe describe a model for choosing the "right" activity for a group at any given time. They call it the GRABBS Modality Checklist (see Figure 2.3 below).

Goals:	How does the activity relate to the group and individual goals that have been set?
Readiness:	This pertains to levels of instruction (skills) and safety capabilities. Is the group ready to do the activity? Will they endanger themselves and others? Do they have the ability to attempt or complete? What do you have to do to change the event to compensate for lack of readiness?
Affect:	What is the feeling of the group? What kinds of sensations are they having? What is the level of empathy or caring in the group?
Behavior:	How is the group acting? Are they resistant? Disruptive? Agreeable? Are they self-involved or group involved? Are there any interactions that are affecting the group, both positive and negative? How cooperative are they?
Body:	What kind of physical shape are they in? How tired are they? Do they abuse substances? Are they on medication? How do they see their own bodies?
Stage:	Which developmental stage [phase] is the group at? Groups will go through levels of functioning, and a schema to describe these levels will provide you with another means of assessment [e.g. Forming, storming/sorting, norming, performing, transforming].

Figure 2.3: GRABBS Modality Checklist[3]

Although cumbersome at first, the GRABBS Modality Checklist becomes internalized with practice. After awhile it will no longer be necessary to think consciously about group development, or to remind yourself to check for affect of the students. With time, one can learn to scan the group and "Grabb" an activity within seconds. Certainly mistakes will be made (bringing the opportunity to learn from those mistakes), but it is all part of learning through experience.

The *science* of sequencing begins with the knowledge of a hypothetically correct sequence and a list of activities drawn up by the teacher. It will be impossible, however, to stick to that list; the needs of the class will affect it. Karl Rohnke and Steve Butler describe sequencing in their book, *Quicksilver,* as:

> ...being *in the right place at the right time.* The same principle applies when leading Adventure activities.... If you happen to know the appropriate activity for a given situation, you're half-way to a successful experience; the other half is recognizing that it fits the needs of the group and the situation.[4]

The interaction between the planned sequence of activities and the class is the "flow." I might have the perfect sequence mapped out on my outline, but if it does not meet the needs of my students, it is useless. This is where knowledge of the stages of group development comes in handy. If the class is sorting through an issue of leadership, for example, you'll need to choose an activity that gives them the opportunity to practice leadership skills. If students are dozing after a heavy lunch, choose an energizer to get the blood pumping. If people are tired of playing "silly" games (a sign that they are ready to move on), jump over the 17 other games that were planned and move into more serious activities. This is the *art* of sequencing.

With experience, the teacher develops a personal instinct about sequencing and the flow of activities. Every Adventure educator can share stories about activities that bombed because each was the wrong activity at the wrong time. Luckily, we can also share the magical moments that came from choosing the right activity at the right time. Karl and Steve remind us that "there are no right and wrong ways to sequence a program. You need to develop your own sequencing instincts."[5] Having the big picture of group development along with the GRABBS Modality Checklist in mind, and connecting it to real experience, makes a powerful combination when trying to meet the needs of your class.

SUMMARY

Community does not just happen; conditions must be right for it to occur. Community is also not magic, although it seems like it at times. Understanding the nature of group development helps a teacher offer experiences that can help a group of students along in their journey. Sequencing activities to conform with the stages of group development requires both knowledge of a hypothetically correct sequence (the *science* of sequencing) and the willingness to alter that sequence (the *art* of sequencing) in order to meet immediate needs and establish a "flow." The science comes with education, while the art is gained through experience.

References
[1] Association for Experiential Education International Conference, Lake Tahoe, 1997.
[2] Schoel, Jim and Michael Stratton. *Gold Nuggets: Readings for Experiential Education.* Hamilton, MA: Project Adventure, Inc., 1990. (p. 76)
[3] Schoel, et al. *Islands of Healing.* (p.80)
[4] Rohnke, Karl and Steve Butler. *QuickSilver.* (p. 41)
[5] Rohnke and Butler. (p. 42)

Chapter 3

MAPPING THE JOURNEY

Once outfitted with an understanding of the developmental stages of a group and an awareness of sequencing, it is time to study our map. The community-building sequence on page 22 (Figure 3.1) loosely follows the group development cycle discussed earlier by highlighting some of the key issues that group members deal with at each phase of development. If these issues are addressed, students can have their needs met at any given stage of the process.

This chapter contains a detailed description of a community-building sequence which can help teachers choose appropriate activities.

A COMMUNITY-BUILDING SEQUENCE

Choosing the right activity to meet students' needs is one important teacher skill. The other is knowing when to stand back while the students work out a conflict, and when to step in to facilitate a discussion—to reflect and process as a group. The Community-Building Model (Figure 3.1) helps provide a structure with which to make decisions about sequencing and processing.

We begin by creating a safe environment within the class. Remember that people are coming with anxiety about what to expect and how they will fit in. It is imperative to create a place where people feel included. Therefore, learning or reinforcing **Cooperation** skills produces an atmosphere where people can work together rather than compete against each other. Put-downs are firmly discouraged, while encouragement is consistently reinforced. Hidden agendas are teased out so that they can be dealt with in the open. Ice Breaker/Acquaintance activities are used to bring students together and help them meet each other.

This is a barrier-breaking time, when people can actually see each other as human beings rather than as objects. A classic example of this is the "us and them" mentality of cliques. Often people do not have the opportunity to meet each other as equals because the "in" and "out" lines are so strongly drawn. Students involved in community-building groups report that they have been able to meet people they never could meet before. It is common to hear "I learned you can't judge a book by its cover" from students who have participated in a community-building process.

If students feel included, can work together, and encourage rather than humiliate each other, they are ready to deal with **Trust** issues. These include the all-important question: Is it OK to make a mistake? Group members delve into the concepts of risk taking and what it means to be trustworthy. Specific activities that help students explore trust are chosen and processed.

Cooperation and trust are the *group formation* parts of the process. They provide the foundation for the next step, **problem solving.** This is a time for members to take on some *group challenges* together. They wrestle with how to make decisions, take leadership and resolve conflicts. This is frequently a time when group goals and individual goals clash. Issues of influence are prevalent during this time, and conflict is evident. There is a switch in focus from participating in activities to taking ownership in solving problems. Communication between people becomes more complex, thus giving rise to concerns about power and control. Processing becomes paramount at this stage of the journey.

Tools
- Full Value Contract
- Challenge by Choice
- Goal setting

CHALLENGE
(Chapter 7)
- Individual goals
- Stating needs
- Encouragement/Support
- Fear/Anxiety
- Success/Failure

Activities
High ropes course
Outdoor pursuits
Urban experience
Presentations/Projects

PROBLEM SOLVING
(Chapter 6)
- Decision making
- Group goals
- Taking turns
- Leadership
- Conflict resolution

Activities
Problem-solving initiatives
Team low ropes elements
Conflict resolution
Academic content

TRUST
(Chapter 5)
- Making mistakes
- Empathy
- Trustworthiness
- Risk taking
- Physical/Emotional trust

Activities
Trust building
Feelings literacy
Behavioral goal setting
Individual low ropes elements

COOPERATION
(Chapter 4)
- Put-ups/Put downs
- Hidden agendas
- Active listening
- Mixing
- Perspective taking

Activities
Ice Breakers/Acquaintance
Deinhibitizer
Challenge by Choice
Full Value Contract

Group formation → Group challenge → Group support/achievement

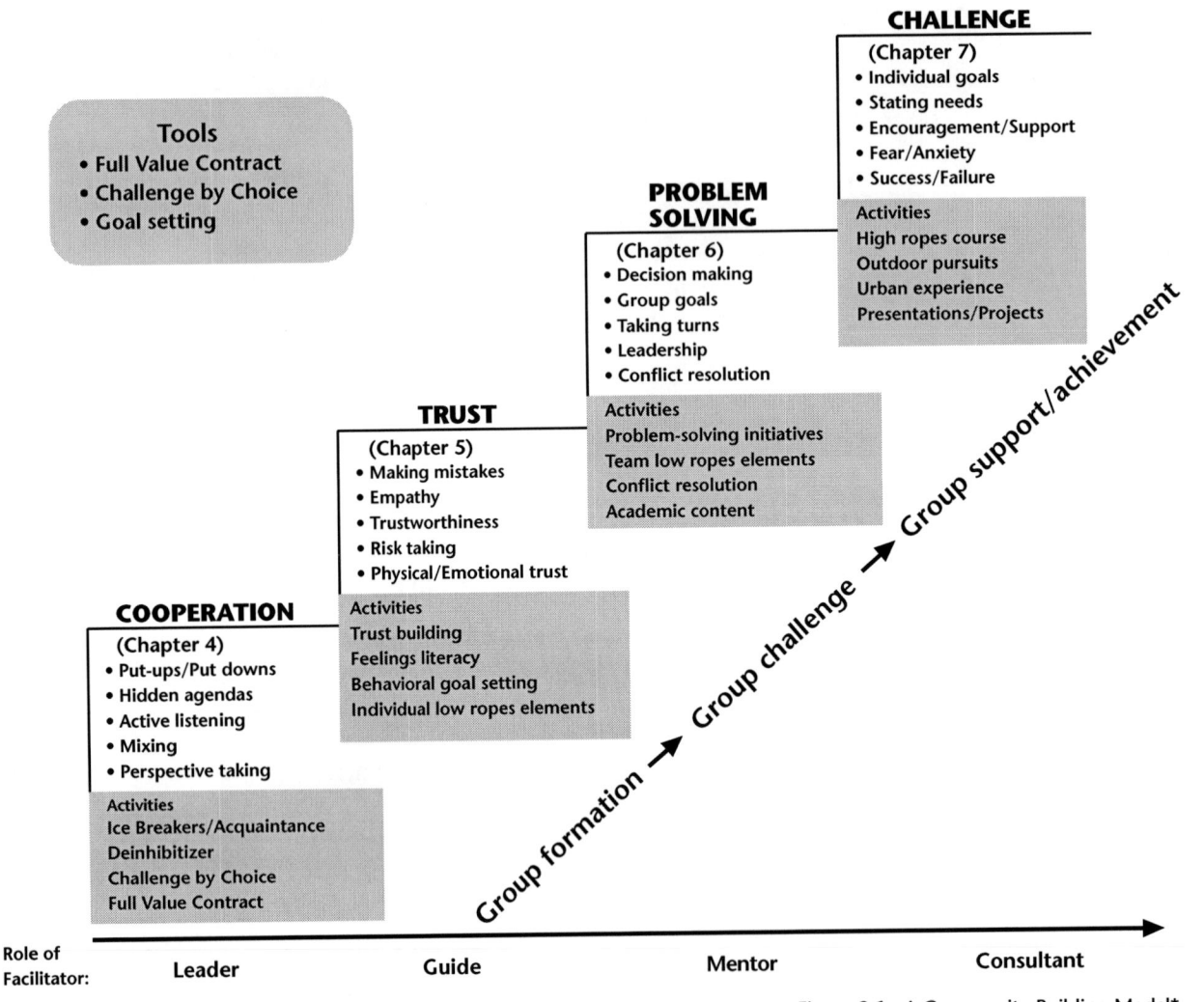

Role of Facilitator: Leader — Guide — Mentor — Consultant

Figure 3.1: A Community-Building Model*

After group members have struggled through conflict, solved problems together, and met group goals, there is generally a sense of group cohesion. Norms are established, and students are ready to take some individual challenges *with the support of their group*. There is a true community feel to the group now. It is safe to be together, but it is also safe to strike out on one's own, knowing that these people will be there for support. Whether the **Challenge** is 30 feet up on a high ropes course, standing in front of a group to give a speech, or planning a service project, the issues are similar. People need to be able to state their needs and ask for help when necessary. They set individual goals and offer mutual support. They experience success and failure. No matter what happens, the community is there to offer support and feedback. To challenge oneself by taking risks is the stuff of growth, and community support is a safety net that allows people to step up to the challenge.

---

* *Group Formation, Group Challenge, Group Support and Group Achievement* are from p. 32 of "A Dissertation of Varying the Sequence of Categories of Adventure Activities on the Development of Group Cohesion," an unpublished dissertation by Christian Bisson, 1997.

◊ COMMUNITY-BUILDING TOOLS: CREATING A SAFE ENVIRONMENT

Throughout the journey, there are tools that can be used first to help a group come together, and then to take care of group needs along the way. When initiating a community-building process, it is necessary to establish certain ground rules. The ultimate goal is to create an environment where everyone feels physically and emotionally safe. Once a safe atmosphere is achieved, participants are more willing to take risks, such as making mistakes and trying new ideas. The act of risk taking encourages emotional growth and aids in building confidence.

There are three main tools that are helpful in the community-building process: Full Value Contract, Challenge by Choice, and Goal Setting. (All of these concepts have been developed by Project Adventure; see Appendices for further information.)

Full Value Contract

Every class consists of individuals who have arrived at that point in time in a unique way; no two people have the exact same history. A person's frame of reference dictates how she or he views the world. One person may feel that teasing someone about his hair is humorous, while another views it as cruel. A Full Value Contract is a starting point for any group. It affords group members an opportunity to establish ground rules to which everyone can agree. It can be as simple as a verbal "Play hard, play safe, play fair, have fun," a concept originally developed by the New Games Foundation in the 1970s, or as complicated as a written document that everyone signs.

A Full Value Contract should contain an agreement that everyone is committed to the physical and emotional safety of all group members. There should also be a mechanism for discussing problems as they arise. (For example, if a participant throws an object at someone during an activity, or calls someone a name, the members should feel that they have the right to stop the activity to call attention to the breach of safety.) In the beginning, the teacher may need to model this behavior, acting as a safety expert until students are more willing to confront the issues themselves.

Another feature of a Full Value Contract is a willingness to work toward group goals and to help others achieve personal goals. In the beginning of a group's life, when the safety parameters are still being set, some students may feel compelled to sabotage the group process in order to meet some personal needs. This is known as a hidden agenda. If, as part of the Full Value Contract, participants agree to work toward group goals, they can be asked to bring hidden agendas out into the open. Many times, a group can help satisfy an individual's agenda while meeting group goals. If an individual's agenda runs counter to the group goals, he or she can be asked to either delay the individual need or to choose to participate in another way. This is known as Challenge by Choice.

Challenge by Choice

The Full Value Contract addresses group needs; Challenge by Choice meets individual needs. In order to feel safe in a community, a person must have control over what she or he will and will not do. There are times when it is appropriate to say no, even in the face of acute peer pressure. This is especially necessary when participants are asked to take risks.

The concept of Challenge by Choice allows each person to be in control of her or his level of participation. This means that someone may *choose* how much personal information to share with the group. It means that someone may choose to be totally involved—

physically and emotionally—in an activity, or may choose to sit back and watch. It does **not** mean that someone may sit and read the newspaper while the group goes about its business. No matter what level of participation an individual chooses, he or she is still part of the group, even if it means being an observer.

Challenge by Choice in action may look like this: During a jump rope activity called Turnstile, a participant says he does not want to jump. At first, the students give him some encouragement, and the teacher asks, "Is there anything we can do to help you jump?" When he says, "No, I just don't want to jump," he is offered the rope to act as a rope turner.

In every group situation there are many roles to take. When planning a project, someone might agree to make phone contacts, while someone else chooses marketing. Still others create artwork, work on logistics or do the note taking. If we practice the art of Challenge by Choice in the beginning stages of community-building, group members will benefit later when asked to engage in real-life projects.

Challenge by Choice is sometimes difficult to conceptualize in a school setting, where students are required to get their work done, be present, and complete a given curriculum. It is helpful to remember that Challenge by Choice is not an "on/off switch," where students make either/or decisions about participating. Rather, students are given choices *within* the school structure. Challenge by Choice, then, does not ask "Will you do this?" Instead it asks, "*How* will you do this?" In keeping with the philosophy of multiple intelligences, students can make choices about how a certain concept will be learned—helping to decide how to best meet their own learning styles. Again, during community-building activities, Challenge by Choice can range from observing to total involvement.

Depending upon the age and maturity level of the students, they need varying degrees of guidance when considering choices, especially if they have very little experience in making informed choices. A common concern for teachers is a scenario where a student chooses (read *refuses*) to participate at all, and a whole group of other students follow that lead. This is a perfect teachable moment about choices and how individual choices affect others. If necessary, you can stop the action for a discussion about choices—what causes people to make the choices they do, internal and external factors and pressures, how individual and group goals sometimes clash, and what can be done to support people's choices while continuing the group process.

As we struggle with the notion of Challenge by Choice in a school setting, other issues arise. As teachers, we must ask ourselves, "Are students *really* being given a choice?" In our zeal to make sure that everyone is included, do we push and prod students into positions where they have virtually no choice? Carla Hacker, an elementary school teacher and Adventure educator, believes that when students are unable, for physical or emotional reasons, to participate in an activity as it is presented, they should be consulted about *how* they want to participate. She has labeled this concept "inclusion by choice." If, for example, the class is involved in a running activity, and a student is on crutches, just handing him a "busy" chore (like cheering everyone on) can be at best pointless, and at worst demeaning. *Ask* students how they want to be included, *respect* their choices, and you will be empowering them to make real choices later on. Being included at all costs is not always the best choice.

Another factor to consider is the need to modify and adapt activities to meet differing levels of physical and cognitive abilities. At the beginning of a group's journey, it is the teacher's role to consider the needs of the class, then to choose appropriate activities and modify them accordingly. As the class becomes more cohesive and accepting, that responsibility can be shared among all community members as issues of inclusivity arise.

Goal Setting

Another tool at the disposal of a community-building group is the art of goal setting. One of the most difficult, never-ending tasks a group must undertake is reconciling individual versus group goals. A Full Value Contract and the Challenge by Choice concept help in dealing with these issues, but students must practice the conscious act of goal setting in order to create a direction for the whole class as well as for themselves. Goal setting offers students the opportunity to define who they are and where they are headed. (Goal setting activities can be found in Chapter 5.)

Group goals can be the most difficult, as everyone may have a different idea about what the group should or could be doing. One strategy is to help students first practice with small goals. For example, when working on a timed initiative (such as Don't Touch Me, where students switch places with partners while being timed), ask participants to agree on a group goal for that particular activity. The goal might be to meet a set time or to reach a faster time. The goal might be to find as many different ways as possible to do the switching, or it could even be to forget about the time and just have some fun.

Once a class has established a way to make decisions about small goals, they graduate to larger goals—such as, "What do you really want to accomplish in this activity?" Finally, students can be encouraged to set goals for larger class projects or school functions.

Individual goals can be behavioral or task-oriented. Each individual can choose a specific behavioral goal that he or she wishes to work toward. One person may wish to speak up more; another might want to be less overbearing or "bossy." The key is for each person to really *want* to work on the goal in order to effect positive personal change. Once a goal is made public, students can support each other in achieving their goals.

A task-oriented goal helps an individual work toward getting a job done. During the Turnstile activity mentioned earlier, someone may state, "I want to jump through three times without stopping the rope." As simple a goal as that may seem, it is an important practice for later, more complex, tasks. During a class project, for example, once a group goal has been established and tasks have been divided among students, an individual may set a timetable for getting her or his part done.

SUMMARY

This community-building process includes a sequence that loosely follows the life cycle of a group. The steps include Cooperation, Trust, Problem Solving and Challenge. Every step builds on the next to address issues and needs of the students. The teacher's role changes as the students form a more cohesive group and become more adept at handling issues that arise.

Communities cannot form in a vacuum, so it is important to have a variety of tools that help create a safe environment. These are used throughout the community-building process to cultivate a safe and respectful work environment. A Full Value Contract is used to help establish norms for the community. While this contract takes care of group needs, Challenge by Choice allows individuals to have control over *how* they will participate in activities. Goal setting helps to set the stage, then provides a structure within which to deal with conflicts and decision making. Later, students use goal setting to create action plans that incorporate both behavioral and academic goals.

Chapter 4

COOPERATION: SETTING THE STAGE

Take yourself back to a time when you were about to join a group. Maybe it was a sports team, a workshop, a party, a committee, or even a community meeting called to deal with a conflict or problem in the neighborhood. Chances are that you tried to find a friend to accompany you so you wouldn't feel so out of place. Dredge up those feelings of anxiety. To one degree or another, they were no doubt there.

These feelings surrounding inclusion always exist in newly forming (or re-forming) groups. There are ways to help people ease into this awkward situation, whether the group's life span is one hour or 20 years. Obviously, the longer a group is together, the deeper its level of community-building. However, even a short-lived group can make people feel included just by allowing them all to introduce themselves.

COOPERATION
- **Put-ups/Put-downs**
- **Hidden agendas**
- **Active listening**
- **Mixing**
- **Perspective taking**

Activities
Ice Breakers/Acquaintance
Deinhibitizer
Challenge by Choice
Full Value Contract

In a classroom situation, where students stay together for a whole semester or a year, this process can go much further. Students arrive anxious and excited. They are dependent upon the teacher for leadership, and they have hopes and expectations for the class. This is a good time to begin setting the stage by informing the class about the journey they will be embarking on together. The classroom is a safe place where everyone is valued and everyone is included. Share your vision by showing them the map for the journey; it's no secret.

Move into a short initial Full Value Contract by asking group members what they can do to make this a safe place, both physically and emotionally. At first, this will be rather superficial, but it is used only as a starting point. Later in the process, the students will develop a more comprehensive and useful Full Value Contract. Make sure that your agenda is incorporated into the contract, and that issues around name calling and put-downs are included.

Mention Challenge by Choice to the group members. Let them know that they have a choice about the level to which they will participate. Tell them that this level runs a continuum from simply watching a given activity all the way to being 100 percent involved—physically, emotionally, cognitively, spiritually.... Participation is not an "on/off switch" where people leave the class to read the newspaper, talk with friends, or do other work. They are still members of the class, and can offer insights just from watching the class in action. Some teachers even provide a list for observers who are choosing to watch an activity so that they can help monitor a class's progress.

At first, you as the teacher will be the main safety expert. As you do activities, watch for instances of physical or emotional tension between group members. Stop the activity to discuss safety issues that arise, if necessary. Do not ignore these issues. They will not go away, and by ignoring them you are sending a powerful signal to the group that safety is unimportant. This discussion does not need to be a diatribe on safety. For example, it may only take a moment to point out that what just happened was an example of a put-down, which is an emotional safety issue. Reminders such as these help students identify what is acceptable and what is not when engaged in conscious community-building. As time goes by, students will begin to identify put-downs and other safety issues without any prompting.

Following are some issues that can arise during the beginning stages of the life of a group. They must be addressed if students are to feel safe and included. These issues can be either formally introduced or simply acknowledged; it all depends on the age, maturity level, and experience of the individuals in the group. A group of at-risk second graders will need to focus on these issues; they might even need to learn them as skills to practice. A group of high-school seniors, on the other hand, may need only the opportunity to introduce themselves through a few Icebreaker activities before they are ready to move on.

> **Have Fun!**
> Although this community-building process sounds like a serious undertaking, it is not as heavy as it seems. There are times to be serious and times to be silly. Life frequently involves this type of balancing act. Create a structure to ensure that safety is taken seriously, and then go out and have some fun. Meeting people should be enjoyable. Give students time to chat, tell stories and laugh. The Icebreaker and Deinhibitizer activities are designed for people to do just that.

COOPERATION ISSUES AND SKILLS

◊ PUT-UPS INSTEAD OF PUT-DOWNS

Teasing is a form of passive violence—passive violence is the root of physical violence.—Gandhi [*]

People love to tease each other. Watch siblings or good friends poke fun at each other's appearance or behavior. Sometimes, one's most embarrassing moments are brought up for public view by a close friend or partner. Sarcastic humor is a favorite form of teasing between friends.

The issue of put-ups and put-downs is probably the most basic for any group to grapple with. A put-down can be a sign of affection between close friends, or it can be a weapon to wield judgment and evoke pain. Since how teasing is interpreted is situational, it is vital to address it when coming together as a community. Sometimes it is necessary to determine what a put-down or a put-up even is. At other times it is enough to agree that students will refrain from using sarcasm to cause pain.

Imagine that a student uses a derogatory term for a homosexual or uses a racial slur. Maybe one student flashes a nonverbal sign to another student that starts a war of words. What do you do? How you, as the teacher, handle these situations speaks volumes to your students. If a community is to develop, it is vital that these episodes be dealt with. Ignoring put-downs implies that they are OK. There are a variety of interventions; the choices you make depend on the situation that unfolds. Here are a few suggestions:

- Engage in a series of activities and discussions to help students appreciate diversity. Allow students to learn about their own commonalities and differences. Then branch out into the world at large. If students can appreciate people as human beings, rather than as labels, it is a step in the direction of preventing future bouts of name calling.

---

[*] Thanks to Dan Creely, Adventure educator at Northeastern Illinois University, for this contribution. Dan also highlights the idea of put-ups and put-downs in this way: "This could be the most critical part of the program. If people know they will not be made fun of, they will try!"

- Stop everything and talk. This can be a short session to check out what's going on, or it can turn into a longer philosophical discussion about how name calling can be hurtful. Even young children can participate in this kind of talk. No matter how long the discussion, it sends the message that this is a serious matter.
- If it is a minor incident and the class is engaged in another activity, make a note on the board as a reminder to talk about it at a later time—either privately with the parties involved, or with the class as a whole.
- Create a "Peace Place" where students can go to de-escalate their anger and talk about the incident—perhaps with a peer, or with yourself as a mediator.[1]

As teacher, you need to be alert for put-ups and put-downs. It may not be possible to know how students will deal with this issue until they have had some experience together. After an activity or two, you will know whether you need to bring it up for further discussion or whether it will take care of itself.

◊ HIDDEN AGENDAS

Hidden agendas frequently surface as saboteurs of the group process. They can manifest themselves as acting-out behaviors, or as an unwillingness to participate. You might see students purposefully putting others down, sitting out, or refusing to "play by the rules." A classic school example has to do with the faculty and administration. Many staff meetings look something like this: An administrator stands in the front of the room talking about her or his agenda, while many teachers sit in the back of the room with their arms crossed. Later, in the parking lot, those same teachers complain about the meeting and the administrator.

These acts of sabotage are usually mere symptoms of an underlying issue: one of inclusion. It is not a matter of being cruel or bad; it is a matter of being excluded from the process. People hide their agendas when they have not had the opportunity to share them or to be involved in decision making. Therefore, if students feel coerced into being part of a group or mission in which they have had no voice, it must be discussed. For example, if, during an activity, a student is rejected or excluded in some way, she or he might pull out of the group, exercising the right to Challenge by Choice. Bringing the agenda out into the open can be a delicate matter. If the student is hurt and unwilling to discuss it, you, as the teacher, can broach the subject with the class by saying something like, "If that had happened to me, I would feel hurt." Later, the excluded student may be willing to discuss it.

An organization called PlayBoard has an initiative called Games Not Names. Based in Northern Ireland, this group offers some "Dos and Don'ts of dealing with sectarianism." *Sectarianism* is defined as the act of being devoted to a sect, "especially a narrow-minded or strongly prejudiced member of a sect" (*The World Book Dictionary*, 1970). Their advice is helpful when dealing with any kind of put down:

- **DO:** Think in advance about strategies that could be used to cope with sectarian behavior.
- **DO:** Probe the children's understanding of what they have said/done.
- **DO:** Promote equality in all aspects of the playscheme.
- **DO:** Provide a supportive atmosphere where children are encouraged to ask questions and discuss their feelings.
- **DO:** Act as a mediator, helping the children to clarify their feelings, fears and concerns.
- **DO:** Promote the understanding that all people have the right to have their opinions respected and help the children to empathize with others—"how would you feel if...?"
- **DO:** Use games promoting good feelings, cooperation and communication.
- **DO:** Help to develop nonviolent conflict resolution skills.

- **DO NOT:** Give children inconsistent messages—always deal with sectarian behavior.
- **DO NOT:** Stop sectarian behavior without explaining **why** it is unacceptable. Further exploration of the incident may also be necessary.
- **DO NOT:** Forget that children are influenced by the behavior which is accepted in the playscheme.
- **DO NOT:** Be afraid to let children discuss issues among themselves—they learn a lot from each other and from the process itself.
- **DO NOT:** Allow any discriminatory practice, language or behavior to go unchallenged. This should cover race, culture, disability and colour as well as religion [gender and sexual orientation].

Even being forced to participate in a community-building process can be cause for a hidden agenda. Think about it: if students feel forced to play "silly games," it is likely that they will play by different rules, or in some other way upset the process. Students are rarely given an opportunity to have a say in their own education. If they have not chosen to be in your class, sit down with them to discuss the community-building process. Fill them in on the underlying rationale and share the sequence. Ask for input about how they might put the plan into action. Set a group goal, such as going to a high ropes course when the group is ready, or working together on a community service project. The important part about planning is that the students are partners in the planning. It is not that they will go to the ropes course if they are "good" enough; it is brainstorming options and having the students create a shared vision. This may take some time, but it is part of "walking the talk." "Facilitating" a community-building sequence as a dictator defeats the whole purpose.

> The beauty of experiential activities is that they offer opportunities in a low-threat environment in which to deal with real situations. Rather than sitting around talking abstractly about a situation that *might* occur, activities provide situations that actually *do* occur. For example, during an activity called Neighbors, where students must find a new spot according to questions asked by a person in the middle of the circle, many students "pretend" that they do not see the empty spaces. Although it may appear that these students are sabotaging the game, thus making it boring for those rushing to the empty spots (and then waiting), the reality is that they wish to have a turn in the middle. Since they are used to sneaking around to get what they want (their individual needs/goals), their hidden agendas cause a group goal (having fun) to fall by the wayside.
>
> By using this "teachable moment" as a topic of discussion to compare the feelings and thoughts of all parties, the hidden agenda can be exposed. The students can then brainstorm ways to create a win-win situation where all people can have their needs met, thus making the game fun and allowing all to have a chance in the middle. This is a simple yet important lesson about stating needs, as well as an exercise in conflict resolution.

◊ ACTIVE LISTENING

Listening is a basic skill that allows people in a community to share ideas and insights. Without the sharing of ideas, the community cannot operate. Without the sharing of insights, it is impossible for students to learn from each other. Active listening is a skill that can be taught and practiced at this early stage of group work. It involves people looking at the speaker and sending cues that show the speaker he or she is being heard.

> Active listening is a useful life skill that can be taught, but it must be practiced as well. There are three strategies to ensure that students learn to use active listening:
> (1) **Modeling:** You must use the skill in your class.
> (2) **Direct Instruction:** Teach the skill through the use of activities such as the 1-1 interview. Go through the steps: (A) Look at the person who is speaking, think about what the speaker is saying; (B) show that you are listening by nodding your head; (C) ask questions if you don't understand; (D) repeat/summarize what the speaker has said.
> (3) **Practice:** Encourage your students to use the skill whenever possible. Offer immediate feedback to students about their active listening skills.

I have witnessed both children and adults sending out messages to the rest of their group, when it appears that everyone else is wearing earplugs. There is no acknowledgment that the speaker even exists, much less has said anything. As a teacher, you can model active listening by looking at each speaker, nodding or making sounds that show you are hearing the message. Follow up with questions, or a summary of what the person said, and thank the speaker for sharing her or his thoughts.

Modeling is one way to show that active listening is important. However, some groups may need to learn active listening skills before being asked to use them. Many activities and subsequent processing sessions can be used to teach active listening.

◊ MIXING

Put a bunch of people in a room together, and they will gravitate to groups where they feel most comfortable. They might hang out with people from their neighborhood, people of the same gender, color, age, or clique. But in a community where everyone is working toward common goals, it is important to be able to work with anybody from the community. It is not necessary to be best friends, just to be able to work with anyone else in the class on any given task.

With some classes, this is no issue whatsoever. In other classes, it is a major focus of the Cooperation step of the community-building process. Sometimes there is one person who is ostracized by everyone else. This person may be a special education student, or may have a history of being scapegoated. You can choose activities that focus on mixing, and foster discussions about what it feels like to be left out of an activity where everyone else is involved. Again, these issues are often delicate, especially if one person is being left out. Many times, however, the larger concepts of inclusion and mixing can be explored without putting anyone on the spot.

> Exclusion can be a severe and vengeful form of put-down. Since most people wish to be part of the group and activities, being left out can be most painful. The scapegoating scenario can be dealt with by using the same approaches that are used with put-downs. These situations often become traditions, occurring over many years where the same person (or family) is treated as an outcast. Breaking the tradition can be difficult, because the culture must change. A healthy community accepts all who wish to be a part, so it is imperative that any scapegoating be addressed promptly.

◊ PERSPECTIVE TAKING

Alfie Kohn discusses the importance of perspective taking in the community-building process:

> A community rests on the knowledge of, and connections among, the individuals who are part of it. This knowledge, in turn, is deepened by helping students imagine how things appear from other people's points of view. What psychologists call "perspective taking" plays a critical role in helping children become generous, caring people...and activities designed to promote an understanding of how others think and feel...have the added advantage of creating the basis for community.[2]

Perspective taking is the precursor of empathy. If individuals can share their perspectives and hear others' perspectives, they are gaining the foundation to be able to actually imagine what it is like to walk in another person's shoes. This can be accomplished by offering activities that require group members to share about themselves—about their families, feelings, cultures, opinions and values. The end results are individuals who can be respected for who they are, and an atmosphere where differing views are accepted.

> Perspective taking can also offer a chance to enrich the social studies. Ask everyone in the class to bring in a special custom or story from his or her own family. Allow time for each person to present the custom or story to the class. Have the students work in groups to brainstorm how these customs might have originated. They can do some research, if possible. Help them compare the different cultures and perspectives represented by your class. (Dan Creely calls this a Cultural Circle.)

COOPERATION ACTIVITIES

◊ ROLE OF THE TEACHER

When a class is just beginning, the teacher takes an active leadership role. There is usually a fair amount of confusion, along with anxiety, as students try to make sense of their environment. The teacher sets the tone, and people welcome the leadership. Anyone walking by the classroom would see the teacher directing the activities. The students would be focused on the rules of each activity, asking many questions to make sure they understand what they are "supposed to do." At this point, the teacher is seen as the expert.

The following activities are designed to give students a chance to learn names, share about themselves, and learn about others. These Ice Breaker/Acquaintance activities and Deinhibitizers are light and do not require people to take large risks. Students have opportunities to laugh and play.

Processing, described in Chapter 8, is kept short and focused. Unless there is a safety issue, many activities can be strung together before a formal processing session occurs. Questions at this stage center around hopes and expectations, safety, and how students think the class as a whole is doing with the issues.

Ice Breakers/Acquaintance Activities

These activities give students an opportunity to meet each other and to loosen up a bit. They are low-threat activities that do not require people to take large risks. They should be light, allowing for some introductory self-disclosure; processing is kept to a minimum.

1. Memory Circle

Focus: Learning names
Materials: Many soft throwable objects such as fleece balls, wadded-up pieces of paper, Nerf™ balls, etc.

<u>Suggested Procedure</u>

1. Clear the desks or tables away and have students stand in a circle. Tell them that this is an activity designed to help people learn names.
2. Pass an object around so that people can introduce themselves. Each person who receives the object says her or his name and gives some personal information—such as number of siblings, something that has happened this week, or something else that other group members don't know.
3. When the object returns to you, go over throwing etiquette: Make sure that the receiver knows the object is coming! This can be accomplished by calling the receiver's name and making eye contact before throwing the item. Model this by calling a group member's name and tossing the item to her or him. That person then continues by calling someone else's name and throwing the item to him, and so on. Anyone can receive the object more than once.
4. After this has gone on for awhile, start throwing an additional object, then another, and another. Pretty soon all the items are being thrown, and the energy and laughter levels have risen exponentially.
5. Continue for awhile. Then stop the action and see if there is anyone who would like to name everyone in the group.

> SAMPLE PROCESSING QUESTIONS FOR MEMORY CIRCLE
>
> - Why might it be important to make an effort to learn the names of people in the class?
> - What does it mean to include others? Why might it be important to be inclusive?
> - How might we make an effort to include everybody in this class?
> - How can each of us make an effort to learn the names of others outside this class?

<u>Facilitation Notes</u>

The element of surprise is effective here. After students get lulled into a sense of ease by having only one item going around, then begin introducing the additional items with increasing frequency. Chaos is bound to reign, which is why the objects must be soft. Wadded-up pieces of paper are not only cost-effective, but they work well in a room full of equipment. Intersperse the paper with a few fun toys (such as rubber chickens or Nerf Slugs™) to add another element of fun. NOTE: **Tennis balls and other objects with hard surfaces can be hazardous. Do not use them.**

If the students already know each other, try this same activity by having them call out a word or phrase that tells something else about themselves, like a favorite story or movie character. You can even use characters from a book the class is reading, or the vocabulary words from social studies. For younger students, try using the sounds of the alphabet or musical notes.

Adaptations for Students with Disabilities: Memory Circle*

Cognitive disabilities	• Adjective Memory Circle may be beneficial to help with memory problems (Adjective Memory Circle uses an adjective with each name (such as "Little Laurie"), and a motion (squatting down to show "little") instead of throwing an object.
Orthopedic impairment	• Orthopedically impaired individuals may have trouble throwing and catching the balls.
	• Use the variation of Adjective Memory Circle, but without the movements.
	• Roll the ball or bounce it.
	• Use a beachball.
Hearing impairment	• For hearing-impaired individuals, you will need an interpreter unless students can lip-read.
	• The person throwing the ball needs to gain eye contact with the hearing-impaired participant before throwing the ball.
Visual impairment	• This is a difficult activity for visually impaired individuals.
	• They could have "catching partners." Each partner could catch the ball and hand it to the visually impaired individual.
	• Use the Adjective Memory Circle as an option.
	• There are balls available that beep to facilitate object location.

MPS: Memory Circle

---

* Thanks to Dave Braby and the Milwaukee Public Schools for use of their *Accessible Curriculum Supplement* for their Adventure program. They have provided the adaptations for many of the activities, which are noted with an "MPS" below the adaptation. Kathy Hellenbrand, a physical education teacher with adaptive P.E. expertise, helped me adapt the rest of the activities.

2. Name Tag

Focus: Hearing and sharing names
Materials: Stopwatch

Suggested Procedure

1. Have students stand or sit in a circle so that everyone can see everyone else. Tell them that this community-building process begins with easy, nonthreatening activities and is designed to get increasingly more difficult. With that in mind, everyone must remember their own first name.
2. Tell the person to your right (or left) that you will say your name, then he will say his, the person next to him will say hers, and so on, until everyone has said his or her name in order. This will be timed. Try it, then announce the time.
3. Do it again, moving in the same direction. Announce the time. Then do the activity in the other direction a couple of times.
4. Now tell the group that, as promised, the task will get more difficult. It will now go in *both* directions. When you say your name, the people on each side say their names, then on down each half of the circle. Everyone will judge which side finishes first. Of course, the two directions will cross in the middle somewhere.
5. Try this dual method a few times, each time holding up your hand for the side that finishes first.

SAMPLE PROCESSING QUESTIONS FOR NAME TAG

- Who won? Why?
- Were you rooting for one side to answer first? Why or why not?
- How did the people caught in the middle feel? Were your classmates supportive of your difficult situation?

Facilitation Notes

This is an activity that does not necessarily need to be processed. It is enough to hear the names and enjoy the activity. There are times, however, when the people caught in the middle are the objects of some teasing if they have trouble with passing the names along. Then this issue can be brought up as a teachable moment to address putting others down instead of supporting each other. For added challenge and fun, try having people say their names backwards (Carol would be Lorac, Jim would be Mij, Bob would be Bob, etc.).

Adaptations for Students with Disabilities: Name Tag

Cognitive disabilities	• Try this first as an untimed activity.
Orthopedic impairment	• No major modifications necessary.
Hearing impairment	• Include a motion to go with each name. Students can either say their name and do their motion together, or they can just do the motion.
	• Use sign-language names for everyone to include when they speak their names.
Visual impairment	• No major modifications necessary.

3. Paired Activities

Focus: Learning about others, mixing with others in the group
Materials: None

<u>Suggested Procedure</u>

1. Clear the desks or tables away and have students stand in a circle. Ask people to find partners (have them do this quickly; they will switch partners later).
2. Have partners look at each other and, according to an attribute (whoever has shorter hair, darker eyes, the most blue on….), separate themselves. The person with the shorter hair (for example) stands on the inside of the circle, facing the longer-haired partner. There are now two circles—one inside the other—with the inside circle facing the outer one.
3. Give the pairs an activity to do (listed on the following pages).
4. After the activity, have partners discuss something about themselves. Possible discussion topics are: Tell your partner about your family, about your favorite place in the world, about your favorite food, a hope or goal in your life, something you hope to learn someday.
5. After the activity and discussion, have *one* of the circles rotate to the right or left by one or two people. Each person will then have a new partner, and a new activity and discussion topic can be done.

Pairing Strategies

Depending on the age and maturity level of your class, you can use a variety of techniques to select pairs for a given activity. Here are a few suggestions:

- Ask everyone to find a partner.
- Tell students to find someone who has the same size thumb (or same eye color), or a different size thumb (eye color, etc.). (Thanks to Pete Albert.)
- Tell students to find someone who was born in a different season.
- Identify each person as a spoon or a fork. When you say "spork," they find the opposite utensil. (Thanks to Mark Roark.)
- Have the group do a lineup. Fold the line in half; the person everyone faces is his/her partner.
- Keep a can of tongue depressors with the name of every student on a depressor. Choose two depressors at a time; they are partners.
- Keep a deck of cards with pairs that number the size of your class. Each person gets one card; students match up their cards with partners.
- Use index cards for this one. Cut each card in half creatively—so that only those two halves match. Each person gets one and finds the matching half.
- Have different well-known songs written on scraps of paper. Make sure there are two of each song. Throw the papers into a hat. Everyone picks one and hums that tune until he or she finds the humming partner.

Sometimes it is important to split up friends, while at other times it may be nice to allow people who know each other well to work together. It is probably beneficial to mix it up so that students can have an opportunity to experience a variety of scenarios.

Activity A: Last Detail

Everyone looks at his or her partner. On a signal, everyone turns around and changes three things about their clothing (turning collars, switching shoes, taking out earrings, untucking shirts, etc.) When each pair is ready, they turn around and try to guess the three things that were switched by the partner.

Adaptations for Students with Disabilities: Last Detail

Cognitive disabilities	• Have students change fewer than three things.
	• Do this as a large group activity, with one person changing things and everyone else guessing.
Orthopedic impairment	• Some students may need assistance.
Hearing impairment	• No major modifications necessary.
Visual impairment	• This may not be an appropriate activity for students who are visually impaired.

Activity B: Tie Your Shoe

Each pair should have at least one person with tied shoes, or the ability to borrow a laced shoe from someone else. The shoe(s) should be untied, and the task is to retie the shoe(s). The problem is that each person in the pair can use only one hand!

Adaptations for Students with Disabilities: Tie Your Shoe

Cognitive disabilities	• Do this activity only if students know how to tie their shoes already.
	• Instead of tying shoes, have students take shoes off and try to put them back on together, using only one hand each.
	• Have students put on a sock instead of tying a shoe.
Orthopedic impairment	• Activity may not be appropriate if students have little fine-motor coordination.
	• Put shoe on a tray, and allow the use of three out of the four hands to tie the shoe.
Hearing impairment	• No major modifications necessary.
Visual impairment	• No major modifications necessary.

Activity C: Me Switch

Teach students a sequence of three motions. It doesn't really matter what they are, but here is an example: Both hands above the eyes, both arms crossed over the chest, and one hand touching the other elbow. Then have each pair designate a person who is "it." This person counts to three, at which point both people simultaneously go into one of the motions. The person who is "it" wants the other person to do the same motion. If the partner does, she or he is now "it," and does the counting. If the partner doesn't do the same motion, the original partner remains "it" and counts again.

Adaptations for Students with Disabilities: Me Switch

Cognitive disabilities	• Use two motions instead of three.
Orthopedic impairment	• Create motions that all people can do in a group.
Hearing impairment	• No major modifications necessary
Visual impairment	• Use sounds or tactile motions (such as a clap, high five, stomp).

Activity D: Macro Rock/Paper/Scissors

Make sure that everyone knows the rules to Rock/Paper/Scissors (Rock = a closed fist; Paper = open hand; Scissors = fingers in a V, like a peace sign): On a signal, the partners do one of the three signals to see who wins. The winning combinations are: Rock beats Scissors, because it crushes the scissors; Scissors beats Paper, because it cuts the paper; Paper beats Rock, because it covers the rock. It is also possible to tie.

For the macro version, substitute these motions: Rock = crouching down with hands over head; Paper = standing with arms at sides; Scissors = standing with arms over head in a V. Have partners stand back to back. Each person must take a step forward to avoid hitting the other. They count to three while jumping up and down, spin around and go into one of the motions. The same winning combinations apply. (Thanks to Dick Jensen and others at Toki Middle School for this variation.)

Adaptations for Students with Disabilities: Macro Rock/Paper/Scissors

Cognitive disabilities	• Use two motions instead of three.
Orthopedic impairment	• Do regular Rock/Paper/Scissors, or make up three motions that all can do. Agree as a group on which motions win over the others.
Hearing impairment	• Stand front to front instead of back to back.
Visual impairment	• Stand front to front instead of back to back.

Activity E: High-Fives

With their partners, students should create three new high-fives. Tell people to be creative, and that it's OK to "cheat" by looking around at others for ideas. Once done, ask each pair to choose their favorite to share with the group.

Adaptations for Students with Disabilities: High-Fives

Cognitive disabilities	• Make up one new high-five instead of three.
	• Students can show a high-five they have done or seen before.
	• Students can take turns showing a new high-five and having everyone else try it, too.
Orthopedic impairment	• No major modifications necessary.
Hearing impairment	• No major modifications necessary.
Visual impairment	• No major modifications necessary.

Activity F: 1-1 Interview
Each person gets a minute or so to tell his or her life story to a partner. Afterward, partners take turns introducing each other to the group and telling as much as they can remember about the partner's "autobiography."

Adaptations for Students with Disabilities: 1-1 Interviews

Cognitive disabilities	• Brainstorm two or three questions that everyone can find out about their partner.
	• Have questions made up in advance for students to use.
Orthopedic impairment	• No major modifications necessary.
Hearing impairment	• Make sure students have an interpreter if necessary.
Visual impairment	• No major modifications necessary.

Activity G: Celebration
Partners create some way to celebrate—high-fives, a dance, a cheer, or some other expression. Then, throughout the day, when someone yells "Celebrate," each student must find his or her partner and celebrate together. (Thanks to Jim Dunn for this activity.)

Adaptations for Students with Disabilities: Celebration

Cognitive disabilities	• Model different ways to celebrate and allow students to choose the ones they want to do, if necessary.
	• Have a large group celebration rather than partner celebrations.
Orthopedic impairment	• No major modifications necessary.
Hearing impairment	• Make sure students have an interpreter if necessary.
Visual impairment	• No major modifications necessary.

SAMPLE PROCESSING QUESTIONS FOR PAIRED ACTIVITIES

- What was it like to work with so many different people?
- Why is it important to be able to work with everyone in this class?
- Is it easy or hard for you to approach someone new?

<u>Facilitation Notes</u>

As you can see, these activities have no deeper, underlying meaning. They are just fun things to do with another person and are rather non-threatening. Some groups need to hear that there is no point to the actual activity, but that there is a purpose to the exercise as a whole.

Depending on the group, it may be necessary to help students find initial partners, especially if you are aware of triads or students who are regularly excluded. See Pairing Strategies on page 35 for some useful techniques to try. Once you have done Celebration, initial partners for other activities can be assigned by having each person find his or her Celebration partner.

4. Group Bingo

Focus: Mixing with others in the group, learning about others, perspective taking
Materials: Premade group bingo cards (see sample on next page for design ideas)

Suggested Procedure

1. Each person gets a group bingo card (see sample on next page).
2. The task for students is to get as many different signatures on their card as possible in the amount of time allotted.

SAMPLE PROCESSING QUESTIONS FOR GROUP BINGO

- Did you learn anything about others in the class? What?
- Does anyone have a personal story to tell about any of the items on the card?
- What other things do you want to know about others in the class?

Facilitation Notes

It is important to take some time after the Group Bingo activity to let students compare notes about class members. Have them find out how many left-handers you have in the room, or how many people have broken a bone. Encourage individuals to share stories so that everyone can learn more about each other.

Rather than using the pre-made bingo card, the class can make up their own. Have them split into small groups and come up with three to five things they want to know about others in the class. Then they can make up cards that include these small groups' questions.

Adaptations for Students with Disabilities: Group Bingo

Cognitive disabilities	• Create a simpler card with fewer categories.
	• Do this in pairs so that those who need help reading are paired with better readers.
	• Do this in small groups. Students can see how many of the squares they can fill in with their group members.
Orthopedic impairment	• Have ink stamps/daubers or allow students to X off each square instead of getting them signed.
Hearing impairment	• Have interpreters available if necessary.
Visual impairment	• Have students do the activity in pairs.

Group Bingo (Sample card)

Someone who was born in the same season as you	Someone who has different-colored eyes than you	Someone who has been west of the Mississippi River	Someone who is left-handed	Someone who likes cats
Someone who has a different number of brothers and sisters than you	Someone who has been (or wants to go) Bungee jumping	Someone who has been out of the United States	Someone who can speak more than one language	Someone who has a pet other than a cat or dog
Someone who has twins in the family	Someone who enjoys reading	FREE SPACE	Someone who plays a team sport	Someone who likes dogs
Someone who was born on a holiday	Someone who can roll his or her tongue	Someone who thinks that 6:00 A.M. is too early to get up	Someone who has broken a bone	Someone who has eaten venison
Someone who has been cross-country skiing	Someone who has gotten stitches	Someone who knows who Maya Angelou is	Someone who belongs to a club	Someone who likes to fish

5. Categories and Lineups

Focus: Mixing with others, learning more about each other, appreciating diversity, perspective taking
Materials: None

<u>Suggested Procedure</u>

1. Clear away an area so that people can move around with ease.
2. Ask the class to line up according to:
    alphabetical order by first name
    alphabetical order by last name
    alphabetical order by mother's first name
    birthday
    shoe size
    height (shortest to tallest)
    hair color (darkest to lightest)
    skin color (darkest to lightest)
    thumb size (shortest to longest)
    etc.
3. Or, have them get into groups according to a certain category:
    number of siblings (count step and half brothers/sisters)
    season in which they were born
    favorite ice cream
    favorite day of the week
    eye color
    types of pets at home
    plans for after high school
    shirt color
    types of holidays they like to celebrate in winter (Hanukkah, Christmas, Kwaanza, Ramadan, none...)
    number of generations born in this country
    etc.
4. For each set of groupings, have students take the time to notice the diversity in the room. Make and take comments about what people observe. Maybe there are a lot of chocolate ice-cream lovers in the room, or everyone seems to like the same day of the week. Why is that?

SAMPLE PROCESSING QUESTIONS FOR CATEGORIES AND LINEUPS

- What do we seem to have in common in this class?
- What are some of our differences?
- How do you like the idea of this kind of diversity?
- What are some of the other things that make each one of us unique?

<u>Facilitation Notes</u>

This activity can be repeated throughout the year. Each time, the categories and lineups can be used to explore diversity issues on a deeper level. Have students create their own categories and lineups. Then use one as a warm-up for class.

Sometimes a student may not know the answer to a question, such as mother's first name, or what generation he or she is in this country. Make sure that students know that Challenge by Choice is in effect; they can choose to observe, use another family member's name, or join any group they wish. The object is not to be legally correct about such things, but to learn more about others.

Adaptations for Students with Disabilities: Categories and Lineups

Cognitive disabilities	• Students can sort themselves into groups by physical attributes, such as shirt color.
	• Do not time the activity.
Orthopedic impairment	• No major modifications necessary.
Hearing impairment	• Write the category or line-up question on the board.
Visual impairment	• Do not do a silent line-up—allow everyone to communicate verbally.

6. Differences and Commonalities

Focus: Perspective taking, mixing with others, appreciating diversity
Materials: None

Suggested Procedure

1. Following the format of the Categories and Lineups activity, ask the students to get into groups according to a number of the criteria listed.
2. Each time groups are formed, give 30–60 seconds to come up with as many things as possible that they all have in common that they **cannot see.**
3. Do the same with differences—have them identify at least one person in the group who is different from the others in some way that is not overtly apparent.
4. Have each group report at least one finding each time the category changes.

SAMPLE PROCESSING QUESTIONS FOR DIFFERENCES AND COMMONALITIES

- How easy or difficult was it for your group to find things in common?
- When you were the only one who was different, how did that feel?
- What can you learn about yourself when comparing yourself with others? What can you learn about others?
- Was it easier or harder to discover differences as opposed to commonalities? Why?
- Have you ever been in a situation where it seems that you have nothing in common with those around you? Does anyone have a situation like this to share?
- When meeting new people, how may you find out more about them?

Facilitation Notes

Keep this activity moving fairly quickly so that students can experience how easy or difficult it is to discover commonalities or differences. With some groups, it may also be necessary to ask that the commonalities and differences be kept "G" rated.

Adaptations for Students with Disabilities: Differences and Commonalities

Cognitive disabilities	• Allow students to use commonalities and differences they can see.
	• Do this activity in pairs.
Orthopedic impairment	• No major modifications necessary.
Hearing impairment	• Write the category or lineup question on the board.
	• Have interpreters available if necessary.
Visual impairment	• Do not do a silent category—allow everyone to communicate verbally.

7. Interactive Video

Focus: Active listening, hidden agendas, perspective taking
Materials: None

Suggested Procedure

1. Ask students to sit in a circle with everyone facing away from the middle.
2. One person stands in the middle and taps another on the shoulder. When the "tapped" person turns around, the person in the middle does a simple visual routine (e.g., hands on hips, tapping toe, with a cheerleading jump at the end).
3. Person #2 taps the next person in the circle and repeats the routine.
4. Person #3 continues by tapping the next person in the circle, etc.
5. When the routine goes all the way around the circle, the first person and the last person face each other. They count to three and do their respective routines (the first person does his or her original routine, the last person does what he or she saw).
6. Once someone has done the routine, she or he may watch the progression around the circle but may not comment on it (other than to laugh when appropriate).

SAMPLE PROCESSING QUESTIONS FOR INTERACTIVE VIDEO

- Did the activity change as it was repeated? What do you think was the cause of the change(s)?
- Do you believe everything you see or hear?
- Have you ever been in a situation where someone has reported seeing another person mishandling your property? Or that they have heard something about someone else? How do you usually react?
- How do you know it's the whole story? What can you do to make sure you are not overreacting?
- How can our own perspectives or abilities cause us to change a message?

Facilitation Notes

As you can see, this is a visual form of the game Telephone (or Operator). Generally, the routines change by becoming simpler, as it is impossible to keep track of all the details that one is witnessing. There is usually much laughing as the audience sees the changes taking place.

In some cases, especially in the elementary grades, students do not wait for the tapped person to turn around before beginning the routine. Obviously, that person will not have the benefit of seeing the full routine and will be at a severe disadvantage. This is a good teachable moment to focus on how one must be tuned in to the person one is trying to communicate with.

Adaptations for Students with Disabilities: Interactive Video

Cognitive disabilities	• Make the motions simple—one or two in a row.
	• Try playing the game Telephone/Operator first (pass along a short phrase).
Orthopedic impairment	• Make sure that the motions can be done by all in the class—sitting instead of standing, for example, or using only upper body.
	• This activity could be performed by an assistant, or with the help of an assistant.
Hearing impairment	• No major modifications necessary.
Visual impairment	• This is not an appropriate activity for visually impaired students.
	• Try the game Telephone/Operator instead.

8. King/Queen Frog

Focus: Active listening
Materials: None

Suggested Procedure

1. Have students sit in a circle.
2. Start by showing the motions of a King or Queen Frog (that is you), and have everyone practice it. The King/Queen frog motion consists of placing one hand in front of you, palm up, and slapping it with the other hand, followed by an upward motion (a jumping motion).
3. The person next to you indicates another animal using motions only. (For example, he could represent a skunk by holding his nose.) The next person might signify a bird by flapping her arms. This continues until everyone has created a unique motion and everyone has practiced them.
4. The game is now ready to begin. You start by showing the King/Queen Frog motion and then another one (say, the skunk—hold your nose). You have just passed it to the person who is the skunk.
5. Skunk now does his own motion, holding his nose; then he flaps his arms, thus passing it to the bird. This continues until someone makes a mistake by taking too long, forgetting a motion, or doing a motion wrong, for example.
6. That person then becomes the King/Queen Frog and takes your chair. Everyone else moves over one chair until the empty chair is filled. This often means that only part of the group moves, while the others stay put.
7. The catch is that the animal motion stays with the chair; it does not move with the person. So, those who have just moved have to learn a new motion.

SAMPLE PROCESSING QUESTIONS FOR KING/QUEEN FROG

- Did you ever feel put "on the spot"? When?
- How much concentration did it take to stay focused on the activity? What strategies did you use?
- Are there things that we all did that helped us stay focused, or distracted us during this game?
- Was this activity communication? How do you know?
- What other forms of nonverbal communication are there? Can you demonstrate some?

Facilitation Notes

Once this activity is started, it is possible to hear a pin drop. Great concentration is required, and students really get drawn into this quiet game. Although it is possible to do this in large groups, it is best done with groups of about 10–15. If you have a large class, teach it in a large group, and practice for awhile. Then have the class split into smaller groups to play.

Generally, making a mistake is of little consequence in this activity because the person just takes a different spot in the circle. If it appears that it may be a problem (for example, where someone is chided for making the mistake, or appears to be making the mistake on purpose), then it may be necessary to have a short discussion about put-downs or hidden agendas.

Other variations are to have someone who knows sign language teach the signs for the various chosen animals, or to use vocabulary words or concepts from your classes for the students to represent with their motions.

This is a good activity to pull out now and again when the class needs to calm down after a loud and rambunctious project.

Adaptations for Students with Disabilities: King/Queen Frog

Cognitive disabilities	• Do this in small groups.
	• Have the motion stay with the person, so that when everyone moves, they all still do the same motion.
Orthopedic impairment	• Make sure that all motions can be done by all students in the class.
	• Allow a longer time to complete motions.
Hearing impairment	• Have everyone learn the sign for their chosen animal and use sign language.
Visual impairment	• Use sounds instead of motions.
	• Do this in smaller groups.

Deinhibitizer Activities

After students have relaxed a bit, learned each others' names, and shared a little about themselves, Deinhibitizer activities can be introduced. These activities require a little more risk taking than Ice Breakers. For example, people may be asked to hold hands for an activity, they might be put on the spot by being in the middle of the class for a game, or the activity may call for people to act silly. Deinhibitizers are meant to get people laughing and relaxed. Ice breakers begin to loosen people up, and Deinhibitizers finish the job.

These activities also allow a group to begin exploring trust issues. Since many of these activities are silly, ask students in which places they would be willing to play the games. Then discuss why they might choose to play here, but not in public. Since this class of individuals has been together for a while, they will probably be willing to risk acting silly because they are no longer with strangers. This is a good distinction when moving into trust issues.

9. 1,2,3 Mississippi

Focus: Being put on the spot, name reminder
Materials: None

Suggested Procedure

1. The group stands in a circle, with you in the middle.
2. Ask students to make sure they know the name of the people to their immediate right and left.
3. Notify them that this game is intended to put people on the spot. Then point to someone and say "right." That person is to say the name of the person on her right.
4. Next point to someone and say "left." He is to say the name of the person on his left.
5. After some practice, tell the class that you are now going to interject something that will mess up their minds. It is the phrase "1,2,3, Mississippi." Now when you say "right" or "left," you will also say "1,2,3 Mississippi." Whoever is being pointed to must say the correct name before you get to the end of the phrase. If not, that person takes your place in the middle.
6. Practice this a few times before putting anyone in the hot seat.
7. For added challenge, add the commands "2-left" or "2-right." Then whoever is being pointed to must say the correct name of the person two away from him or her in the correct direction.
8. You can also say "you" or "me." If "you" is stated, then whoever is being pointed to must say his or her own name. If "me" is stated, then whoever is being pointed to must say the pointer's name.

SAMPLE PROCESSING QUESTIONS FOR 1,2,3 MISSISSIPPI

- How did it feel to be put on the spot?
- Did it seem as if people were able to laugh at themselves, or was that too risky? Why do you think this is?
- Why do you think it was so difficult to focus when someone was yelling "1,2,3 Mississippi" at you?
- Are there other situations when it is difficult to focus at school? Does anyone want to share one?

Facilitation Notes

Depending on the age of your class, you can use the basic version, or you can add more challenges. It is also possible to start with the basic game and make it harder as you progress through the year. If the class knows each others' names already, try having people assume a persona from your studies, or a favorite book character.

It is important that the class be prepared to be put on the spot, and ready to laugh at themselves and with others. This is generally not a problem, unless there is some active antagonism in the class. If so, this activity should be avoided for the time being.

If you have a large class, try having more than one person in the middle at a time.

Adaptations for Students with Disabilities: 1,2,3 Mississippi

Cognitive disabilities	• Use only "you" and "me."
	• Point first to the person who is calling the name, then to the person you want named.
	• Count to 10 instead of saying "1,2,3 Mississippi."
	• You stay in the middle throughout the activity.
Orthopedic impairment	• Allow students more time to call each name.
Hearing impairment	• Teach everyone the sign for "right" and "left" so all can use it.
	• Count by putting up fingers 1–5, or 1–10.
	• Allow for signing of names.
Visual impairment	• Give people time to learn who is next to them whenever anyone moves.

10. ¿Como Estás?

Focus: Acting silly, name reminder
Materials: None

Suggested Procedure

1. This can be an active game, so it is best done outside, or in a large room such as a gym or all-purpose room. It can be done in the classroom if people move slowly—walking instead of running.
2. Have the class stand in a circle. Two people stand outside the circle.
3. The two people outside are "it." They decide on a way to "locomote." They can walk, skip, gallop, etc. Then they use this locomotion as they go around the circle together.
4. They choose two people standing next to each other and tap them on the shoulder. The two new people turn around to face the ones who are "it."
5. Each person from one pair shakes hands with someone from the other pair. Simultaneously each person says, "¿Como estás?" Then, simultaneously each one answers, "Me llamo *(name)*." They then shake hands with the other person in the opposite pair and repeat the niceties.
6. Now each pair, using the original locomotion, takes off in opposite directions around the circle. (The empty spot left by the second pair should stay open.)
7. When the pairs meet on the other side, they go through the whole "¿como estás?" routine again, after which they continue on their separate ways around the circle.
8. The pair that gets back to the empty spot first stays. The other team is "it." They decide on a new form of locomotion, and the whole thing starts over again.

> **SAMPLE PROCESSING QUESTIONS FOR ¿COMO ESTÁS?**
>
> • Were there winners and losers in this game? Why or why not?
> • Did you feel silly playing this game? Why or why not?
> • What if we did this in a public place? Would you have played? Why or why not?
> • Why might you be willing to do this activity here, but not in another place?

Facilitation Notes

As with most Icebreakers and Deinhibitizers, it is not usually necessary to spend a great deal of time processing this activity. If there are issues that arise—like someone putting another down, or people not wanting to stand next to someone (a mixing issue)—then it may be necessary to spend some time talking about what happened during the activity. For the most part, though, the point is to have fun and create an atmosphere where people can feel comfortable with each other—to "connect."

⚠️ One safety note with this activity: If a pair decides to "locomote" backwards, other group members must watch out for their safety by warning them when they are approaching the other pair (who are also going backwards) when they meet on the other side of the circle.

Adaptations for Students with Disabilities: ¿Como Estás?

Cognitive disabilities	• Have students say "¿Como Estás?" and their names only once each time.
Orthopedic impairment	• This may not be appropriate for students who are orthopedically impaired.
	• Use only walking for this activity.
	• Ask the class how to make it fair for everyone; choose a type of locomotion that evens the playing field.
Hearing impairment	• Students can shake hands only.
	• Teach and do a short patty-cake rhythm instead of "¿Como estás?"
Visual impairment	• Have students walk only.

11. Morphing

Focus: Acting silly, mixing
Materials: Stopwatch (optional)

Suggested Procedure

1. Clear a small area in the room. Have everyone stand in a circle.
2. Make sure that everyone knows the game Rock/Paper/Scissors, and agree on the rules for that game.
3. Show everyone the following motions: egg (squatting down), chicken (hands under armpits squawking like a chicken), dinosaur (arms up, making roaring noises), superhero (flying through the air), know-it-all smartypants (arms crossed, looking smug).
4. The object is to get as high up in the chain as possible in a given amount of time (I usually go for two minutes or so).
5. Everyone begins as an egg. Everyone then finds another egg and does Rock/Paper/Scissors until a winner is established. Whoever wins gets to move up the chain to chicken. He or she must then find another chicken with whom to do Rock/Paper/Scissors.
6. The winner moves up to the next step (dinosaur), while the loser goes down a step (back to egg).
7. This continues for the allotted time. When someone makes it up to know-it-all smartypants, that person then stands outside the circle, arms crossed, looking smug.
8. In other words, if you win, you're out.

> **SAMPLE PROCESSING QUESTIONS FOR MORPHING**
>
> - How do you feel about where you ended up in the sequence?
> - Did you think this game was fun? Why or why not?
> - How did you like acting like a chicken/dinosaur with everyone else?

<u>Facilitation Notes</u>

This game can be played with any group larger than eight or so. It has been played with hundreds. People seem to love it because it is funny, and there is an element of challenge injected by having to beat the clock. I like to tell people that wherever they end up, they must walk that way for the rest of the day....

Also try making up your own motions. We have done the history of candy: licorice, taffy, lollipop, chewing gum and chocolate bar. Or, have the students make up the sequence and motions with a connection to a sequence or chronology from their studies.

Adaptations for Students with Disabilities: Morphing

Cognitive disabilities	• Use fewer stages in the chain.
	• Teach Rock/Paper/Scissors first and play it for awhile before attempting to add this variation.
Orthopedic impairment	• Create motions that all students can do.
Hearing impairment	• No major modifications necessary.
Visual impairment	• Do this in pairs; each partner takes a turn doing the Rock/Paper/Scissors.

12. Screaming Toes

Focus: Acting silly, mixing
Materials: None

<u>Suggested Procedure</u>

1. Clear away a space and have the class stand in a circle.
2. Tell everyone that they should look down at someone else's shoes. When you say "look up," they should look that person in the face.
3. If that person is looking at someone else, nothing happens.
4. If that person is looking directly back (i.e., making eye contact), then both parties act surprised by letting out a little scream or yell.
5. Those who make eye contact then meet in the middle for a high-five, and switch places in the circle.

> **SAMPLE PROCESSING QUESTIONS FOR SCREAMING TOES**
>
> - How did you like screaming during this activity?
> - Did you try to avoid eye contact or to get eye contact? Why?
> - What made this game fun/not fun?

Facilitation Notes

If you have a large class, teach the activity as written above, then try the following variations. (1) Have each person identify a partner across the circle (they should know that they are each other's partner). When you say to look down, they can then look either at the shoes of their partner, **or at the shoes of the person to their own left or right.** The choices are now narrowed down to three, and more action will take place. Even after they change places with someone, they should keep their same partner. (2) Have the class make two or three smaller circles. They can look at anyone in their circle. If eye contact is made, they both scream, and then join a different circle. (Sometimes it is necessary to practice screaming with the entire group before asking them to scream solo.)

Adaptations for Students with Disabilities: Screaming Toes

Cognitive disabilities	• Explain directions slowly with a demonstration if necessary.
Orthopedic impairment	• No major modifications necessary.
Hearing impairment	• No major modifications necessary.
Visual impairment	• This is not a good activity for students with visual impairment.

MPS: Connecting Eyes*

13. Get the Point

Focus: Unselfconscious touch
Materials: None

Suggested Procedure

1. Clear a space and have the class stand in a circle.
2. Ask everyone to put out their right hand, palm up.
3. Then have everyone put the pointer finger of their left hand in the palm of the person to their left.
4. When you say "go," people should try to catch the neighbor's finger in their palm, but not let their own finger get caught.
5. Try this a few times, then switch hands.

SAMPLE PROCESSING QUESTIONS FOR GET THE POINT

- Was it difficult to touch (or be touched by) someone else in this activity? Why or why not?
- What kinds of touching can be threatening?
- If you do not want to be touched in this class during an activity, how should you (and we) respond to that?
- Are there any guidelines we could make about touching, to make sure it is a safe/acceptable thing for everyone?

Facilitation Notes

This is a short activity that can be used as an energizer, or if you only have a few minutes left in class. Try mixing up the "Go" signal to keep people a little off balance. For example, say "Go" a couple of times, then say, "On your mark, get set...." People will jump in before you say "Go." Or, try "On your mark, go!"

---

* See footnote on page 33.

This is a good activity to use if you are concerned about touching issues. It allows people to touch each other in a very nonthreatening way, which then allows you to talk about it.

Adaptations for Students with Disabilities: Get the point

Cognitive disabilities	• Students can try this with partners first, using only one hand to begin with, then two hands. Then try the whole class together.
Orthopedic impairment	• This activity may not be appropriate for students with an orthopedic impairment.
Hearing impairment	• Use a visual signal or a drumbeat to signal "Go."
Visual impairment	• No major modifications necessary.

14. Speed Rabbit

Focus: Acting silly, being put on the spot, mixing
Materials: None

<u>Suggested Procedure</u>

1. Clear a space and stand in a circle. You take the middle.
2. Teach a variety of motions, to be made by three people as described below.
3. Point to someone and say *"elephant"*: The person you point to makes the trunk by clasping her hands together, arms held straight, pointed at the ground, while the people on either side make ears (one hand up near the middle person's head, the other hand near his or her hip).
4. Point to someone and say *"moose"*: That person puts both hands up by her eyes and sticks her elbows out in front of her (this is the nose of the moose), the people on either side turn their backs to her and put their arms in the air (antlers).
5. Point to someone and say, *"flight attendant"*: That person mimes putting on an oxygen mask, while the people on either side smile and point to the "exits."
6. Once these have been established and practiced, the game can begin. Tell students that you will point to someone, say "elephant" or "moose" or "flight attendant," and count to 10 as fast as you can. If they go through their motions before you get to 10, you continue. If not, the slowest person takes your place in the middle.
7. After doing this for awhile, add more. Here are some suggestions: *Cow:* middle—holds hands out with thumbs down; sides—pull on thumbs. *Roller coaster:* middle—puts hands on face/cheeks and pulls back to simulate g-force; sides—put hands in air and scream. *Rabbit:* middle—hands on head to make ears; sides—stomp a foot like Thumper. *Palm Tree:* middle—arms over head and swaying; sides—do hula dance. *Ostrich:* sides—hold hands to make a circle; middle—put head in circle to simulate putting head in sand. *Jello:* sides—hold hands around middle person; middle—jiggle.
8. Students can try making up their own.

SAMPLE PROCESSING QUESTIONS FOR SPEED RABBIT

- What is the point to this game?
- Did you have fun playing it? Why or why not?
- How did you feel about being put in the middle? Did you feel put on the spot, or were you looking forward to it? Why?

Facilitation Notes

This is a classic Deinhibitizer activity. As with most of these games, there is not much of a point in and of itself. They are designed to be silly, funny, and fun if people are ready to let their guard down a bit. This game has helped many classes finally break down and laugh. Other classes see some students exercise their choice to observe because they are not ready to be quite this silly yet. Whatever happens, you will have more information about your class by doing this activity. By the way, unless you are working with young children, I recommend that you do not do this on the first day.

If you don't like the slowest person being forced into the middle, try having the person who is pointed to go in the middle if the team doesn't do the motion in time. This changes the dynamic. You can also have the pointer in the middle pick one of the three to go into the middle.

The book *Adventures in Peacemaking* has a nice variation on this game that involves making up motions to go along with feelings. For example, the group agrees how "anger" would look (middle person frowning, side people raising fists), or excited, scared, and so on, and use these in the game.

Adaptations for Students with Disabilities: Speed Rabbit

Cognitive disabilities	• Create motions that require one person or pairs only (e.g., *frog*: one person squatting down).
	• Only do two different motions at first. Add more later.
	• Don't count at first.
	• You stay in the middle.
Orthopedic impairment	• Make sure that all students can do the motions—ask for help from the students about how to modify them.
Hearing impairment	• Use your fingers to count.
	• Stay with the student in the middle to help say the name of the animal or thing.
Visual impairment	• Teach the motions verbally, and allow practice time for the motions.
	• Stay with the student in the middle to help with pointing.

15. Elbow Tag

Focus: Unselfconscious touch, acting silly, hidden agendas, mixing
Materials: None

Suggested Procedure

1. This activity should be done in a large room or outside. People will be running.
2. Have the class get into pairs.
3. Students should stand in a large circle, or scattered about, and interlock elbows with their partner. They do not move unless tagged.
4. One pair is chosen to unlock elbows. One person in this pair is "it," while the other is chased. They run around.
5. If the person being chased doesn't want to be caught, then she or he can lock elbows with someone else.
6. Since three is a crowd, the person on the other end of the trio must now unlock his or her elbow and become the one who is chased. For example, if the "chasee" (A) locks elbows with B, who is attached to C, then C is now chased.

7. This continues until time is up or people fall down from exhaustion.

SAMPLE PROCESSING QUESTIONS FOR ELBOW TAG

- Would you rather be "it" or be chased? Why?
- Did it matter to you whom you were partnered up with? Why or why not? How did you feel about changing partners?
- Why is it important to be able to work with everyone in the class? When is it appropriate to expect mixing, and when might it be unrealistic?

<u>Facilitation Notes</u>

Once people understand how this game works, it is a favorite of all ages. It is helpful to show this in slow motion at first. Later there will inevitably be some confusion—when, for example, someone thinks that a partner has been tagged and takes off. (Suddenly there will be three people running around instead of two.) The students will figure it out eventually, and it is good practice for later problem solving. Watching their strategies during the confusion can give you some insight into the decision-making style of this particular group of students.

A few issues tend to come up during elbow tag. One is when someone gets stuck being "it" for a long time and is obviously getting tired. One strategy to deal with this situation is for the person who is "it" to hook on to someone else, thus creating a new "it." Another issue is when someone is enjoying being chased, and doesn't hook on to anyone, but keeps running around. This scenario offers an opportunity to talk about hidden agendas, since the rest of the class will be getting fidgety, frustrated, or bored by standing around and watching the action instead of being part of it.

Another issue that can arise in some groups is being paired with others. This is a great activity in which to have people choose their own partners, because they will be mixed up anyway by the end of the game. It is also obvious when students will only latch onto their friends, or if girls hook onto girls, and boys to boys (a classic issue in grades 4 and 5). This is not necessarily a bad thing, but it offers an opportunity to talk about mixing and why it is important to be able to work with everyone in the class. It can also be a time for the students to relate how difficult it is to mix, and how it might be unreasonable to expect them to do it all of the time (a valid point that I have discussed with many groups).

Here's a variation for elbow tag: Have the person who is being chased spontaneously choose a form of movement (skipping, crab walk, hopping, doing the twist, etc.). The person who is "it" must copy that movement when chasing. The next person who is chased can change the movement. This adds a new dimension to the game.

Another variation is what I call the "graduate school" level. When someone links up to an established pair, the person released is now "it" (the tagger). This variation causes quite a bit of confusion, which can be fun if the students are ready for it.

When working on inclusion in class, it is important to "frontload" the topic—especially for upper-elementary through middle-school students. Discuss the concept of how being able to work with everyone is the sign of a healthy community. Remind them that we are not asking people to be best friends, but only to work together on specified tasks. Ask students to give examples of how one's reaction to a new partner might be a put-down, and how one can react in a way that is welcoming. Then have them **practice.**

Adaptations for Students with Disabilities: Elbow Tag

Cognitive disabilities	• Reiterate rules. Practice game one time before beginning, talk about it, and then go on.
Orthopedic impairment	• In the case of a nonambulatory person, the partner can put a hand on the wheelchair handle or tray instead of hooking elbows.
Hearing impairment	• No major modifications are necessary.
Visual impairment	• Make the play area smaller.
	• Make a defined area on the floor by using a rope, mat, etc., so that students can feel the boundary when moving around.

MPS: Elbow Tag

16. Little Bert

Focus: Acting Silly

Materials: Little Bert story (see below)

Suggested Procedure

1. Clear a space in the room; put chairs (one for each student) in the middle. Chairs should be in two rows, back to back. (You can also do this outside by sitting or standing in two lines, back to back.)
2. From a hat, each person picks a persona from the story below. Depending on the number of students in your class, each character will probably have more than one person playing the part.
3. Students should sit randomly in the chairs.
4. Read the Little Bert story. Each time a character's name is called, those representing the character stand up, run clockwise around the chairs, and sit back down in their own chairs.
5. If "everyone," or "the whole family" is said, everyone stands up, runs around the chairs, and sits back down.

LITTLE BERT

This is a story about Little Bert. He lived with his younger sister, Victoria, Mom, Dad and Grandma. They lived in an apartment in the city with a cat, C'mere, and a parrot named Geraldine. One day Little Bert and Victoria wanted to ride their bikes to the park. Mom and Dad thought it was too dangerous, but Grandma told them that the kids had to have some freedom. C'mere just sat watching Geraldine. Geraldine was nervous.

Finally Mom and Dad relented, so Little Bert and Victoria put on their helmets, and away they rode. About an hour later, Victoria came running into the house yelling that Little Bert was nowhere to be found. So, everyone but Bert went running to the park. Even C'mere and Geraldine got into the act.

Grandma called, "Little Bert, where are you?" Victoria looked in all their secret hiding places, and Mom and Dad just walked around acting worried. Geraldine flew up into the trees and spied Little Bert across the street in the ice cream shop. Geraldine flew down to Grandma and tried to land in her hair as a signal. Grandma just got angry. Finally, Geraldine called, "C'mere, C'mere, I found him!" Understanding the universal animal language, C'mere got Victoria's attention and led her to the store.

Little Bert and Victoria came running across the street, and the whole family was united once again. Mom and Dad took everyone out for ice cream.

> **SAMPLE PROCESSING QUESTIONS FOR LITTLE BERT**
>
> - Were you happy with the character you portrayed? Why or why not?
> - Were you hoping that your character would have a large part or a small one? Why?
> - How did you deal with the movement part of this activity—how did you keep things safe?

Facilitation Notes

This is just a fun activity that gets people moving around and acting spontaneously. It is a good activity to do in conjunction with the Night at the Improv activity described below.

Rather than using the random method of assigning characters, try having people choose their character. This may mean that you have more of one than another, but it can offer some fun discussion about why people chose the characters they did. Sometimes everyone wants to be the title character because it seemingly is the most glamorous. If this occurs, then the idea of sharing responsibility can be discussed, because not all parts of a task are glamorous, but they must still be done.

Adaptations for Students with Disabilities: Little Bert

Cognitive disabilities	• Have people simply stand up and sit down again when their character's name is called.
Orthopedic impairment	• Have a special sound or motion that is done when a character's name is called.
Hearing impairment	• This may not be appropriate for students who are hearing-impaired.
Visual impairment	• Have people simply stand up and sit down again when their character's name is called.

17. Night at the Improv[*]

Focus: Spontaneity, being put on the spot, active listening
Materials: None

Suggested Procedure

1. Clear a space and have people get into pairs.
2. *Phase I:* With a partner, show how you can create a sentence by having the partners alternate words. The trick is to listen to what your partner is saying, rather than jump to conclusions about what you think he or she will say. For example—You: *"Once..."* Partner: *"there..."* You: *"was..."* Partner: *"a..."* You: *"yellow..."* Partner: *"jacket..."* You: *"that..."* Partner: *"flew..."* You: *"up..."* Partner: *"under..."* You: *"your..."* Partner: *"shirt..."* You: *"period."*
3. Have partners practice for awhile.
4. *Phase II:* Now have the group form a circle.
5. Create sentences with the whole group by having each person contribute a word around the circle. Do this for awhile.
6. *Phase III:* Designate a stage area. Create a whole story as described below.
7. Have someone contribute a sentence that is the beginning of a story. Examples might include: "Once upon a time there was a little goblin" or "Call me Ishmael" or "The whole

---

[*] Thanks to Michael Popowits of Michael T. Popowits & Associates for these ideas.

thing was a big mess." This person stands at the stage area at one end.

8. Then have someone contribute the ending sentence of the story. Examples might include: "And they lived miserably ever after" or "They rode off into the sunset" or "The whole thing was a big mess." This person stands at the other end of the stage area. Have the two people on the stage say their parts of the story in order.

9. Now have someone give the middle of the story. This could be, "We thought the truth was out there" or "He fell asleep for a long, long time" or "The whole thing was a big mess." This person stands between the beginning and end people. In turn, they should say their lines of the whole story, as is.

10. Now, have people begin putting themselves into the story with their own lines, one or two people at a time. Then, repeat the story as it stands.

11. Finally, the whole class should be lined up in the stage area. The entire story should be recited with emotion.

SAMPLE PROCESSING QUESTIONS FOR NIGHT AT THE IMPROV

- At the beginning of this activity, how did you like being put on the spot to come up with a word or phrase so quickly?
- During the story, did you wait until the story unfolded or did you jump in right away? Why did you use that particular strategy?
- Was this difficult or easy for you? Why do you think so?

Facilitation Notes

If the students are ready to be spontaneous, this can be a wonderfully fun activity. Even if they aren't feeling very spontaneous at the beginning, try doing this periodically throughout the year. It provides good listening practice, and the creativity level rises each time it is attempted.

During the story, some people stand back for awhile to reflect more on the story, while others jump in right away. This can open the door to a discussion about people who are more action-oriented versus people who prefer to reflect before taking action.

Of course, some classes might need to be reminded to keep the language "G" rated.

Adaptations for Students with Disabilities: Night at the Improv

Cognitive disabilities	• Do this in small groups. Have students write down each word.
Orthopedic impairment	• No major modifications necessary.
Hearing impairment	• Write down the words and sentences.
Visual impairment	• No major modifications necessary.

Challenge by Choice Activities

It is one thing to talk about Challenge by Choice; it is another to experience it. A main goal for any group is for its members to be as independent as possible, with people getting their needs met because they are able to *ask* for what they need. In the beginning, when norms are not yet established, many people are willing to subjugate their own needs in order to fit into the group. Challenge by Choice cannot be overemphasized in these cases. An atmosphere where choice is honored is empowering; it allows students to take the first steps away from dependence.

These activities are Ice Breakers and Deinhibitizers that lend themselves to a beginning exploration of Challenge by Choice. They are not the only possible activities. Moreover, when an issue of choice is brought up during any activity, a teachable moment exists.

18. Neighbors

Focus: Challenge by Choice, being put on the spot, hidden agendas, perspective taking
Materials: Place markers for everyone (poly dots, scrap paper, pieces of cloth, etc.)

<u>Suggested Procedure</u>

1. Clear a space and have students stand in a circle. You take the middle.
2. Each person stands on a place marker.
3. The person in the middle (you at this point) asks a question that is already **true for him or her.** For example, I can ask, "Is there anyone here who has a brother?" because I have a brother. But I cannot ask, "Is there anyone here who has been to Hawaii?" because I have not been to Hawaii.
4. Once the question is asked, anyone who can answer "yes" steps forward into the middle of the circle. Then, each of these people should move to find any empty place that is not their own.
5. The person in the middle also finds an empty place—thus leaving someone without a spot, which makes this new person take the middle to ask the next question.
6. Some rules you may wish to interject after the game gets going: (1) No one can move to the place next to him or her; everyone must skip at least one place marker. (2) To add another dynamic, you can have anyone who says "no" to a question be allowed to fill an empty spot next to him or her if available.

SAMPLE PROCESSING QUESTIONS FOR NEIGHBORS

- Would it have been possible to *not* move even if you answered "yes" to the question? How would we know? Would it matter?
- What kind of choices did you make? For example, how did you interpret number of brothers and sisters (if this was asked)? Did you include step- or half-siblings? Is one interpretation right and another wrong?
- What happened when you were challenged about your interpretation? How did you—and the group—handle that?
- How should we handle choices that people make, even if we don't agree with them? When is it necessary to intervene or challenge a choice that someone is making?

<u>Facilitation Notes</u>

This activity provides a non-threatening way to bring up the issue of choice. Sometimes there are disagreements of interpretation about questions. Is one wrong and the other right? Or are they just different? This can lead to a larger discussion about choices, and when to question the choices that a peer or friend is making, especially if it seems to cause harm. Challenge by Choice is also "fuzzy" because people genuinely want others to succeed. Success, in itself, is open to many different interpretations. The only way to come to mutual understanding about these issues is to discuss the varying points of view.

A nice variation to this game is to do it in pairs.* Each marker is occupied by two people who stay together for the whole activity. Two people are in the middle and must

---
* Thanks to Jim Dunn for this variation.

decide on something that is true for **both** of them. In order to move to a new place marker, the question must be true for both people in a pair. They then run together to a different marker.

Adaptations for Students with Disabilities: Neighbors

Cognitive disabilities	• Reiterate rules and provide several examples.
	• Create some generic prompt cards that say: "I wonder if any of my neighbors…" (have shoes on, like pizza, watch TV, etc.).
	• Smaller group may work better.
Orthopedic impairment	• Have another participant assist in pushing the wheelchair if necessary.
Hearing impairment	• Use another participant or interpreter to indicate the hearing-impaired student's questions and explain others' statements.
	• Have students make up cards ahead of time that they can use to ask their questions.
Visual impairment	• Have another participant act as a guide to assist the visually impaired person to a poly-spot (plastic place marker).
	• Do this activity in pairs.
Notes	• Play the entire game with all participants working as partners.

MPS: My Neighbor

19. Everybody's It

Focus: Challenge by Choice
Materials: None

Suggested Procedure

1. This is an outside or gym activity. Create boundaries of which everyone is aware.
2. The only rule for this game is that *everybody* is "it."
3. Once the game starts, if a person gets tagged, he or she must squat down.
4. If two people tag each other, they both squat down.
5. When only a few people are left, count down from 10 and start again. This goes quickly.
6. Try playing a few times before talking about it. Then play it again after your discussion.

SAMPLE PROCESSING QUESTIONS FOR EVERYBODY'S IT

- Did you find yourself backing away from others or going after people? Did you do both?
- When did you use these strategies, and how effective were they?
- Are there times in your life (school, home, teams, organizations) when you go after something?
- Are there times in your life (school, home, teams, organizations) when you sit back and wait?
- What are some choices you have made in your life (even today)?
- Did some people choose to be tagged quickly so they didn't have to keep playing? Is that an acceptable choice? Why or why not?

Facilitation Notes

This activity offers an opportunity to talk about other choices during the year, because the game itself is the picture of choices—sometimes running after someone, sometimes backing away.

A variation on this theme is Hospital Tag. The same rules apply, except that each person must be tagged three times before squatting down. Each time someone is tagged, he or she puts a hand over the spot that was touched. A cautionary statement should be made that tagging with the feet is not acceptable, as it can cause someone to be kicked or tripped.

Adaptations for Students with Disabilities: Everybody's It

Cognitive disabilities	• For safety reasons, you may want participants to move out of the defined area after they are tagged.
Orthopedic impairment	• For safety reasons, you may want participants to move out of the defined area after they are tagged.
	• Don't say "squat down," only say "freeze."
Hearing impairment	• No major modifications necessary.
Visual impairment	• Play the game with auditory feedback (bells, clapping, talking). Boundaries should be physically marked (with rope, mats, etc...).
	• When tagged, these students need to move out of the defined area so that others do not trip over them.

MPS: Everyone Is It

20. Growth Circles

Focus: Challenge by Choice, perspective taking
Materials: Ropes or tape on the floor—in three concentric circles (see Figure 4.1)[3]

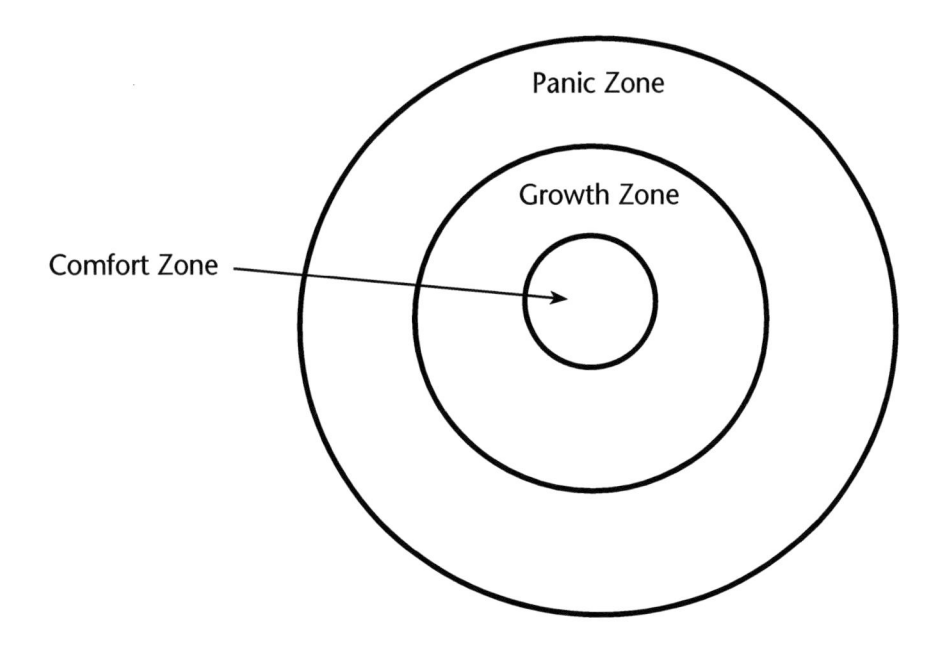

Figure 4.1

<u>Suggested Procedure</u>

1. Outline the growth circles on the floor and discuss their meaning (see facilitation notes).
2. Ask questions like those below, and have people put themselves into the circles they feel most appropriate.
   How do you feel about:
   • spiders?
   • speaking in front of a large group?

- singing solo in front of a large group?
- singing in a choir?
- Bungee jumping?
- telling a family member that you love him or her?
- heights?
- confronting a friend about something he or she did or said?
- snakes?
- taking a math test?
- introducing yourself to someone new?
- taking a driver's test?

3. After each question is asked and people have moved into position, give the students a chance to comment on why they put themselves in their particular spots. Is there a story to share? Who is sharing a point of view?
4. After a few of your questions, allow students to ask any questions they have for the class.

SAMPLE PROCESSING QUESTIONS FOR GROWTH CIRCLES

- Were you surprised by where you ended up compared with others?
- How can we support the choices each of us makes?
- How can we encourage you to step into your growth zone without putting too much pressure on you? What kind of encouragement is useful to you?
- What can we do to respectfully tell people when the encouragement they are giving is too much?

Facilitation Notes

When considering the idea of Challenge by Choice, it is helpful to talk about the idea of challenge as well as choice. The Growth Circles game allows this. When we are in our comfort zones, each of us is in a place that is safe and secure. By choosing to step out of the comfort zone to the growth zone, we are open to new ideas and experiences. We are, in essence, breaking new ground. Although not always comfortable, this is a place for optimum learning.

What we try to avoid is going beyond the growth zone into the panic zone. The panic zone is a place where learning cannot take place because the threat is too great.

Challenge by Choice affords the opportunity for students (and teachers) to make the decisions that are right for them. It is a delicate balancing act for each individual—how to take advantage of challenging opportunities without going over the edge.

This activity helps the class to explore these issues. Through the discussion, boundaries can begin to be established about how much to encourage people to push themselves, and how to support the choices each person makes.

Adaptations for Students with Disabilities: Growth Circles

Cognitive disabilities	• Focus on one area at a time (comfort zone first, then growth zone, then panic zone), so that students can more easily distinguish their feelings.
Orthopedic impairment	• Make sure there is enough room for wheelchairs in each zone.
Hearing impairment	• Have an interpreter available if necessary.
Visual impairment	• Have a partner help the student to the area of his or her choice.
	• Make sure the boundaries are well defined.

21. Song Tag

Focus: Challenge by Choice, being put on the spot, acting silly, perspective taking
Materials: None

Suggested Procedure

1. Clear an area and have students stand in a circle. You stand in the middle.
2. Tell the class that you will start singing a song.
3. When someone thinks of a song that connects with your song in any way, then that person steps in and starts singing that song.
4. You will then take that person's place in the circle.
5. This continues for awhile; people choose to step into the middle and sing, but not everyone is expected to take a turn. In fact, some people will take more than one turn.

SAMPLE PROCESSING QUESTIONS FOR SONG TAG

- Why did you choose to either step into the middle and sing or stay back and observe for the whole time?
- Was it possible to participate in the activity without taking a turn in the middle? How?
- What does Challenge by Choice mean to you?

Facilitation Notes

This activity can be highly threatening for some people. Others can't wait to get in the middle and sing. It is a good way to explore the issue of choice, because all participants feel involved in the activity even if they are observers. It is also possible to branch off into a discussion of individual strengths. Some love to sing, others to dance, read, participate in athletics, communicate, and so on.

Adaptations for Students with Disabilities: Song Tag

Cognitive disabilities	• Brainstorm a list of songs in advance on a given topic. Practice them all first, then try the activity.
Orthopedic impairment	• No major modifications necessary.
Hearing impairment	• This activity may not be appropriate for people with hearing impairments.
Visual impairment	• Have well-defined boundaries.
	• Start off sitting, and have people stand up when they wish.

22. Group Interview

Focus: Challenge by Choice, being put on the spot, active listening, perspective taking
Materials: None

Suggested Procedure

1. Have students sit in a circle. Ask for a volunteer to be interviewed by the whole group.
2. The idea is for this person to be questioned by the others and to answer as honestly as possible.
3. If the person being interviewed doesn't want to answer a question, she or he can pass.

4. Be prepared with your own questions to help get the process going.
5. Allow yourself to be interviewed as well.

SAMPLE PROCESSING QUESTIONS FOR GROUP INTERVIEW

- How did it feel to be the center of attention?
- Did it seem as if you really had a choice about answering the questions? Why or why not?
- How did your classmates treat you when you were being interviewed?

<u>Facilitation Notes</u>

Group Interview is an activity that can be revisited throughout the school year so that everyone who wants to be interviewed can do so. It is a great activity to do when there are 10 minutes left at the end of a class.

Generally, students are respectful of the difficult position the interviewee is in and will ask respectful questions. With practice, the questions become deeper and more thoughtful.

If it is early in the year and a student who has a history of being teased by others is being interviewed, you may need to be alert to questions with hidden put-downs. If this occurs, it needs to be talked about so students understand that a community is a place that is both physically and emotionally safe.

Adaptations for Students with Disabilities: Group Interview

Cognitive disabilities	• Brainstorm a list of questions first.
Orthopedic impairment	• No major modifications necessary.
Hearing impairment	• Have an interpreter available if necessary.
Visual impairment	• No major modifications necessary.

Full Value Contract Activities

As with Challenge by Choice, Full Value Contract (FVC) is better experienced than only talked about. There are many ways and times to introduce FVC. Some facilitators like to begin their community-building with a FVC, while others prefer to wait until the group has some history together. I like to begin with one that lays a foundation for the beginning of group norms around safety. Later, when students are more willing to share their thoughts with people who are no longer strangers, we develop a more extensive FVC that is put in place for the life of the community.

No matter what your preference as a facilitator is, it is important to have FVC in place before a group heads into trust issues. In this way, students have established ownership of their class by helping to set the ground rules. Make sure you also commit to the FVC.

Once a FVC is established, it is seen as a working document to which everyone has made a commitment. The qualities that are agreed upon provide a structure for the operation of this particular class. During processing sessions, the FVC can be referred to when discussing how group members are interacting. If one or more of the qualities are disregarded, it can be discussed. The qualities that are written are *ideals*—something to work toward. Every time one is ignored, it is an opportunity to learn. One pitfall of a Full Value Contract is that it is sometimes used as a weapon with which to metaphorically beat someone over the head if he or she does not live up to the community standards. Remember that it is a *guide*. If the same quality is consistently being violated, then it must be discussed.

Finally, the FVC needs to be re-evaluated periodically in order to keep it up-to-date with the developing community. With experience, group members may choose to add a quality to the FVC, or they may even choose to remove one if it is no longer relevant.

23. Five Finger Contract

Focus: Initiating and exploring a Full Value Contract, establishing norms
Materials: Writing materials (optional)

<u>Suggested Procedure</u>

1. Teach the class the five-finger contract as described below.

FIVE FINGER CONTRACT

Each of these fingers is a reminder to us about points that will make this class a safe and respectful place for everybody:

- **Pinky:** *Safety*—it's the smallest and most vulnerable finger
- **Ring finger:** *Commitment*—willingness to let things go (and not hold grudges)
- **Middle finger:** Awareness of *put-downs*
- **Pointer finger:** *Taking responsibility* instead of pointing blame
- **Thumb:** Agreement to work toward *group goals*

2. Write about or discuss each one to agree on what it means to this class at this time.
3. Have small groups address each point with a pie chart and report to the class.
4. Another strategy is to write these on posterboard and ask everyone to add their thumb-print to denote agreement (once everyone indicates that they understand them).
5. Revisit the Five Finger Contract periodically to learn more about what each point means. For example, talk about one or more points after an activity or as an evaluation at the end of a class. Talk about one or more points before a class begins to remind students about creating a safe environment.

It is difficult to reach consensus in large groups. Here are a few strategies for dealing with Full Value Contracts with large classes:

- Have students do a Full Value Contract in groups of 4–6. Then share their process and discussion with the whole class. Generally, there is quite a bit of overlap of ideas. Tape all ideas together into a large scroll or mural. The contract will be referred to over time, and certain ideals will become more pertinent to the class than others.
- Brainstorm 10–15 ideals. Each week, focus on one and add it to the Full Value Contract, which is hanging in the room.
- Create a group history mural/scroll using butcher paper. Every so often, ask the students what they have learned about their community, and have some students depict it on the scroll. This group history becomes the Full Value Contract for the class.
- Using sticky notes, have each student write what is important to her or him in this community. Post the notes; over time, give people a chance to explain their messages.
- Create a puzzle by taking poster board and cutting it into different shapes. In small groups, the students draw or write their ideals, and put them back together into a complete puzzle. Maybe hold a couple blank pieces out, so that the class can add more to the puzzle as they go along.

One of the difficulties in discussing issues with students is that they may try to give the "correct answers" without giving them much thought. Another concern is knowing whether or not the words carry much real meaning for the students. One strategy is to ask the students what a particular action looks like, sounds like and feels like. Chart it so that everyone can see the results. It may look like this:

Topic: Cooperation

LOOKS LIKE
- reaching out to help someone
- sitting close together
- looking at each other
- not talking when someone else is talking
- etc.

SOUNDS LIKE
- saying "thank you"
- saying "I'm sorry"
- one person talking at a time
- saying "I'll help"
- etc.

FEELS LIKE
- safe
- not crazy
- comfortable
- happy
- etc.

> **SAMPLE PROCESSING QUESTIONS FOR FIVE FINGER CONTRACT**
>
> - How would you define each of these five points?
> - Considering that no one is perfect, and that we are working toward these goals, what should we do when one (or more) of these points is ignored?
> - How can we celebrate when we are adhering to these goals?

Facilitation Notes

Many times it is difficult to know where to begin when attempting to create a safe and respectful community. The Five Finger Contract is a good place to start. It is important to set the right tone at the beginning of the process, and this can help. After the class has been together for awhile, students can move into another phase where they create a Full Value Contract of their own.

Adaptations for Students with Disabilities: Five Finger Contract

Cognitive disabilities	• No major modifications necessary.
Orthopedic impairment	• No major modifications necessary.
Hearing impairment	• Have an interpreter available if necessary.
Visual impairment	• Reread/review the contract at regular intervals to act as a reminder.

24. PEEP

Focus: Initiating and exploring a Full Value Contract, establishing norms, sharing responsibility
Materials: Writing materials (optional)

Suggested Procedure

1. Teach the class about safety using PEEP as described below.
   - **Personal:** Take off jewelry, dangling earrings; wear appropriate clothing for the task (if outside, wear closed toe shoes, for example); nothing in mouth, etc. (In some programs this can also focus on refraining from use of drugs or alcohol).
   - **Emotional:** Use and respect Challenge by Choice; only volunteer yourself; no put-downs.
   - **Environmental:** Move in a controlled manner; follow safety protocols/directions; be aware of weather, insects, etc. Take care of the environment. When inside, be aware of furniture.
   - **Physical:** Be aware of physical limitations; take care of yourself. When outside, use sunscreen, drink water, wear appropriate clothing.
2. Write about or discuss each point to agree on what it means to this class at this time.
3. Have small groups address each point with a chart and report to the class.
4. Another strategy is to write these on posterboard and ask everyone to add a thumbprint to denote agreement (once everyone indicates that they understand them).
5. Revisit PEEP periodically to learn more about what each point means. For example, talk about one or more points after an activity or as an evaluation at the end of a class. Talk about one or more points before a class begins to remind students about creating a safe environment.

> **SAMPLE PROCESSING QUESTIONS FOR PEEP**
>
> - How would you define each of these four points?
> - What are some situations that can be "PEEPED"?
> - How should we handle it when a "PEEP" is heard?

<u>Facilitation Notes</u>

PEEP is a wonderful way to involve everyone in personal and group safety. Explain that, as the teacher, you are ultimately responsible for everyone's safety and will step in when a situation seems unsafe. This applies to emotional as well as physical safety. As one person, however, it is impossible for you to monitor all situations all of the time. Therefore, it is important that each member of the class take responsibility for safety, and not always wait for the teacher to step in. If an unsafe situation presents itself, all one has to do is say "PEEP." At that point, everything stops until the matter is dealt with.

Here are three examples:

(1) Someone in the class calls another student a name. Those who hear it say "PEEP." Action stops, and the students are questioned. One says, "She called me a name!" The other says, "I was just teasing." You ask, "Did you think she was teasing?" "No, it seemed as if she meant it." The first student then says that she won't do it again.

Although this may not solve the problem, it is a beginning. Having those around *recognize* the put-down, and then having a short discussion, allows all to learn from the incident.

(2) Someone in the class calls another student a name. Those who hear it say "PEEP." Continue with the activity. It might be enough just to publicly recognize the put-down for this behavior to stop.

(3) The class has moved the furniture to do the activity Neighbors. There is a table right behind one of the place markers. Just as the activity is about to start, someone says "PEEP." Action stops, and that person (who is across the circle from the table) says, "That table is really close to the place marker; I'm concerned that we'll run into it." The table is moved and action continues.

This is all about sharing responsibility. Generally, people are reluctant to "PEEP" others at first. You can model this response to unsafe situations. Later, "PEEPING" becomes more shared as students become more comfortable. A norm has been established.

Adaptations for Students with Disabilities: PEEP

Cognitive disabilities	• Modify PEEP to just **Physical** (body) and **Emotional** (feelings) at first.
Orthopedic impairment	• No major modifications necessary.
Hearing impairment	• Have an interpreter available if necessary.
Visual impairment	• Use tactile representatives for each part of PEEP.

25. Play Hard, Play Safe, Play Fair, Have Fun*

Focus: Full Value Contract, creating definitions for each concept, perspective taking
Materials: Writing materials

Suggested Procedure

1. Divide the class into smaller groups.
2. Give each group one of the phrases, and ask them to define it.
3. Have each small group present their definition to the class.
4. Discuss the definition—make any additions or changes as the discussion progresses.
5. Post and revisit the definitions periodically to revise the contract.

SAMPLE PROCESSING QUESTIONS FOR PLAY HARD, PLAY SAFE, PLAY FAIR, HAVE FUN

- Why might different people have different concepts of "fun" or playing "hard"?
- How would you define "cheating" (a concept that regularly comes up when discussing playing fair) or "playing by the rules"?
- What are some examples of playing safe?

Facilitation Notes

The definitions for these concepts are extremely important. I might think "fun" means using sarcastic humor; the receiver of that humor may think otherwise. As the class spends more time interacting, these definitions will change.

With elementary classes, it might be necessary to take these concepts one at a time. Explore each one in depth over a few weeks, and then add the next one.

Adaptations for Students with Disabilities: Play Hard, Play Safe, Play Fair, Have Fun

Cognitive disabilities	• Deal with only one concept at a time.
Orthopedic impairment	• Use cutouts with Velcro™ backing to stick to the board.
	• Instead of using tagboard, use magnets to make words. Or, write words on small pieces of paper and put them up with small magnets.
	• Use magnetic strips that can be stuck to the back of paper.
Hearing impairment	• No major modifications necessary.
Visual impairment	• Come up with a symbolic tactile representation for each value/concept being discussed.

MPS: Full Value Contract

26. The Being[4]

Focus: Full Value Contract, describing attributes
Materials: Butcher paper and markers

Suggested Procedure

1. Divide the class into groups of 4–6.
2. Give each group a long piece of butcher paper and various markers.
3. Have each group trace the body of one person in their group.

---

* Thanks to the New Games Foundation for this concept.

4. On **the inside** of the outline, they should draw or write behaviors or qualities that are safe and respectful of self, others and the class (e.g., sharing, humor, a picture of people shaking hands, etc.).
5. On **the outside** of the outline, they draw or write behaviors or qualities that damage people's sense of respect and safety (e.g., prejudice, a picture of someone hitting another, etc.).
6. Post the Beings and have each group present theirs to the class.
7. Have all students sign their work. Refer to these Beings over time.

SAMPLE PROCESSING QUESTIONS FOR THE BEING

- What is the class like when it is peaceful?
- What is the class like when it is not peaceful?
- How might these Beings help remind us about making this a safe and respectful class?
- When there are issues that occur from outside your Beings, how should we handle it?
- How can the class use the inside attributes, while working to diminish the outside attributes?

Facilitation Notes

The Being is a nice activity because it allows people to be physically engaged while discussing the qualities of a safe and respectful place. Encourage people to be creative with their outlines—dress them up a bit. Of course, the person who is being traced must volunteer. The students must have some trust built up before allowing themselves to be traced by others.

Adaptations for Students with Disabilities: The Being

Cognitive disabilities	• Create and use a bank of words for values, impediments to our goals, etc.
Orthopedic impairment	• Use cutouts with Velcro™ baking to stick to the board.
	• Instead of using tagboard, use magnets to make words. Or, write words on small pieces of paper and put them up with small magnets.
	• Use magnetic strips that can be stuck to the back of paper.
Hearing impairment	• No major modifications necessary.
Visual impairment	• Come up with a symbolic tactile representation for each value/concept being discussed.

MPS: Full Value Contract

27. The Village

Focus: Full Value Contract, determining goals and ideals
Materials: Flip-chart paper or butcher paper, markers

Suggested Procedure

1. Split the class into groups of 4–6. Have each group follow these directions to create a "village."
2. Determine, **at most,** 20 ideals that your village will use to make it work well (respect, sharing, etc.). You should write, draw, or otherwise mark these ideals inside your village.
3. Decide on what hinders you from sticking to your ideals, or drags your village down (racism, hate, etc.). These go on the outside of your village.
4. Each person should draw his or her own dwelling (a.k.a. personal goal) on the village map.

This is a goal for how each student wants to act in class. For example, if I think I talk too much, I may draw a mouth that says, "Let others talk."
5. Each group should be prepared to present their village to the class.

> **SAMPLE PROCESSING QUESTIONS FOR THE VILLAGE**
>
> - What process did you use to decide on how to do your village?
> - Did you have agreement on what the ideals should be? Why do you think it was so easy/difficult to reach agreement?
> - Are there some ideals that we already are achieving?
> - Which ideals do you think we need to work on more?

Facilitation Notes

The Village is best used with classes at the upper-middle to high-school level. It takes considerable discussion about what students envision their class ideals to be.

Encourage groups to use drawn symbols as well as written words to describe their ideals and hindrances. Each of the villages will look different, and many times a group will use their village as a metaphor. For example, a group may draw a river around their village to keep the hindrances out, and then draw paths between the dwellings to represent communication and shared goals.

Adaptations for Students with Disabilities: The Village

Cognitive disabilities	• Create and use a bank of words for values, impediments to our goals, etc.
Orthopedic impairment	• Use cutouts with Velcro™ backing to stick to the board.
	• Instead of using tagboard, use magnets to make words. Or, write words on small pieces of paper and put them up with small magnets.
	• Use magnetic strips that can be stuck to the back of paper.
Hearing impairment	• No major modifications necessary.
Visual impairment	• Come up with a symbolic tactile representation for each value/concept being discussed.

MPS: Full Value Contract

28. Hands All Around

Focus: Full Value Contract, identifying attributes and vocabulary
Materials: Flip-chart paper or butcher paper, **water-soluble** markers or crayons

Suggested Procedure

1. Break the class into groups of 4–6. Direct students as follows:
2. Brainstorm a list of words or phrases that describe how you want to be treated—and how you want to treat each other—in order to make your class a safe and respectful place to be.
3. From this list, choose 10 that are most important to you as a class.
4. Make sure that everyone understands what each of the words means. For example, if someone says "cooperation," define it so that everyone agrees on what cooperation means for your group.
5. On a large piece of paper, have everyone trace their hands around the edge (feel free to decorate your traced hands).

6. Write your 10 words in the middle of the paper, so that your traced hands form a frame around them.
7. Read the 10 words out loud, and decide if you can agree to live by these ideas while in this group.
8. If so, sign your hands. If not, discuss your concerns and modify your words to make it possible for everyone in your group to sign.
9. Choose one or more spokespersons to share your contract with the larger group.

> **SAMPLE PROCESSING QUESTIONS FOR HANDS ALL AROUND**
>
> - Did you all agree on how to create your product? What worked and did not work for you?
> - How did you decide on which words to use? Was it easy to agree?
> - Do you understand all of the words that are used here?
> - Give an example of each word. What do these actions look like, sound like, feel like?

Facilitation Notes

For younger students, the brainstorming can take place as a whole class. Then have each small group pick their top 5 or 10 to put on their group sheet. Older students can have more time in their small groups to discuss what is important to them. It is also possible to be less structured and more creative with older students about what to draw on the paper.

Adaptations for Students with Disabilities: Hands All Around

Cognitive disabilities	• Create and use a bank of words for values, impediments to our goals, etc.
	• Deal with one concept at a time.
Orthopedic impairment	• Use cutouts with Velcro™ backing to stick to the board.
	• Instead of using tagboard, use magnets to make words. Or, write words on small pieces of paper and put them up with small magnets.
	• Use magnetic strips that can be stuck to the back of paper.
Hearing impairment	• No major modifications necessary.
Visual impairment	• Come up with a symbolic tactile representation for each value/concept being discussed.

MPS: Full Value Contract

29. What Do I Need? What Can I Give?

Focus: Full Value Contract, creating rules
Materials: Flip-chart or butcher paper, adhesive notes

Suggested Procedure

1. Hand two sticky notes to each student.
2. Ask students to think about what they need in order to feel safe and respected in this class. This should be written on one note.
3. Ask them to think about what they can give to make others feel safe and respected in this class. This should be written on the other note.
4. Give them time to think and write.

5. Divide the class into groups of 4–6.
6. Ask students to share what they wrote on their sticky notes.
7. Have them combine their ideas. For example, if two or more people wrote something like, "I need people to take me seriously" or "I need people not to laugh at me," these can be combined.
8. Give each group a turn to share one of their ideas. If an idea has already been suggested, they do not need to repeat it. As each idea is stated, write it on the flipchart or butcher paper.
9. After all the combined ideas are written publicly, ask students to read them out loud. Ask them to think about three things: (1) Do they need clarification about any of the ideas? (2) Can they agree to work toward doing what's written? (3) Is there anything missing?
10. Hold a discussion to clarify, negotiate and add.

> SAMPLE PROCESSING QUESTIONS FOR WHAT DO I NEED? WHAT CAN I GIVE?
>
> - How did you like this process? Was it helpful?
> - Are you surprised about anything on our list?
> - What will it take for us to live by these ground rules?
> - How will we handle it when there is a problem—when one or more of the ground rules is ignored?

<u>Facilitation Notes</u>

This process is best used with upper-middle and high-school students. It gives them an opportunity to discuss not only external rules but also what they can give and receive internally to make the classroom a good teaching and learning environment.

This is also a process that does not take a huge amount of time. It can be done in 45 minutes to an hour. Encourage discussion about clarifying the ideas. Sometimes students are reticent about asking what they think are obvious questions. Model how this might be done by choosing one that is unclear to you and asking for clarification. This usually gets the discussion rolling. Also, make sure you fill out your own sticky notes and add them to the mix.

Adaptations for Students with Disabilities: What Do I Need? What Can I Give?

Cognitive disabilities	• Brainstorm as a large group.
Orthopedic impairment	• Use cutouts with Velcro™ backing to stick to the board.
	• Instead of using tagboard, use magnets to make words. Or, write words on small pieces of paper and put them up with small magnets.
	• Use magnetic strips that can be stuck to the back of paper.
Hearing impairment	• No major modifications necessary.
Visual impairment	• Come up with a symbolic tactile representation for each value/concept being discussed.

MPS: Full Value Contract

Summary: When to Move on to Trust

Assessment of a group is both an art and a science. You can look to the Cooperation issues in the Community-Building Model (page 22) as a guide to determine if group members have made progress. With time together, students will have the opportunity to know which cooperation issues need to be addressed and which ones are already in place. When students are encouraging of each other, rather than degrading—in essence, *kind* to each other—then it is possible to move into issues of trust.

It is not necessary to be 100 percent successful with every issue. There will always be times when people put themselves or others down, for example. Having some history with the issues, though, offers a frame of reference for dealing with them later. Many times, all it takes is a reminder to help students get back on track. At other times, it may be necessary to back up and do more cooperation activities in order to deal with specific issues.

It is important to include your students in the decision to move on. Talk about what attributes they need to make sure that trust can, in fact, flourish in the class. Ask them if they are ready to meet the challenges in order to make it safe for everyone to build trust.

One way to approach moving from one step to another is to decide to try a low-level trust activity. There are many trust activities that do not put people at risk for injury if group members prove to be unprepared. Once you try the activity, the group can assess how it felt to put trust in other group members. Your observations can be added to the mix to determine if the students are ready to "dive" into Trust.

Codes, Missions and Values

Many organizations have mission statements, codes of conduct or value statements. The YMCA, for example, holds dear the values of "caring, honesty, responsibility and respect." Create a Full Value Contract by presenting the mission statement, values declarations or code of conduct. Ask group members to define what it means to them.

Community Standards

Older students might not enjoy an activity that seems "juvenile." If this is the case, ask them to create community standards. These are standards that make the class a place for everyone to feel safe and be respected. These might begin as general qualities that the students define and agree on (honesty, sharing, listening). Later they may get more specific (taking turns when speaking, spending time discussing before diving into a project, etc.).

Signing a Contract?

A contract denotes a legal obligation to fulfill the terms of the said contract. We ask students to indicate an agreement to the Full Value Contract in a variety of ways: nodding, thumbs up, signatures, thumbprints, initials, etc. The reason for requesting an active token of agreement is to make the process concrete and show that it is important to the process as a whole.

What about those who do not wish to sign? Although this is a rare occurrence, these folks generally have valid reasons for not wanting to put their mark on the FVC. Usually it means that they are taking the process quite seriously and truly believe that they cannot live up to the spirit of the contract.

My experience includes a student who was diagnosed with attention deficit disorder. His history included little success with behavior programs, and he saw his signature as a symbol of future failure. Since I already had a rapport with the student, we were able to talk privately about the matter. We discussed that these were goals—not reasons for punishment—and that messing up meant we could learn from the situation. We agreed that he would participate without a signature for awhile, and check in after two weeks. Within a month he felt comfortable enough to sign the contract.

Another way to deal with this situation is to spend time as a group negotiating about the ideals and points on the contract until everyone feels comfortable signing it. This can take awhile, especially with a large class, so it may take many small discussions over a longer period of time to establish the contract. We must remember that it is not the product but the discussion process that allows each of us to learn and understand the ideals. It is time well worth taking.

As the contract develops, the students gain a deeper appreciation for individual needs and create a document that is useful for all involved.

◊ MOVING TO TRUST: SOME OBSERVATIONS

	Class Can Move On	**Class Should Stay with Cooperation**
Put-ups/Put-downs	• You notice a decrease in put-downs over time. • Students notice when a put-down occurs. • When a put-down occurs, students are willing to discuss it, then let it go. • You notice an increase in put-ups, both verbal ("thank you," compliments) and physical (more sharing, helping others). • Laughter is shared, and people can laugh at themselves.	• You notice no change in the number and kind of put-downs. • Students seem to ignore put-downs altogether, as if it's just part of the way things are. • Students seem to say only "the right things" so that they can avoid talking about put-ups/put-downs. • Put-ups, when they do occur, seem superficial. Although a beginning, it may not be time to move to Trust. • Students laugh at each other, especially when someone makes a mistake.
Hidden agendas	• Students are able to state their needs rather than sneak to get an individual need met. • No matter who is in the class, people are willing to participate and discuss issues. • You notice that people are more willing to take turns, rather than monopolize playing and talking time.	• You find students opting out of activities in the name of Challenge by Choice on a regular basis. • You notice that students are more willing to participate and talk when one or more individuals are gone. (This can indicate fear of reprisal or bullying outside of class.)
Active listening	• Active listening skills have been taught and practiced. • You notice that active listening skills are being used (at least sporadically) at other times.	• Students constantly talk out of turn. • There is an unwillingness to "hear" another person's point of view. • Even when focusing on active listening, students cannot seem to use the skills.
Mixing	• Students are willing to work with everyone in the class on an activity. • Students notice when there is a segregation (e.g., all the boys on one side, all the girls on the other) even if they do nothing about it. • When gathering spontaneously, there is not always a gender, race, or clique segregation.	• There is a student who is constantly scapegoated, and no one will work with her/him. • Students complain about their partners when paired with others. • Students refuse to mix, even when it is focused on.
Perspective taking	• Students have had an opportunity to explore other perspectives besides their own. • Students are willing to compromise when necessary. • When someone is hurt or upset, students are able to show concern. • People are willing to solve conflicts when they occur. • Students are willing to take responsibility for their actions.	• Students hold grudges and seek revenge. • When someone is hurt or upset, students tease or show little concern for the individual. • Students constantly blame others. • Students make fun of others' cultures or customs.

References

[1] Kreidler and Furlong. *Adventures in Peacemaking.* (p. 8)
[2] Kohn, Alfie. *Beyond Discipline.* (pp. 113–114)
[3] Luckner and Nadler. *Processing the Experience.* (p. 20)
[4] Kreidler and Furlong. *Adventures in Peacemaking.* (p. 14)

Chapter 5

TRUST: THE CORNERSTONE OF COMMUNITY

Without trust, a community can not survive. It is the foundation on which relationships are built, and community is all about building and maintaining relationships. Trust is also a fragile commodity, in that it is painstaking to establish, yet easily broken. Once broken, it is even more difficult to reestablish.

By necessity, after the laughing, joking and good-natured teasing of Deinhibitizers, the mood of the class must change. Students need to switch gears to a more thoughtful frame of mind. Trust building has to be taken seriously if it is to be a safe experience.

Students are now asked to become partners in keeping track of safety. Everyone is responsible for speaking up if a potential or actual safety hazard is spotted. At this stage, too, they must use humor with care. If, for example, someone jokes that she is going to run her partner into a wall during a blind Trust Walk, trust is already on shaky ground. If no one speaks up to protect a class member, trust can easily be shattered, and the class may have to go back to square one.

TRUST
- Making mistakes
- Empathy
- Trustworthiness
- Risk taking
- Physical/Emotional trust

Activities
Trust building

Feelings literacy

Behavioral goal setting

Individual low ropes elements

Along with this added group responsibility is a focus on personal responsibility. People are encouraged to make "I" statements and reflect on their own behavior, especially as it relates to being trustworthy. It is also a time to delve into the world of feelings so as to become more self-aware. Goleman states that "self awareness—recognizing a feeling *as it happens*—is the keystone of emotional intelligence…. An inability to notice our true feelings leaves us at their mercy."[1] The myriad of emotions that we feel during an activity that requires giving up some of our own control to others is fertile ground for the development of a feelings vocabulary. The more we can identify our feelings, the more literate we are when working through conflict and the other dynamics of relationships.

Challenge by Choice is highlighted during trust building. Choosing to trust others is a personal decision. An individual's past experience has a huge effect on his or her willingness to trust others. It is risky to varying degrees, depending upon history and frame of reference. Personal goal setting can also be initiated at this point, as students begin to explore the meaning of risk taking and setting personal goals. These goals can be self-monitored with support from other students.

Trust Issues and Skills

◊ Making Mistakes

Every group must ask itself the question, "Is it OK to make a mistake?" Invariably, students answer in the affirmative. "Of course it's OK. Everyone makes mistakes, and we can learn from our mistakes!" The trouble is, when someone actually does make a mistake, the first reaction from many is to tease or degrade that person. Therefore, it is necessary to ask this question outright and then to have some practice with it. The ultimate goal is to have people's actions be consistent with their words.

If students work through this issue, there is a tangible change in the atmosphere of the group. People are able to take greater risks without fear of reprisal. The level of trust among students soars, because people don't have to worry that others are lying in wait to catch them in a mistake. Once a class gets over this bump, it can truly thrive.

Activities can help you focus on this question of making mistakes. My favorite is Turnstile, described in the Trust activity section later in this chapter.

> The ability to make mistakes is vital not only to establishing trust within a class, but also to learning. Learning from one's mistakes is a powerful way to gain experience. It can be encouraged during community-building time—and all the time. Spend time talking about mistakes from which you have learned, and invite students to tell stories about their mistakes. Create an environment where learning from mistakes is a norm, not something to hide.
>
> As students become more comfortable with making mistakes, emphasize a few points:
> - Making mistakes is meaningless unless we can glean learning from them.
> - There is a difference between making a mistake and gross negligence. It is the difference between forgetting to turn on your turn signal and getting into the driver's seat after drinking. Spend time clarifying the difference and brainstorming examples.
> - Making mistakes implies consequences. If I stay up too late and sleep through my alarm, I will have to deal with the consequences of being late to work or school. The idea is to learn from this mistake in order to prevent others like it in the future.
> - Along with the consequences comes responsibility. Sometimes it is enough to throw up one's hands and say, "oops!" At other times the mistake may have caused hurt feelings—like forgetting someone's birthday, or borrowing something and losing it. In these cases it is important to find a way to "make things right."

◊ Empathy

To truly identify with someone else's feelings is to care. It makes sense to trust someone who cares about you. This is why focusing on empathy is so important at this stage of community-building. We display empathy by taking care of each other, by asking questions about how people want to be treated during the trust activities, and by making sure we all take responsibility for everyone's physical and emotional safety. If someone is uncomfortable, we try to make it right, because that person's discomfort causes us discomfort. "I feel your pain" is more than a cliché.

Perspective taking is a precursor to empathy. The first step is to understand that others have different perspectives from one's own. The next step, empathy, allows people to recognize the feelings of others. Daniel Goleman calls it the fundamental people skill. The beauty of using activities to explore these concepts is that real things happen. When someone reports that he could not keep his eyes closed during the Trust Walk, there is real fodder for discussing emotional safety. Since everyone has an easier time with some activities and a harder time with others, your class can investigate how people have different reactions to different experiences. Being blindfolded can be difficult for one person and easy for another. The roles may be reversed, however, when choosing to fall backwards and be caught by others.

Since 90 percent or more of an emotional message is nonverbal, reading another's feelings accurately requires noticing nonverbal cues. *How* a message is conveyed can be more telling than the actual words. Help students key into tone of voice, gestures and facial expressions—the body language we all transmit.

Process what it feels like to be cared for by another person to whom we have entrusted our safety. Discuss what it is like to be responsible for another's well-being. Discover what it is like to empathize and care about another's welfare.

◊ TRUSTWORTHINESS

One way to show empathy is to be trustworthy in taking care of another's needs. To be "worthy of trust" means that one's behavior toward another is consistent and caring.

Consistency is a key factor in establishing trust. When giving up some of our control, and entrusting our personal safety to another, it is important to know what to expect. If, on the other hand, that other person behaves in unpredictable ways, it is difficult for us to trust.

Clear communication is another way to engender trust and prove trustworthiness. For example, encourage participants who are guiding others during a blind Trust Walk to paint pictures with words about the environment they are entering. There is no need for them to withhold information. This can lead to a discussion about keeping secrets, or sharing information so that everyone is included. These are big trust issues for a community.

Another trust-related behavior involves consulting with a person who appears to be in need. Before simply assuming that someone has needs to be met (or needs rescuing), it is important to ask if he or she *wants* help. It can be maladaptive to encourage everyone to jump in to help others without invitation. Conversely, we want students to recognize when someone is in danger and to act to keep that person from getting hurt. Encourage students to ask for help if they need it. Yet, as with so many other instances in life, we must learn to deal with ambiguity. The important thing is to bring this issue out into the open so that people can grapple with it.

◊ RISK TAKING

In our quest to make life as safe (and as litigation-free) as possible, we sometimes err on the side of encouraging *less* risk taking. Certainly, the words *safe* and *safety* are used frequently in this book. Yet, risk taking is the stuff of growth. To risk is to push one's limits, to expand boundaries, to learn.

What Do We Do Now?

You have just spent the last month creating a place where trust can be built. You have developed a Full Value Contract and have worked through **cooperation** issues. Now it is time to "step up" to **trust,** so you choose a beginning activity like the Trust Walk to begin this part of the journey. After talking about how to lead someone with closed eyes and how to get into pairs, students lead each other around tables, desks and bookcases. Then it happens: One student leads another into the wall. Now what?

After checking if everyone is OK, you can frame this incident as a higher level of put-down and deal with it accordingly. As with put-downs, it *must* be acknowledged and processed. Was it on purpose or was it an accident? No matter what the motive is, how does it affect a student's ability to trust or be trusted?

This can take a minute or the rest of class, depending on the severity of the incident and the hurt feelings involved. If there is time after the discussion, ask the person who was being led if she or he feels up to trying it again, and then respect the decision. Next time, revisit the incident briefly as a way to learn from a mistake, then try the whole activity again. Usually the person who was run into the wall will be ready to try again after some time has passed, and the person who was leading will be ready to be more alert.

During this stage of trust building, it is your responsibility to be alert to possible safety issues. Watch the students' body languages to ascertain their empathy level. Offer reminders to those who are moving too fast or seem to be unaware of how their partner will fit through a door or between tables. Sometimes shorter students forget to look up for the barriers that only affect taller students.

This incident provides an after-the-fact way to discuss empathy. Empathy is best taught through experience, and although we have been learning these lessons since we were toddlers, it is something that cannot be overemphasized. Choosing activities carefully is a way to make sure that students can learn about empathy without being put at undo risk. Address the mistakes that occur at the lower levels so that everyone will be prepared to care for each other's physical and emotional safety as you introduce higher-level activities.

It's All About Behavior

Being trustworthy has everything to do with behavior. Saying one thing and doing another is a sure way to break trust, while aligning one's beliefs and deeds proves that one can be trusted. It means looking at the big picture to work toward positive outcomes and then matching those intentions with actions. Sounds like an exercise in ethics....

There are two main schools of thought about risk taking. One is to push people outside their comfort zones. By doing so, it is believed people will learn and grow from the experience. The other approach is to create an environment where it is safe for people to *step* outside their comfort zones. Within the context of Challenge by Choice, people are given opportunities to try things they never thought possible. The group encourages and supports the goals that individuals set for themselves. The second approach is much more conducive to the creation of community, where the empowering aspects of self-determination and personal responsibility are highly valued and reinforced.

To trust is to risk. What better time to begin an exploration of risk taking than when involved in a series of trust-building activities? Themes around risk taking include: What is a safe or unsafe risk? What does "healthy" risk taking mean? When is it appropriate to say no? What role does peer pressure play in risk taking, and what is the difference between peer pressure and encouragement? All of these questions—and more—will emanate from the activities described in this chapter and subsequent discussions of trust building.

> **BLINDFOLDS?**
> Pete Albert, a social worker, longtime Adventure educator and originator of the Madison Metropolitan School District Stress/Challenge program in Wisconsin, tells a story about the use of blindfolds when he was working with a group of high-school English as a Second Language students some time ago. At least a half-dozen cultures were represented in this group, including students from Mexico, Laos, Viet Nam and the United States. When the blindfolds were brought out to use for a trust activity, Pete describes the atmosphere in the room as getting suddenly colder. Not understanding what was going on, he put them away and went on to another activity. Later, he learned that the last time many of the students had seen blindfolds, they had been on the faces of people about to be executed. Pete brought in strips of white cloth for the students to decorate as their own, thus turning them into personal works of art that happened to be eye coverings, instead of blindfolds.
>
> Many of our trust activities involve the use of blindfolds. Pete's story prompted me to reassess my use of them. I now offer blindfolds for those who wish to use them, with the other option being to close one's eyes. If people peek, it is just another exercise in Challenge by Choice.

◊ PHYSICAL AND EMOTIONAL TRUST

Most of the activities we do involve some sort of physical trust—blindfold activities, falling and catching, walking on cables and spotting. These concrete examples open doors to the abstract concepts around emotional trust. Although there may be an apparent difference between trusting someone to keep your body safe and trusting that same person to keep your feelings safe, they are really two sides of the same coin. As issues come up for discussion around physical trust, they can be used as metaphors for other emotional trust issues such as entrusting someone with confidential information, helping someone meet personal goals, or not passing on rumors.

TRUST ACTIVITIES

The following trust activities must be chosen carefully, with much thought given to sequence. Each class will need to follow its own path of trust. Some classes take baby steps, while others leap through the activities as if it is no problem at all. Whatever pace your class takes on, it can be enlightening for all involved.

◊ ROLE OF THE TEACHER

The teacher's role changes from leader to guide at this point. On an expedition, a guide is needed because the group of people going on the trek are unfamiliar with the area, or they may not have the necessary experience to undertake the journey on their own, and it is understood that the guide has been down this path before. A guide teaches the necessary skills to accomplish the tasks required for the trek. The guide helps the group decide which route to take, works with participants to take care of their own needs, and watches out for the general safety of the group.

During trust activities, the teacher takes the guide role by planning a sequence of activities to help the students develop a history that will engender trust. He or she teaches the necessary spotting skills, along with appropriate communication to make the activities safe, and discusses behavior that is consistent with trustworthiness. The teacher/guide helps the students develop a feelings vocabulary with which to communicate and take care of their emotional needs. These physical and behavioral skills will be used during the rest of the journey.

While in the middle of the sequence, the teacher may consult with the students about which activity to move to next. Although the sequence is important, it is not so hard and fast that it is inflexible. Giving students an opportunity to make some decisions encourages them to begin the transition into becoming a more self-determining body.

Processing is important during the trust phase. People need a chance to discuss their feelings about trusting others and being trusted. What does trust even mean? When might trusting someone be appropriate, and when might it be too risky? All students must have the opportunity to answer questions like these for themselves. The answers will differ for each person, depending on background and personal experiences with trust.

Trust Activities

These activities require people to give up a little control while entrusting others to keep them safe, both physically and emotionally. Care must be taken to brief your class about the activities in such a way that everyone knows what is expected and how to keep their colleagues safe. Discussion about behaviors that prove trustworthiness is essential before embarking on these activities.

30. Turnstile

Focus: Making mistakes, aligning beliefs and actions, dealing with frustration, emotional trust
Materials: Long jump rope (20 feet or longer)

Suggested Procedure

1. This activity can be done in a classroom if the furniture is moved out of the way. However, more room is desirable, so a gym, all-purpose room, hallway or outside area is a better option.
2. Ask the class how they feel about making mistakes. Is it OK? Why or why not? Discuss how to show support when someone makes a mistake.
3. Ask for two volunteers to turn the rope. These people can also jump, or they can choose only to turn. Everyone else is asked to stand on one side of the rope. *The turners spin the rope "front door," or toward the jumpers as it arcs over the top.*
4. The object is to get everyone from one side of the rope to the other. Tell them that they are trying to get everyone to graduate from high school. Once they get everyone through one level, they will advance to the next, more challenging level.
5. *Level I: Pre-school*—Everyone must get through the rope without it stopping or touching them (this means that some people may choose to run through without jumping). If the rope stops or touches them, then the person who has missed goes back to try it again.
6. *Level II: Kindergarten*—One person at a time runs in, jumps once and runs out. If the rope stops, or the person does not jump, then that person goes back to try it again.
7. *Level III: Elementary School*—People jump through in groups of two or three—run in

together, jump once and run out. If even only one person misses, the little group of two or three goes back to try again.

8. *Level IV: Middle/Junior High School*—Same as Level II, *except* that if anyone misses the *whole group* goes back and tries again.
9. *Level V: High School*—Same as Level IV *except* that each time the rope hits the ground, another person must be jumping. This means that people continuously follow each other in and out of the jump rope setup. If the rope stops, or no one is in the rope when it comes around, then the whole group must start over.

Sample Processing Questions for Turnstile

- Is it *really* OK to make a mistake in this class? How do you know?
- How did you feel when you missed?
- What did you say and do when someone else missed?
- How can making mistakes help us?
- What kinds of mistakes are OK to make? Give some examples.
- Did you ever feel like quitting this activity? Why did you choose to continue?
- Which level was the most satisfying to complete? Why?

Facilitation Notes

It is important to have a discussion about making mistakes before attempting this activity, because someone *will* miss. Being prepared for this inevitability helps develop the norm that making mistakes is acceptable. Ask the students if it is OK to make a mistake. With few exceptions, they will answer as expected: "Yes, because we learn from our mistakes" or "Nobody's perfect." We are taught to pay lip service to this notion, yet we rarely see that making mistakes is truly fine. Adults model this inconsistency by chiding others (and themselves) or laughing at people when mistakes are made.

Turnstile is perfect for dealing with this very issue, because mistakes will be made. This activity can be presented as a way to practice both making mistakes and reacting to others who have made mistakes. It can set the tone for the rest of the year. Later, if students tease or blame others for mistakes, all you need say is, "Is it *really* OK to make a mistake?" That phrase alone will act as a reminder.

Another nice element of Turnstile is the built-in sequence. If students are struggling with one level, then stop at the end of that level. Later, return to the activity and continue with the sequence when students are ready for a bigger challenge.

This activity almost guarantees a struggle. Few groups can accomplish every level of the Turnstile without missing more than a few times. Once worked through, students celebrate getting through the challenge, and the stage is set to discuss tenacity and dealing with frustration.

Another issue that arises during the Turnstile (especially with elementary students) is one of taking turns. Developmentally, these younger students are more concerned about getting a turn than in accomplishing the group task. If the group must all come back, there can be varying levels of pushing and shoving as students jockey for position. Ask them to develop a ground rule for this so that the need for pushing and shoving is diminished. Generally they will institute a norm assuming that those who have just gone through go to the back of the line to give others the next chance.

Turnstile can also be done by students in wheelchairs; they can be required to get through the rope without it touching them. These students can either do it themselves or have someone help by pushing them through on their signal.

Once a group "graduates," you can offer them "postgraduate" challenges: Everyone can try to jump once at the same time, do Level V in pairs, or repeat Level V—except that everyone should run back to the end of the line after jumping to see how many in a row can make it back before the rope stops.

Adaptations for Students with Disabilities: Turnstile

Cognitive disabilities	• Use the rope-swinging method, where the rope does not make full circles, but only swings back and forth (cradles).
	• Make sure that the rope is swinging at a slow pace.
Orthopedic impairment	• This activity may not be appropriate for individuals with an orthopedic impairment.
	• People in wheelchairs can either try to figure out the timing of this activity themselves, or have someone push them on their signal to try and get through the rope without it touching them.
	• These students could turn the rope.
Hearing impairment	• No modifications necessary.
Visual impairment	• Use brightly colored rope or something that makes noise when it hits the ground.
	• This activity may not be appropriate for anyone with a severe visual impairment.

MPS: Turnstile

31. Paired Blindfold Trust Activities

Focus: Physical and emotional trust, trustworthiness, empathy, risk taking
Materials: Blindfolds (optional), soft throwable objects

Suggested Procedure

1. Depending on the age and maturity level of your students, these activities can be done inside or outside (see facilitation notes).
2. Have your students get into pairs, either by choice or by a random method (see page 35 for pairing strategies).
3. Describe the activity (see below) and go over all safety guidelines: speed, making sure both people can fit through a space, looking up for obstacles, giving one's partner as much information as possible, making sure people know what is around them before asking them to bend down, etc.
4. Teach the "bumpers up" position: hands out in front.
5. At any time either person in the partnership can stop the activity if she or he feels too much discomfort. This must, of course, be communicated to the partner before stopping.
6. Offer blindfolds to those who want them; others can close their eyes.
7. Set up boundaries.
8. Allow enough time for each person to have a turn guiding and being led.

Activity A: Blindfold Trust Walk

The partner who is guiding can give both verbal and nonverbal directions.

Show the class different methods for leading someone who cannot see. The blindfolded partner can hold hands with the guide, hold the elbow of the guide, or have the guide hold his or her elbow. Or, he or she may not wish to be touched at all, but opt for verbal directions only. The important thing is that this be discussed. Each person *must* be given the opportunity to choose if or how to be touched.

Remind students that there are no secrets about what is in the area. Partners should feel free to describe what or who is around the people they are leading. Encourage them to take their partners to an object (tree, chair, etc.) and have them feel it. Later they can try to guess what it was.

Adaptations for Students with Disabilities: Blindfold Trust Walk

Cognitive disabilities	• Keep the space open, with few barriers, such as in a gym.
Orthopedic impairment	• Make sure there is a large amount of space.
	• Remind students to hold on to blindfolded individuals, as balance is more difficult when sight is taken away.
Hearing impairment	• Have students with hearing impairments be the guides; they should only be led if they choose.
Visual impairment	• Do this in groups of threes, with at least two sighted people per group.

Activity B: Search and Rescue

The partner who is guiding can only give verbal instructions. Make sure each pair has a soft throwable object.

Once the partner has closed eyes or is blindfolded, the guide throws the object. After the object is thrown, only the blindfolded person can touch it. Her or his task is to retrieve the object and get it to the "hospital" (spot on the floor, trash can, bag…). When that has been achieved, the two partners switch roles.

A word of caution: If the object is thrown near a wall or other barrier, the guide *must* tell the partner that the barrier is there *before* asking the person to bend down.

Adaptations for Students with Disabilities: Search and Rescue

Cognitive disabilities	• Teach a few concrete verbal directions that can be used.
	• Keep the space open, with few barriers, such as in a gym.
Orthopedic impairment	• Make sure there is a large amount of space.
	• Allow students to help their partners keep their balance.
Hearing impairment	• Have students with hearing impairments be the guides; they should only be led if they choose.
	• Students can use physical guidance to lead hearing-impaired partners.
Visual impairment	• Do this in groups of threes, with at least two sighted people per group.

Activity C: Drive My Car

The partner who is guiding can only give non-verbal instructions.

The person who is blindfolded is the "car," and the guide is the "driver." Since we do not talk to our cars when we drive them, the same applies here. The "car" stands in bumpers-up position, and the driver stands behind him or her. The signals go like this:

- Hands on shoulders: **stop**
- Hands off shoulders: **go**
- Hand on right shoulder: **turn right**
- Hand on left shoulder: **turn left**
- Two taps on shoulder: **reverse**

⚠ Speed is an issue here since the driver's hands are off the shoulders when the car is moving. It is important that the car not outrun the driver. Also remind drivers *not* to wait until the last minute before avoiding a collision, and to look behind them when reversing.

If someone does not wish to be touched at all, offer the option of having the driver give verbal directions.

Adaptations for Students with Disabilities: Drive My Car

Cognitive disabilities	• Keep the space open, with few barriers, such as in a gym.
Orthopedic impairment	• Make sure there is a large amount of space.
	• Change the rules so that hands on shoulders means "go" to aid in balance.
Hearing impairment	• Have students with hearing impairments be the guides; they should only be led if they choose.
Visual impairment	• Do this in groups of threes, with at least two sighted people per group.

SAMPLE PROCESSING QUESTIONS FOR PAIRED BLINDFOLD TRUST ACTIVITIES

- What did your guide do to gain your trust? Be specific.
- Did you feel your guide took care of your safety? Why or why not?
- Did your guide do anything to make you nervous? What?
- Were you more comfortable being led or being the guide?
- When you were guiding, did you feel responsible for your partner? Why or why not?
- Did you feel the need to peek? What caused you to choose to look?
- How risky was this for you? What would have made it more/less risky?

<u>Facilitation Notes</u>

At first, have your students try a blindfold activity in a large open area like a gym or empty lunch room. It will give them an opportunity to understand all that is expected. It will also give you the opportunity to assess their readiness to accept the responsibilities that go along with building trust. Next, add obstacles in the large room. Then try these activities in a smaller space, like your classroom, or outside, where the terrain is uneven and less predictable.

It is also important to think about how you want your students to pair up. In the beginning, it may be helpful to have your students pick their own partners, so that they are comfortable with their guides. As their comfort level increases, have them pair up in a more random fashion so that they have an opportunity to build trust with people they do not know (or even like) as well.

It is not necessary to do all of these paired activities. Age and developmental level play a huge part in the decisions you make during this step in the sequence. Elementary students will need more practice because they are at a different developmental level (and thus more egocentric) than high-school students. Since each activity requires something different from the students (nonverbal versus verbal directions, for example), you may choose to combine all into a mini-sequence, or choose one that you feel will challenge the students at the highest level.

During the debriefing, students generally talk about how it helped to know that their partners were there by hearing a voice or feeling a hand on their shoulder. This is a good metaphor for communication. Good communication can give rise to a higher level of trust.

32. Hog Call

Focus: Risk taking, physical/emotional trust, trustworthiness
Materials: Blindfolds (optional)

Suggested Procedure

1. Find a large open area, like a gym or field.
2. Have the students get into pairs.
3. Ask each pair to create two words that go together, like *salt* and *pepper*, or *fire* and *hydrant*.
4. Ask students to share their words out loud to make sure that no two pairs are alike.
5. Tell students that they will be split up, and that they must all find their partners without using their sense of sight. They can only call the "name" of their partner (e.g., *salt* calls *"pepper"*).
6. Split the pairs up so that one person from each pair is lined up on one side of the large space and the other person from each pair is lined up on the other side.
7. Explain that everyone will have closed eyes or will be blindfolded, and that your job is to make sure no one runs into a wall or barrier.
8. Remind everyone to move slowly and with bumpers up.
9. Everyone closes their eyes or puts on a blindfold.
10. On a signal, they start calling their partner's name.
11. Continue until all partners are reunited.

SAMPLE PROCESSING QUESTIONS FOR HOG CALL

- Was it necessary to trust everyone around you? Why or why not?
- Did you feel at risk during this activity? How?
- What strategies did you use to find your partner? Did you plan in advance?
- What did you do to keep yourself safe?
- What did you do to keep those around you safe?

Facilitation Notes

Hog Call is a nice, albeit less structured, way to begin looking at issues of trust. It is less intimate than having one person lead another, offering a more gamelike atmosphere. Students must be cautioned about moving too fast.

A more challenging variation of Hog Call is to have people spread out around the designated area, instead of lining up in straight lines.

Adaptations for Students with Disabilities: Hog Call

Cognitive disabilities	• Keep the space open, with few barriers, such as in a gym.
Orthopedic impairment	• Make sure there is a large amount of space.
	• Allow students to help their partners keep their balance.
Hearing impairment	• Make this a partner activity for hearing-impaired students.
	• Make sure that students with a hearing impairment are *choosing* to close their eyes or be blindfolded.
Visual impairment	• No major modifications necessary.

33. Shakers

Focus: Risk taking, physical/emotional trust, spotting

Materials: Blindfolds (optional), noisemakers (maracas, juice cans containing beans, whistles), soft item for tagging (soft foam ball, stuffed animal)

<u>Suggested Procedure</u>

1. Clear desks away and have students form a circle.
2. Ask for one volunteer to be "the bat" and another volunteer to be "the moth." These two stand in the middle of the circle. Everyone else is a spotter.
3. The bat and the moth each get a noisemaker. They should both choose either to close their eyes or put on a blindfold. Also, give the bat the soft item so that she or he can tag the moth without fear of violating the other person's space.
4. The object is for the bat to tag the moth by using echolocation. To do this, the bat shakes her noisemaker. At this point, the moth must respond by shaking his noisemaker.

SAMPLE PROCESSING QUESTIONS FOR SHAKERS

- Did you have to think much about your own safety, or did you feel comfortable with your spotters? Why or why not?
- When you were the bat, what strategies did you use to find the moth?
- When you were the moth, what strategies did you use to stay away from the bat?
- What did you do when you were spotting to keep the players safe?

<u>Facilitation Notes</u>

This is a good starting activity for younger students. It is very controlled, and it offers the opportunity to try out moving without sight. It also puts the rest of the class in a position to act as spotters. If the class size is large (over 15), try splitting into two groups so more people get an opportunity to be in the middle. You can also set a time limit for each pair.

Caution people to move slowly. The spotters should put their hands up to keep the players from straying outside the circle.

Adaptations for Students with Disabilities: Shakers

Cognitive disabilities	• These students can practice making sounds and responding to sounds before trying the activity.
Orthopedic impairment	• Make the circle big enough to accommodate a wheelchair.
	• Assign a partner if help with balance is needed.
Hearing impairment	• Use drums as the noisemakers.
Visual impairment	• No major modifications necessary.

34. Everybody Up

Focus: Risk taking, physical/emotional trust, trustworthiness
Materials: None

Suggested Procedure

1. Clear an area and have people get into pairs.
2. Ask for two volunteers so that you can show how this is to be done.
3. Ask the volunteers to sit down on the floor facing each other. They should put the bottoms of their feet together.
4. Have them get a good grip with their hands (this looks as if they are going to do the rowboat stretch).
5. Now ask for two spotters; one should stand behind each seated person. The spotters' job is to protect the two in the middle in case something goes wrong; they need to especially make sure that their heads do not touch the floor. (Although this rarely happens, it is important to have spotters ready.) Spotters stand with one foot behind the other, knees bent and hands out behind the person they are spotting. They are not to help, only to protect.
6. Tell the two who are sitting that their responsibility is to **not let go of their partner's hands.** After a count to three, they should pull with their hands and push with their feet. In this way, they will use tension to stand up.
7. Once these volunteers have successfully stood up, have pairs join together to stand and spot for each other.
8. Once everyone has tried this with a partner, have students mix up and try it with different people.

SAMPLE PROCESSING QUESTIONS FOR EVERYBODY UP

- What worked and didn't work for you and your partners?
- Were your partners trustworthy? What did they do to make sure you were safe?
- Were you trustworthy? How do you know?
- What responsibility did the spotters have? Why do you think it was important to have them there, even if they did not have to act?
- Can you think of other times when we prepare for trouble and hope to not use the skills (CPR, first aid…)? Why do this?

Facilitation Notes

This is another activity that can be tried early on to assess the students' commitment level. It is also a nice warmup activity for Dream Catcher, described on the following page.

One issue that can occur with Everybody Up is body image and size. Larger individuals have a more difficult time with this. If there are some comparatively large people in the class, ask them to pair up with people about the same size. Generally this is not a problem, because the students figure out quickly that the smaller folks compensate by leaning farther out. Larger students who may really have difficulty with this are welcome to act as spotters for others.

Adaptations for Students with Disabilities: Everybody Up

Cognitive disabilities	• Give hints as necessary to facilitate success.
Orthopedic impairment	• Play could be on mats, soft grass, etc.
	• Participants in wheelchairs can stay in their chairs. They can lean forward with their partner and sit back up as their partner stands.
	• Participants who are not in wheelchairs need the ability to hold onto their partner's hands and stand up with assistance from the group.
Hearing impairment	• Agree on visual signals for the group to use ahead of time to indicate when they will be sitting and standing.
Visual impairment	• Design tactile signals for the group to use ahead of time (for example, "I will take my hand off your shoulder when we should stand up").

MPS: Everybody Up

35. Dream Catcher*

Focus: Risk taking, physical/emotional trust, trustworthiness, goal setting

Materials: 1-inch tubular webbing in 10- or 12-foot pieces (can be found in sports stores with rock-climbing departments)

Suggested Procedure

1. Find a large space free of furniture, and have everyone pair up.
2. Give each pair a piece of webbing. This should be pre-tied in a circle using a water knot, or you can teach the participants to tie the water knot themselves (see Figure 5.1). As an alternative, they can overlap the ends and tie an overhand around each end so that the knots back onto each other when tension is pulled (see photo).
3. Have some extra webbing circles available.
4. After doing Everybody Up, ask students to figure out at least three new ways to sit down and stand up together by using tension. They may choose to use the webbing as a prop. Teach the girth hitch as a way to put two or more pieces of webbing together (see photo).
5. After people have tried this for awhile, have volunteers show their creations to the class.
6. Then take one of the webbing circles, and girth-hitch enough pieces of webbing to it so that everyone has a place to hang on—one or two people per piece of webbing. This now will look like a circle with spokes extending from it.
7. On an agreed-upon count, everyone should sit down and stand up together.

SAMPLE PROCESSING QUESTIONS FOR DREAM CATCHER

- How difficult was it for you to trust the large group as opposed to just your one partner?
- Did your responsibility change when more people were added to the dream catcher?
- What would have happened if even one person had let go in the middle of the activity?
- Have you ever been affected by the actions of someone else? Have you affected others by your actions?
- What dreams do you have? What are your goals?
- What are some goals for this class? What do we want this place to be like, and what do we want to accomplish?

---

* Dream Catcher is an adaptation of Dr. Tom Smith's Raccoon Circles, which are described in Karl Rohnke's *FUNNStuff III* on page 60 under the title Miniature Yurt Circles.

Facilitation Notes

During a Project Adventure workshop one day in Vermont, we were doing an activity called Raccoon Circles (developed by Dr. Tom Smith). Without warning, the participants took their pieces of webbing and girth-hitched them all to one other circle, so that it looked like a wheel with spokes. Then everyone hung on to a spoke and we all sat down together. It looked like a Native American dream catcher, so the name stuck.

There is a natural sequence to Dream Catcher which is quite engaging. Once everyone gets the hang of sitting down and standing up together, come up with a cheer that can be yelled while doing the activity. You can also use the cheer as a transition after a debriefing session later on. After a period of talking, bring out the dream catcher. Yell your cheer as you sit down and stand up. Now you're ready for another activity.

This activity offers a wonderful time to talk about dreams and goals. What are students' goals, both here in class and later on in life? What do we want to accomplish as a class?

⚠ As with Everybody Up, remind students never to let go of their webbing while doing the activity. Cause and effect are very real here. If someone lets go, the others will have no way to hold themselves up. This is a great metaphor for community—what one person does affects everyone else.

Water knot   Overhand knot

Girth hitch (Step 1)   Girth hitch (Step 2)

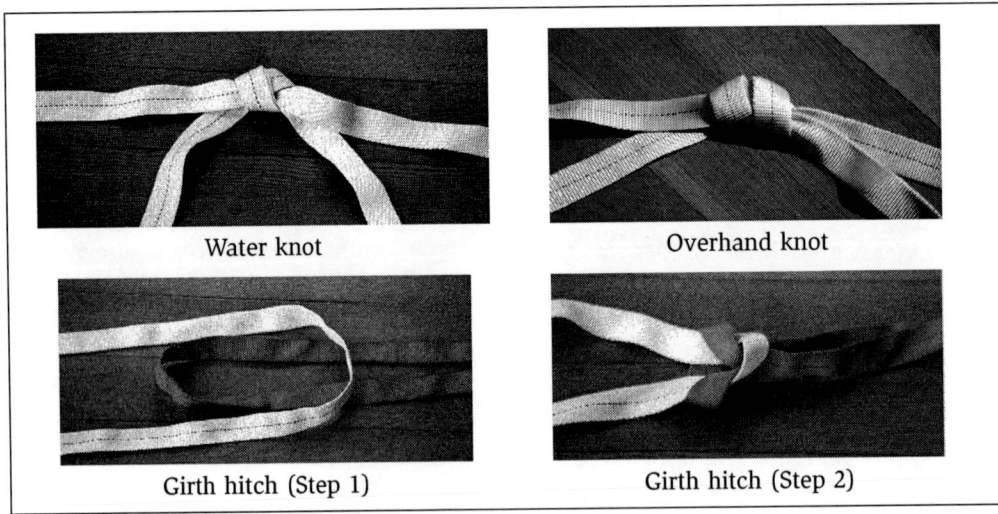

Figure 5.1

Adaptations for Students with Disabilities: Dream Catcher

Cognitive disabilities	• Give hints as necessary to facilitate success.
Orthopedic impairment	• Play could be on mats, soft grass, etc.
	• Participants in wheelchairs can stay in their chairs. They could lean forward with the group and lean back as the group stands.
	• Participants who are not in wheelchairs need the ability to hold onto their partner's hands and stand up with assistance from the group.
Hearing impairment	• Agree on visual signals for the group to use ahead of time to indicate when they will be sitting and standing.
Visual impairment	• Design tactile signals for the group to use ahead of time (for example, "I will take my hand off your shoulder when we should stand up").

MPS: Everybody Up

36. Yurt Circle

Focus: Risk taking, physical/emotional trust, trustworthiness
Materials: None

Suggested Procedure

1. Find a space that is big enough to accommodate the whole class standing in a circle, with some room to spare. Have everyone then take a step back so that the circle isn't too tight.
2. There must be an even number of people in the group. If there isn't, then you should step out to make the number even.
3. Determine what your state bird and state flower are. (In Wisconsin they are the robin and the wood violet.)
4. Every other person would be labeled a bird (in the Wisconsin case, a robin); all the others are the flowers (wood violets, in this case).
5. The object of this activity is for all of the birds to lean in one direction while all of the flowers lean in the other direction. You will determine which group leans in and which group leans out.
6. When people lean, they should keep their bodies as stiff as possible, trying not to bend at the waist.
7. Ask everyone to hold hands so that they have a good grip. Remind everyone to not let go during the activity.
8. Count to three, then have people slowly lean in their given direction—either in or out.
9. Try this a couple of times, then have them reverse directions. When people get really good at this, they can start leaning in one direction, then switch to the other direction seamlessly.

SAMPLE PROCESSING QUESTIONS FOR YURT CIRCLE

- What made this work?
- What would happen if someone let go?
- Was it easier for you to lean in or out? Why?
- How might a community work in this way—where everyone is connected, even though it might not be obvious?
- How did you work with the people around you to make sure no one was pulling too hard? What adjustments did you make?
- What kind of adjustments do we make with members of our class to make sure they are taken care of?

Facilitation Notes

It may be necessary to address the issue of squeezing hands. Students are often embarrassed to hold one another's hands, so you must first determine if they are ready to do so. Another outcome is for someone to squeeze his or her partners' hands too tightly, causing them to cringe. Ask students, or remind them, about trust. You might also suggest that they try holding each others' wrists, which gives a better grip.

As with the Dream Catcher activity, this one demonstrates how people are connected even when they do not think they are. If one person moves too fast, or is not in sync, then everyone feels it. It usually takes a few tries to get the Yurt Circle to work well. Once people get it, then it seems almost easy.

Adaptations for Students with Disabilities: Yurt Circle

Cognitive disabilities	• Use smaller groups (4–6 students each).
	• Have every other person turn around. Then have them all lean back (they will be leaning in opposite directions but facing each other).
Orthopedic impairment	• Play area could be on mats, soft grass, etc.
	• Participants in wheelchairs can stay in their chairs. Have someone hold each chair.
	• Participants not in wheelchairs need the ability to hold onto someone's hand tightly.
Hearing impairment	• Agree on visual signals for the group to use ahead of time to indicate when they will be leaning.
Visual impairment	• No major modifications necessary.

37. 60-Second Speeches

Focus: Risk taking, emotional trust, empathy
Materials: 3" x 5" note cards and writing utensils

Suggested Procedure

1. Everyone is given a set amount of time (5–15 minutes) to prepare a 60-second speech of his or her choosing.
2. Offer note cards to anyone who wishes to take advantage of them.
3. Set up a forum for the speeches—auditorium-like, circle, etc.
4. Students are given 60 seconds each for their speeches, no more and no less.

One year I did the 60-Second Speech activity with a sixth-grade class. One student was terrified and said that he could not do it. Challenge by Choice was, of course, in effect, and I asked him to talk with me after class. He shared that he would really like to do the activity, but it was too much of a risk for him, so we talked about alternatives: taping it, speaking in front of a smaller group, or giving the speech to one other person. None of those options seemed to work, so he remained part of the audience and did not give a speech.

Later in the year, we had a high ropes course experience. Climbing was easy for the student who had had so much difficulty giving a speech. During the last week of school, this student asked if he could give his speech to the class. He stood up there and stammered his way through it. We cheered.

SAMPLE PROCESSING QUESTIONS FOR 60-SECOND SPEECHES

- What was the most difficult part of this activity for you?
- How did the audience treat you? Were they helpful?
- What strategies did you use to get through this challenge?
- Did you consider this a risk or not? What do you think makes it risky for some and not so risky for others?
- What things do you find risky?
- Did you want to get this over with, or were you content to put it off as long as possible? How do you usually handle situations that are difficult or risky for you?

Facilitation Notes

Speaking in front of a group is one of the riskiest endeavors for people in our society. Take the time to acknowledge this fact, and then talk about what the class can do to make it easier for each speaker. To give a speech is to risk embarrassment. How do people show their trustworthiness with other people's feelings?

Since this activity can take some time, split it up over a few days. Have a few people give a speech at the end of a class period, or as a warmup to another activity. It is a great change-of-pace activity.

Adaptations for Students with Disabilities: 60-Second Speeches

Cognitive disabilities	• Have these students work with partners.
	• Do not hold fast to the time limit.
	• Consider having them tell a story together instead of giving a speech.
Orthopedic impairment	• No major modifications necessary.
Hearing impairment	• Have an interpreter if necessary.
Visual impairment	• No major modifications necessary.

38. Sherpa Walk

Focus: Risk taking, physical/emotional trust, trustworthiness
Materials: Long rope like clothesline (optional), blindfolds (optional)

Suggested Procedure

1. Outside in a wooded area is the most interesting place for a Sherpa Walk, but it can be done almost anywhere.
2. Have the entire class line up one behind the other.
3. Either have students put their hands on the shoulders of the person in front of them, or have them all hold onto one long rope.
4. Ask for two volunteers to be the guides, or have the class choose two people to act as guides. These people leave the line.
5. Everyone in the line either puts on a blindfold or closes her or his eyes.
6. One of the guides stays toward the front, while the other takes up the rear.
7. The guides lead the line of blindfolded people through a course that is either predetermined or made up as they go along.
8. You act as a spotter, but you may not talk.

SAMPLE PROCESSING QUESTIONS FOR SHERPA WALK

- How much did you rely on the guides? On those around you? On yourself?
- How did it feel not to be in control of where you were going?
- Whom did you have to trust in this situation?
- What did the guide have to do to make sure everyone was taken care of?

Facilitation Notes

There are many variations to a Sherpa Walk. Try having the guides lead without being able to talk. Set up an obstacle course in a gym, or string clothesline around a bunch of trees for people to follow. The more people must go through, under, over or around, the more interesting the activity will be. You can also fill a hat with pieces of paper, some of which are blank and others of which have an *X*. Whoever draws an *X* is able to talk. Whoever draws a blank must be silent. This can produce some good discussion about dealing with different challenges.

Adaptations for Students with Disabilities: Sherpa Walk

Cognitive disabilities	• Have extra spotters for these students. Give them practice with a "hands-on" experience first.
Orthopedic impairment	• The rope should be attached or arranged so that participants can feel the rope, yet still have both hands free to use manual wheelchairs.
	• Any participant in a wheelchair should be in the front of the line, or should have an individual spotter.
	• The guide can use verbal cues to warn people in advance to stop.
	• The guide can first give a hand sign to the individual spotter before actually stopping.
Hearing impairment	• The spotter should be readily available to give tactile cues to stop, go, etc.
Visual impairment	• No major modifications necessary.

MPS: Incredible Journey (i.e., Trust Walk)

39. Trust Lean

Focus: Risk taking, physical/emotional trust, trustworthiness, empathy
Materials: None

Suggested Procedure

1. You will need space for many groups. Use the hallway, school lawn, gym or all-purpose room if possible. A classroom is feasible but tight.
2. Have students get into groups of three or four. Ask for one group to volunteer as models. Make sure to show the whole activity before having everybody do it.
3. One person in the small group is the "faller." This person assumes the falling position:
   - Stand with feet together.
   - Arms are crossed over the chest.
   - Hold body stiff as a board (squeeze the buttocks—not only is this good exercise, but it keeps the body from bending).
4. The other two or three people are spotters and stand behind the faller. They assume the spotting position:
   - Stand shoulder to shoulder.
   - Put one foot in front of the other to provide a stable base. (If two people, their outside foot goes in front. If there is a third spotter, the middle person can use either foot in front).
   - Keep knees bent.
   - Keep hands up, with fingers pointing toward the sky.
5. The spotters stand very close to the faller.
6. Teach a communication sequence between faller and spotters:
   - *Faller:* "Spotters ready?"
   - *Spotters:* "Ready!"
   - *Faller:* "Falling!"
   - *Spotters:* "Fall on!"
7. At this point, the faller tips backward into the waiting hands of the spotters, who gently set the faller upright.
8. If everyone feels comfortable, then the faller chooses to step a bit forward, and the whole process is repeated a couple more times.

9. Remind the spotters that each time the faller steps forward she or he will fall back lower, so they should squat down a little more. They should **not** turn their hands so that their fingers face the floor. This creates poor leverage and does not work well.
10. If something should go wrong (faller bends or tilts to the side), the spotters' responsibility is to keep the faller's head, neck and shoulders from touching the floor.

SAMPLE PROCESSING QUESTIONS FOR TRUST LEAN

- Were you more nervous as a spotter or as a faller? Why?
- What did the spotters do that helped keep the faller safe and as comfortable as possible?
- Did you feel your spotters were serious about keeping you safe?
- What were some of the things that went through your head when you were falling/spotting?
- How did you choose how far to step each time? Did you think about it?
- Did you trust your spotters? Why or why not?
- Did you trust yourself? Why or why not?

Facilitation Notes

The Trust Lean is the beginning of a classic sequence that signals a quantum leap when dealing with issues of trust. Up to this point you have focused on situations that are more controlled. Now you are sure that students truly care about each others' safety, and are able to make choices freely about what they are willing to do and not do.

⚠️ Spotting is now very active. Spotters truly have someone's welfare in their hands, and it must be taken seriously. This is no time for joking about dropping someone or pretending not to be there. These types of jokes can break trust as surely as allowing someone to fall. It is also good to remind people that not all accidents can be prevented. Sometimes people bend, and the spotters cannot do anything about that. What spotters can do, though, is to keep people from hurting themselves by always protecting the head, neck and shoulders.

One point to make with students is to remind them that anyone—faller or spotter—can stop the activity at any time. If someone is not comfortable falling or catching, he or she can stop and the group moves on to the next person.

Some teachers prefer to do this activity on mats as an extra safety precaution.

Adaptations for Students with Disabilities: Trust Lean

Cognitive disabilities	• Make sure that spotters understand their role. Stand nearby, ready to assist, when this activity is first tried.
Orthopedic impairment	• An adult can tip the wheelchair if it is a manageable weight and the participant feels comfortable about being tipped.
	• Check to see if the participant can come out of the wheelchair with assistance to more fully experience the activity.
Hearing impairment	• Use tapping cues to indicate when the participant should "fall on."
Visual impairment	• These spotters should touch the back of the faller so that they know how far away the faller is.
	• When spotting, these students should be paired up with others who are comfortable spotting.
	• Add an extra spotter, if necessary.

MPS: Trio Spotting

40. Pendulum Trust Lean

Focus: Risk taking, physical/emotional trust, trustworthiness, empathy
Materials: None

Suggested Procedure

1. You will need space for many groups. Use the hallway, school lawn, gym or all-purpose room if possible. A classroom is feasible but tight.
2. Have students get into groups of five or six. Ask for one group to volunteer as models. Make sure to show the whole activity before having everybody do it.
3. One person in the small group is the "faller." This person assumes falling position:
   - Stand with feet together.
   - Arms are crossed over the chest.
   - Hold body stiff as a board (squeeze the buttocks—not only is this good exercise, but it keeps the body from bending).
4. The other four or five people are spotters. Two stand in front of the faller, and the other two or three stand behind the faller. They assume the spotting position:
   - Stand shoulder to shoulder.
   - Put one foot in front of the other to provide a stable base. (If two people, the outside foot goes in front. If there is a third spotter, the middle person can use either foot in front.)
   - Keep knees bent.
   - Keep hands up, with fingers pointing toward the sky.
5. The spotters stand very close to the faller. The faller indicates in which direction she or he will fall first—forward or backward.
6. Teach a communication sequence between faller and spotters:
   - *Faller:* "Spotters ready?"
   - *Spotters:* "Ready!"
   - *Faller:* "Falling!"
   - *Spotters:* "Fall on!"
7. At this point, the faller tips into the hands of the spotters, who gently push the faller back into the waiting hands of the other spotters—very much like Bozo™ dolls which never fall down no matter in which direction they are pushed.
8. This swaying back and forth stops when the faller stands up and says, "I'm on my own."
9. If everyone feels comfortable, the faller asks the spotters to take a step back, and the whole process is repeated a couple of times more.
10. Remind spotters that each time they step farther away from the faller, she or he will fall lower, so they should squat down a little more. They should **not** turn their hands so that their fingers face the floor. This creates poor leverage and does not work well.
11. If something should go wrong (faller bends or tilts to the side), the spotters' responsibility is to keep the faller's head, neck and shoulders from touching the floor.

SAMPLE PROCESSING QUESTIONS FOR PENDULUM TRUST LEAN

- How did this activity compare with the one-direction trust lean?
- How did your role as a spotter change?
- What does it take to trust others with your physical safety?
- What did you do as a spotter to help the person in the middle?

Facilitation Notes

⚠️ The Pendulum Trust Lean ups the ante by having the faller go in two directions. Caution students about the urge to push too hard, thus almost throwing the faller back and forth. This can be unsettling for the faller.

It is also helpful to talk with the class about where to touch a person when spotting in the front. The faller has her arms over her chest. This means that the elbows and upper arms are good places to touch.

Adaptations for Students with Disabilities: Pendulum Trust Lean

Cognitive disabilities	• Reiterate directions to ensure understanding.
	• Make sure that participants are in correct spotting positions.
Orthopedic impairment	• This activity may not be appropriate for students with an orthopedic impairment.
Hearing impairment	• Use visual cues to indicate when the participant in the middle is going to "fall on."
Visual impairment	• Have assistants help place these students in the middle.
	• When these students are spotting, have them stand behind the faller and touch the faller's back to see how far away she or he is.
	• Add an extra spotter if necessary.

MPS: Willow in the Wind

41. Willow in the Wind

Focus: Risk taking, physical/emotional trust, trustworthiness, empathy
Materials: None

Suggested Procedure

1. You will need space for one, two or three groups. Use the hallway, school lawn, gym or all-purpose room if possible. A classroom is feasible but tight.
2. Have students get into groups of 8 to 10. Ask for one group to volunteer as models. Make sure to show the whole activity before having everybody do it.
3. One person in the small group is the "faller." This person assumes the falling position:
   • Stand with feet together.
   • Arms are crossed over the chest.
   • Hold body stiff as a board (squeeze the buttocks—not only is this good exercise, but it keeps the body from bending).
4. The other people are spotters and stand in a tight (shoulder-to-shoulder) circle around the faller. They assume the spotting position:
   • Stand shoulder-to-shoulder.
   • Put one foot in front of the other to provide a stable base (it doesn't matter which foot).
   • Keep knees bent.
   • Keep hands up, with fingers pointing toward the sky.

> **E**ric Borgwardt and company at Bethel Horizons Adventure Center use the following communication sequence whenever a student is engaged in trust, low or high ropes activities:
> *Faller:* "I'm going for it!"
> *Spotters:* "We're here for you ____, (name)."
> *Faller:* "Falling."
> *Spotters:* "Fall on, _____, (name)."
>
> This helps students make a more concrete connection between what they are doing and how it relates to the others.

5. Teach a communication sequence between faller and spotters:
   - *Faller:* "Spotters ready?"
   - *Spotters:* "Ready!"
   - *Faller:* "Falling!"
   - *Spotters:* "Fall on!"
6. At this point, the faller tips backward into the waiting hands of the spotters, who gently push the faller to another part of the circle. This continues until the faller chooses to stand and says, "I'm on my own."
7. There should be at least three hands on the faller, which means that nobody is having to hold the entire weight of the faller by him or herself. (The more the better!)
8. Remind spotters that they should *not* turn their hands so that their fingers face the floor. This creates poor leverage and does not work well.
9. If something should go wrong (faller bends or tilts to the side), the spotters' responsibility is to keep the faller's head, neck and shoulders from touching the floor.

SAMPLE PROCESSING QUESTIONS FOR WILLOW IN THE WIND

- How did it feel to be surrounded by so many people during this activity?
- Did you feel that the spotters were taking care of your safety? How could you tell?
- Compared with the other leaning activities, how was this one?

<u>Facilitation Notes</u>

At this point in the sequence, people are asked to fall in all directions. Willow in the Wind can be very difficult for some students because of all the touching that is involved. Make sure to remind people about Challenge by Choice; individuals must be sure to make the choice that is right for them. It can also help to acknowledge that touching is an issue for some people.

For the most part, though, students enjoy this activity. Encourage people to close their eyes, which offers a different dimension to the activity. As with the Pendulum Trust Lean, remind students to monitor how hard they are pushing people. It can get out of hand very quickly.

With some classes, it may be useful to have an adult join each of the groups for the first couple of tries until students understand exactly what is expected of them.

Adaptations for Students with Disabilities: Willow in he Wind

Cognitive disabilities	• Reiterate directions to ensure understanding.
	• Make sure that participants are in correct spotting positions.
Orthopedic impairment	• This activity may not be appropriate for students with an orthopedic impairment.
Hearing impairment	• Use visual cues to indicate when the participant in the middle is going to "fall on."
Visual impairment	• Have assistants help place these students in the circle.
	• Tighten up the circle.

MPS: Willow in the Wind

Emotional Self-Awareness: Feelings Literacy

People can learn to be more self-aware of their emotions by developing a feelings vocabulary. Here are some activities* that encourage students to learn the names of a variety of emotions so that they can begin identifying them when they occur.

42. Feelings Speed Rabbit

Focus: Feelings literacy, acting silly, being put on the spot
Materials: None

Suggested Procedure

1. Clear a space and have students stand in a circle. You take the middle.
2. Teach a variety of motions/emotions, each of which will be acted out by three people.
3. Point to someone and say "scared." Ask the class how someone who is scared might show it on his or her face. Have the person you're pointing to do that. Then ask how someone who is scared might show it on his or her body. The person on each side of the person you pointed to do that motion. Together, the three people embody the word *scared*.
4. Point to someone and say "angry." Have students create the face and body language to show anger, with the person you pointed to showing the face and the side people showing the body signals.
5. Point to someone and say "excited." Have students create the face and body language to show excitement.
6. Once these have been established and practiced, the game can begin. Tell them that you will point to someone, say "scared," "angry," or "excited," and count to 10 as fast as you can. If the threesome make it before you get to 10, you continue. If not, the slowest person of the threesome takes your place in the middle.
7. After doing this for awhile, try some new emotions to act out. Ask the class to give their suggestions.

SAMPLE PROCESSING QUESTIONS FOR FEELINGS SPEED RABBIT

- Why is it important to learn about different feelings?
- How can you tell if someone is feeling a certain way?
- What are other ways to express your feelings?

Facilitation Notes

Sometimes it helps to begin this activity using some of the classic Speed Rabbit animal motions (see p. 51), and then build in the feelings motions as the activity progresses. This strategy allows students to get into the groove of the activity without adding new content right away. This is also a wonderful activity to repeat throughout the year, adding more feelings to the vocabulary list.

---

* These are adapted from *Adventures in Peacemaking* by Bill Kreidler and Lisa Furlong.

Adaptations for Students with Disabilities: Feelings Speed Rabbit

Cognitive disabilities	• Create motions that require one person or pairs only.
	• Only do two different emotions/motions at first. Add more later.
	• Don't time students at first.
	• You stay in the middle.
Orthopedic impairment	• Make sure all students can do the motions; ask for help from the students about how to modify them.
Hearing impairment	• Use your fingers to count.
	• Stay with these students when they are in the middle to help say the animal, being or emotion.
Visual impairment	• Teach motions verbally and allow students time to practice them.
	• Stay with these students when they are in the middle to help with pointing.

43. Feelings Cards: Charades

Focus: Feelings literacy

Materials: Feelings cards—homemade or commercially made

Suggested Procedure

1. Divide the class into groups of 4–6.
2. Give each group a stack of feelings cards set face down.
3. The object is for students to take turns choosing a card and acting it out for their group members to guess. When the feeling is guessed, another person takes a turn.
4. If the group is having a hard time guessing the feeling, the person doing the charade can show them the card and pick a new one, or ask someone in the group for help.
5. Continue this for 5 minutes or so.

SAMPLE PROCESSING QUESTIONS FOR FEELINGS CARDS: CHARADES

- How easy/difficult was it to act out the feelings on the cards? Why?
- Is it possible to misinterpret what someone is feeling? How does that happen?
- What body language do you use to show how you are feeling?

Facilitation Notes

It is easy for this activity to become competitive, with each small group trying to get more cards than the next. Obviously, this detracts from the true focus of the activity, which is to practice and learn about feelings. It is possible to minimize the competitive nature of the activity by publicly stating that each group has a different set of cards and de-emphasizing the competition. Of course, if competition becomes a factor in the activity, it is a topic that is worth processing.

Adaptations for Students with Disabilities: Feelings Cards Charades

Cognitive disabilities	• Choose 3–6 feelings to start with and have them repeated in the piles of cards. Practice them in advance. Add more later.
	• Have a list of feelings posted for students to choose from.
Orthopedic impairment	• No major modifications necessary.
Hearing impairment	• Teach the signs for all the emotions so that people can guess by using signs as well as verbally.
Visual impairment	• Have the cards written in Braille.
	• Use words or sounds instead of pantomime.

44. Feelings Cards: Stories

Focus: Feelings literacy

Materials: Feelings cards—homemade or commercially made

Suggested Procedure

1. Divide the class into pairs.
2. Give each pair three feelings cards.
3. Ask them to create a short story (one paragraph) using those feelings words.
4. Have each pair read and/or act out their story.

> Feelings cards can either be made by the class or purchased (see Adventure/Experiential Education Resources in the Appendices). Try brainstorming a list of feelings (supplementing the list with other common emotions) and having students create the cards with markers and paper. Another strategy is to bring in an "instant" camera and photograph students showing feelings, then labeling them. It may be necessary for the students to do some research on what a particular feeling is by asking other students and adults how they would describe it.

SAMPLE PROCESSING QUESTIONS FOR FEELINGS CARDS: STORIES

- Which feelings were easier to write about? Why do you think they were easier?
- Which ones were more difficult? Why do you think they were more difficult?
- What are different ways to express how you feel? Writing is one way.

Facilitation Notes

This is just one way to do this activity. Try giving each pair just one card and having individual students create a story about that single feeling. Or, give each person a card and go around the circle asking individual students to create a sentence using that feeling word, or describe an event (real or created) in which that feeling occurred. The idea is to encourage students to examine a myriad of feelings so that they can better communicate their feelings and needs.

Adaptations for Students with Disabilities: Feelings Cards Stories

Cognitive disabilities	• Make sure everyone knows what each feeling is before starting.
	• Give assistance as needed.
Orthopedic impairment	• No major modifications necessary.
Hearing impairment	• Provide interpreters as needed.
Visual impairment	• Have the cards written in Braille.

45. Crossing the Feelings Line

Focus: Feelings literacy, communicating feelings
Materials: Rope or tape to make a large circle on the floor

Suggested Procedure

1. Clear an area. Place the rope or tape in a large circle so that everyone can stand around it.
2. Tell the class that each person is going to cross the line **differently** than anyone else.
3. Each person is to cross the line by showing either (a) a different feeling or (b) the same feeling as someone else, but exhibited in a different way.
4. Demonstrate by stepping over the line with hands clenched and a scowl on your face, then step back.
5. Either have each student tell the class what the emotion is when it is being shown, or have the class try to guess.
6. After everyone has had a turn, have students pair up.
7. This time, each pair is to cross the line differently than any other pair. Give them 30 seconds or so to plan.
8. After pairs, go in groups of four, then groups of eight, and so on, until the entire class is crossing the line together.

SAMPLE PROCESSING QUESTIONS FOR CROSSING THE FEELINGS LINE

- Were you concerned about running out of feelings to share? Did that happen? Why or why not?
- How was it working with other people on this? Were the ideas easier or more difficult to come by?
- Which feelings do you see as "positive," and which do you see as "negative"? Why?
- What ways did you use to express each feeling? What are other ways you could have used?
- Which are the feelings that seem to be the most commonly mentioned? What are some other feelings that we have?
- How might it be risky to express your feelings to others? What can we do to reduce the risk so that people feel comfortable sharing their feelings here?

Facilitation Notes

Generally, as the groups get bigger in this activity, the students have an easier time coming up with ideas. With the addition of people, options are expanded. The first time around, it may be necessary to help individual students come up with ideas toward the end of the activity, so make sure you have a few feelings ideas available. For example, suggest the following: "concerned," "shy," or "hysterical." These are feelings that are usually forgotten in favor of the more common "mad," "sad," "glad."

Adaptations for Students with Disabilities: Crossing the Feelings Line

Cognitive disabilities	• No major modifications necessary.
Orthopedic impairment	• No major modifications necessary.
Hearing impairment	• No major modifications necessary.
Visual impairment	• Have the boundary clearly defined.

46. Emotion Motions

Focus: Feelings literacy, active listening
Materials: None

Suggested Procedure

1. Have students sit in a circle.
2. Start by showing—through motions—only an emotion (hitting your hand in your fist, for example, to show frustration). Then have everyone practice it.
3. The person next to you shows another feeling using motions only. For example, he may represent "pride" by crossing his arms and sitting tall. The next person may signify "bored" by placing her chin in her hand and sighing. This continues until everyone has a unique motion and everyone has practiced them.
4. The game is now ready to begin. You start by showing your motion (fist in hand), then showing another one (say, "pride"—crossing your arms and sitting tall). You have just passed to the person who is "pride."
5. "Pride" now does his own motion, crossing arms and sitting tall. Then he puts his chin in his hand and sighs, thus passing to "bored." This continues until someone makes a mistake (by taking too long, forgetting a motion, doing a motion incorrectly, etc.).
6. That person then becomes your motion ("frustration") and takes your spot. Everyone else moves over one spot until the empty spot is filled. Many times this means that only part of the group moves, while the others stay put.
7. The catch is that the feeling motion stays in the same spot; it does not move with the person. So, those who have just moved have to take on a new motion.

SAMPLE PROCESSING QUESTIONS FOR EMOTION MOTIONS

- What are some nonverbal signals that show how someone might be feeling?
- How might you treat someone differently depending on the nonverbal signals he or she is sending out?
- What are some actions you can take when you are feeling mad, sad, anxious, etc., to help your situation?

Facilitation Notes

This activity helps open the door to talk about nonverbal communication and body language. You can then transition the discussion into what to do when feeling depressed, angry and so on. Encourage students to talk to others and seek out help when they are feeling hurt, angry, frustrated or depressed. Creating different strategies for these situations helps students become more aware of their feelings and how to take appropriate actions.

Before trying this activity, it is important to make sure that students feel OK about being put on the spot, and that it is OK to make mistakes in this class.

This is a variation on King/Queen Frog (Activity 8 under Ice Breakers/Acquaintance Activities in Chapter 4). Try that activity first to lead into this one.

Adaptations for Students with Disabilities: Emotion Motions

Cognitive disabilities	• Do this in small groups.
	• Have the motion stay with the person, so that when everyone moves, they all still do the same motion.
Orthopedic impairment	• Make sure all motions can be done by all students in the class.
	• Allow a longer time to complete motions.
Hearing impairment	• Have everyone learn the sign for their chosen emotion and use sign language.
Visual impairment	• Use sounds instead of motions.
	• Do this in smaller groups.

Behavioral Goal Setting

The Trust phase of the sequence is a great time to begin looking at personal goal setting. Goals are better achieved when people have help and encouragement from the outside. It is risky to entrust others with the contents of a personal goal that is near and dear to one's heart. These trust activities give people experience with the art of goal setting, and strategies to use in order to try to meet those goals.

A behavioral goal has to do with just that: behavior. Ask students to assess their own behavior in class. What might they want to change or reinforce? What personal goals do they have in regard to trusting other students and being trustworthy? Have them first write up a goal that can be accomplished in a very short period of time—maybe even one that can be accomplished in an hour or less. After processing what worked and did not work with that goal, try another goal-setting exercise that requires a longer period of time. This type of goal setting is invaluable as a way to encourage self-reflection, a skill that can be used for an entire lifetime.

47. The River of Life

Focus: Personal goal setting, risk taking, physical/emotional trust, trustworthiness
Materials: Two long ropes for boundaries (clothesline works fine), lots of "stuff" to put inside the boundaries (wadded-up pieces of paper, stuffed animals, shoes, etc.), a sticky note and writing utensil for each person, blindfolds (optional)

<u>Suggested Procedure</u>

1. Clear out the middle of the room or find a large area like a gym or all-purpose room. You can also go outside.
2. Place the two ropes on the ground parallel to each other, about 10–15 feet apart. Make them wavy to simulate a river.
3. Distribute the "stuff" randomly inside the river boundaries.
4. After presenting the concept of SMART goals (p. 101), ask each student to think about a personal behavioral goal—something to work toward in this class. For example, maybe someone is very quiet in a large group and wishes to be more vocal. That person may set a goal to contribute to a group discussion at least once per day. Another student may have trouble getting her homework in on time. Her goal may be to finish all her homework, and hand it in, at least 27 of the next 30 school days.
5. Have them write their goals on their sticky notes.
6. Divide the class into pairs and have them stand around the "river of life."
7. Explain that the river of life is full of accomplishments and frustrations. One way to

navigate through the river of life is to set goals for oneself. This helps to provide direction. Many times, though, there are obstacles to achieving goals—some external, some self-imposed. For example, if a goal is to get one's homework in on time, some obstacles would be: procrastinating by choosing first to do other things (like playing games or watching TV), other responsibilities at home or leaving it at school by mistake. The obstacles are represented by the "stuff" that is strewn about.

8. Have each pair choose someone to be the goal-getters first. The other is the guide. The goal-getters place their goals in the river of life. The object is to get to the goal, pick it up, and get out on the other side of the river while touching as few obstacles as possible.

9. Goal-getters then don blindfolds or close their eyes. The guides then *verbally* direct the goal-getters to their goals. If the goal-getters touch an obstacle, then they must tell their guides about an obstacle that might be encountered when trying to achieve this particular goal.

10. After goal-getters get out on the other side, they switch roles with the guides.

> **M**ary Henton, in *Adventure in the Classroom*, describes "SMART" goals. A SMART goal is:
> - **S**pecific: Goals are not either/or situations. They should focus on one behavior that a person wants to increase, decrease or change in some way.
> - **M**easurable: In order to know if a goal has been achieved, it must be measurable according to quantity and time.
> - **A**chievable: A goal needs to be realistic. If we continually make goals that cannot be accomplished, it is more an exercise in frustration than goal setting.
> - **R**elevant: This refers to the larger group. The goal must offer an overall positive outcome within the context of the group. Although the goal may carry over into a person's life outside of the group, it cannot be damaging or harmful to the person, group or society as a whole.
> - **T**rackable: It must be possible to see if you are heading toward your goal at any particular time. If half of the time has expired to your stated goal, you should be able to see how far you have come, and what else you need to do to achieve the goal.
>
> (Adapted from *Adventure in the Classroom*, p. 81, as adapted from Blanchard, and Sharp and Cox).

SAMPLE PROCESSING QUESTIONS FOR THE RIVER OF LIFE

- What did your guide do to help you achieve your goal?
- What are some resources that can help you achieve your goal? (These can be things or people.)
- What are some obstacles you are likely to encounter when working toward your goal? What can you do to deal with the obstacles so that they don't prevent you from achieving your goal?
- How will you know when you have achieved your goal? How will you keep track? Is there anyone who can help you track your goal?

<u>Facilitation Notes</u>

Make sure you have done some blindfold activities before this one so that students are already used to the concept of being guided by someone else. Also, remind goal-getters to keep their hands in the bumpers-up position.

This activity can get loud and confusing for the students. Some teachers prefer to have the guides stay on the outside of the boundaries, while others permit the guides to accompany the goal-getters into the river. This decision will be based upon the maturity and experience of the students. Also, the amount of "stuff" in the river will be determined by the ability of each class. The more items, the more difficult the activity.

After the activity, create a way for students to report on how they are doing with their goals. Maybe have them check in with their partner every day, or have them chart their progress. When someone achieves a goal, have a celebration. Then have that student create a new goal. If someone is not progressing with his or her goal, have a private conference to ascertain the issues. Revisit the SMART goals checklist to make sure the goal is appropriate; help the student decide on strategies to either re-create a goal or make progress on the given goal.

Adaptations for Students with Disabilities: River of Life

Cognitive disabilities	• Try to make partners a "safe" match (i.e., one partner should be responsible).
Orthopedic impairment	• Leave more space between obstacles for participants in wheelchairs.
	• Use poly-spots (or other flat objects) for participants in wheelchairs (poly-spots work well for ambulatory participants as well).
Hearing impairment	• The partner can give directions using hand taps, hands on the shoulders, etc.
	• Make sure the student with the hearing impairment feels comfortable closing her or his eyes.
Visual impairment	• These individuals would not be able to give directions, but could be the goal-getter.
NOTES	• Consider using an alternate version where objects are hung from the ceiling, for example.

MPS: Minefield

48. Three-Person Trust Walk

Focus: Personal goal setting, risk taking, physical/emotional trust, trustworthiness
Materials: Blindfolds (optional)

Suggested Procedure

1. After discussing SMART goals (p. 101), have each person create a personal goal for him or herself.
2. Find a large open area, like a gym or field.
3. Have the students get into groups of three.
4. Tell them that each person will have a turn to be led (blindfolded or with eyes closed) by the two other people in the group, who are the guides and will keep their eyes open. The person being led will be in the middle. Each group should discuss how the person in the middle wishes to be led (holding hands, walking next to each other, holding onto the guides' elbows...).
5. State the boundaries. Give each group at least three minutes. During that time, the person being led is the center of attention for the guides. The one being led should share his or her goal and discuss with the guides how he or she expects to accomplish it, what obstacles may occur, how to celebrate achieving the goal, and what to do if it turns out that the goal is unrealistic. All during this time, their guides are leading this person inside the stated boundaries.
6. After three minutes, give a signal for people to switch. Do this a third time to make sure everyone in the group gets a turn.
7. Have students write and post their goals in the classroom.

> **SAMPLE PROCESSING QUESTIONS FOR THREE-PERSON TRUST WALK**
>
> - How did it feel to be led by two people?
> - What did your partners do to keep you safe and prove that they were trustworthy?
> - As guides, how did it feel to both lead and listen to your teammate? How did you deal with the safety aspects of this situation?
> - How did it feel being the center of attention?
> - What were some things you shared with your group about your goal?
> - What will you do if you find that your goal is unrealistic?

Facilitation Notes

Make sure that students have had some practice with other blindfold activities before attempting this one, since the combination of leading and listening can be difficult.

Try having students create personal goals that relate to their academic work. For example, if the class is working on a research project, what do they want the outcome to be? How might it look? What quality level are they aiming for? If, on the other hand, they are working on some multiplication concepts, what level of accuracy do they wish to accomplish? Or, if their handwriting needs work, what goal can they set to begin the process of improving it?

Adaptations for Students with Disabilities: Three-Person Trust Walk

Cognitive disabilities	• Discuss goals in advance and offer suggestions when needed.
	• Use an open area, such as a gym, and add obstacles (cones) for a greater challenge.
Orthopedic impairment	• Make sure there is a large amount of space.
	• Remind students to hold on to blindfolded individuals as balance is more difficult when sight is taken away.
Hearing impairment	• Have students with hearing impairments be the guides; they should only be led if they choose to do so.
Visual impairment	• Do this in groups of threes, with at least two sighted people per group.

49. Anonymous Goals

Focus: Personal goal setting
Materials: Paper and pens for each student

Suggested Procedure

1. Hand out paper and pen to each student.
2. Tell them *not* to write their names on their papers.
3. After discussing SMART goals (p. 101), ask each person to write an example of a SMART goal. It does not need to have personal meaning for them, but it can if they wish.
4. When done, they should crumple their papers and throw them in a pile on the floor.
5. Mix the papers up, then have each person take one at random. It does not matter if students get their own.
6. Divide the class into groups of 3–4 students.
7. Each group's task is to read the goals and evaluate them in relation to how SMART they are. Students then make any corrections necessary.
8. Each group presents one of their SMART goals to the class.

> **SAMPLE PROCESSING QUESTIONS FOR ANONYMOUS GOALS**
>
> - Why is it helpful to create goals for yourself?
> - How might SMART goals help you?
> - What part of SMART goals is most difficult for you to create? Why is that?

<u>Facilitation Notes</u>

Although less action-oriented, Anonymous Goals is a low-risk, experiential method to determine if students understand the concept of SMART goals. Not only do they practice writing goals, they also practice evaluating them. This is a good activity to use as an assessment tool to see if your students understand the notion of goal setting.

Adaptations for Students with Disabilities: Anonymous Goals

Cognitive disabilities	• Help these students with their writing.
Orthopedic impairment	• These students can use computers or scribes to write their goals.
Hearing impairment	• No major modifications necessary.
Visual impairment	• These students can use scribes to help write their goals.

Low Challenge Ropes Course

A low challenge course contains activities that develop trust between students. Ropes courses can be indoors or outdoors and require personnel who have specific training on the use of the elements. Many school districts are building their own courses, but if there is no course in your district, there are many that are privately run in most areas of the United States.*

> **T**he term *challenge course* is commonly used to refer to a low ropes course. These courses involve using special equipment designed to encourage the development of trust and group problem-solving skills. These elements are secured to trees, poles, or walls or are designed to be free-standing. Some are even portable.
>
> When building any challenge course, it is important to make sure that the elements are safe and built to industry standards. The Association for Challenge Course Technology (ACCT)† has developed challenge course standards in the areas of installation, operations and ethics, and is an integral resource for any organization interested in building a low or high ropes course.

Generally, any activity that involves spotting of participants involves trust. (Later Problem-Solving activities involve trust, too, but they also require the group to solve a dilemma in the process.) The following low challenge ropes activities focus on an individual taking a risk to trust the other students to act as his or her safety net. Each of these elements is described below, along with sample processing questions. **NOTE: It is necessary to have the proper training before doing any ropes course elements. If you do not have the necessary training, contract with a reputable provider of ropes course services** (see Appendices). This book is not a substitute for proper training and does not give you enough information to safely run these activities.

These activities are included here so that, if used, a class can continue the community-building process at the challenge level. In this way, the ropes course does not become an isolated event or an end in itself, but rather part of the existing program. If your group is using outside facilitators, make sure to communicate with them about

---

* For more information on ropes courses in your area, contact AEE or Project Adventure (see Adventure/Experiential Education Resources in the Appendices).

† See Adventure/Experiential Education Resources in the Appendices.

what has already been accomplished, including the stage of group development. Also, bring your Full Value Contract to the course. You may also wish to talk with the facilitators about your level of involvement during the experience. Are you interested in bringing in classroom issues during processing time; do you wish to participate with the students; or are you more interested in observing? These decisions will be made according to the maturation level of both the individuals and the class in their group process, along with the goals that you and they have set.

If you choose to participate with the students, it can be a rich experience for all involved. Seeing you take some risks, express nervousness and share feelings models these very attributes for the students. The danger,of course, is that they see you as the person with the answers, and fall back on your experience. If your participation is in the plan, make sure you communicate your motives and vision of your involvement. The most difficult part of the day could just be keeping thoughts and ideas to yourself.

50. Wild Woosey

Focus: Risk taking, physical/emotional trust, trustworthiness, spotting and support

Description

Sometimes called the Commitment Bridge, the Wild Woosey consists of two cables strung between three trees or poles in the shape of a V (Figure 5.2). Two participants stand on the narrow (pointed) end of the cables (one per cable) and support each other as they move down the cables. As the cables move further apart, they must adjust their strategy to get as far as possible.

As a pair works together to get as far down the cables as possible, the rest of the group acts as spotters. They are taught special spotting techniques to ensure a safe experience for the students on the wire.

> **SAMPLE PROCESSING QUESTIONS FOR WILD WOOSEY**
>
> - What did you do to support your partner on the cable? What worked? What didn't work?
> - How did the rest of your group support you and make sure that you were safe?
> - How can you support each other in class? What are some examples of ways to support each other?
> - How can you ask for help if you need it?
> - For you, is it easy or difficult to ask for help? How can we make it easier to ask for help in our class?

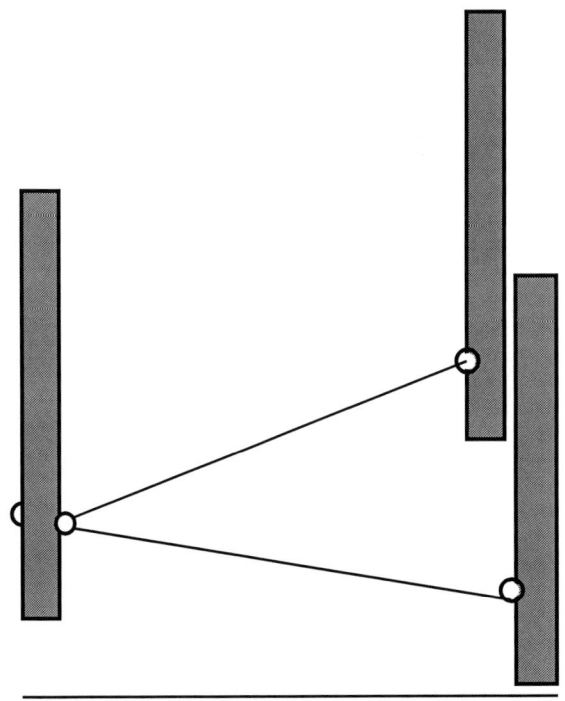

Figure 5.2

Facilitation Notes

Participants on the Wild Woosey generally go farther down the cables when they resist the urge to pull away from their partners, and instead lean in on them. This reality creates a nice metaphor for support by talking about how we can "lean" on others and, in turn, allow others to "lean" on us. When is it appropriate to offer help to others? How does one ask for help when it is needed? To whom does one go for help? **It is necessary to have the proper training before doing any ropes course elements. If you do not have the necessary training, contract with a reputable provider of ropes course services.**

51. Walk of Life (AKA: Mohawk Walk)

Focus: Risk taking, physical/emotional trust, trustworthiness, spotting and support

Description

The Walk of Life is a series of cables strung between poles or trees (Figure 5.3). These cables vary in length, and some have different types of ropes nearby to be used as support. The object is to get the entire group safely from one end of the series to the other. This generally is accomplished in two ways: Either half the group attempts the entire element while the other half spots, *or* each leg of the element is accomplished together—whoever is not on the cable spots the others. Once everyone finishes one leg, the entire group moves to the next.

> **SAMPLE PROCESSING QUESTIONS FOR WALK OF LIFE**
>
> - What did you need to do to help each other across the cables?
> - What did you do to communicate your needs? How did you ask for what you needed?
> - Is it risky to ask for help or to communicate personal need? What are the risks?
> - Given the risks, what can we do to help people risk asking for help in our class?
> - Given the risks, what can you do to reduce your personal risks?

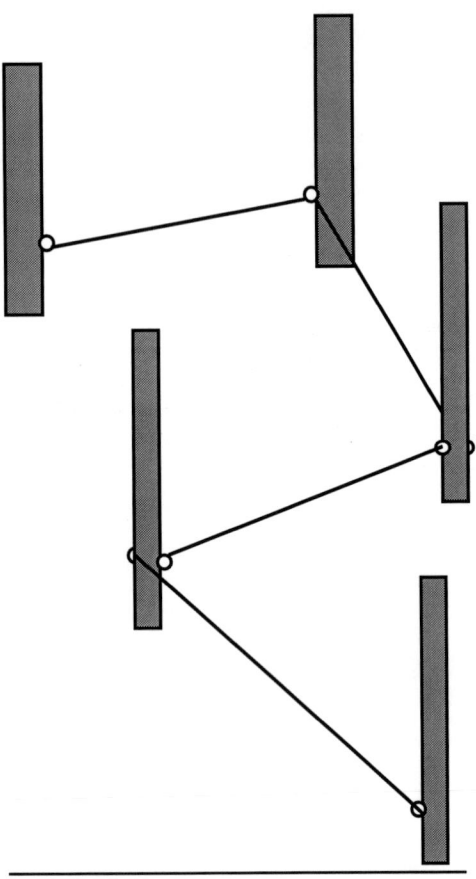

Figure 5.3

Facilitation Notes

It is common for students to begin this activity by trying to walk the cables alone. Although some of the shorter cables allow for this solution, it does not take long for students to figure out that they need to give and receive help to get across the longer cables.

The Walk of Life version of this element involves a metaphor for our journey through life. Each leg of the cable series can be identified with a stage of life. The first can be Birth, the second Preschool, etc. The final cable might be Graduation, with a stated goal that we are working to help everyone graduate. **As with any ropes course activity, do not try the Walk of Life without proper training.**

52. Tension Traverse

Focus: Risk taking, physical/emotional trust, trustworthiness, spotting and support

Description

The Tension Traverse is another cable activity that can either stand alone or be part of a Mohawk Walk. It incorporates one cable attached between two trees or poles, with a long rope attached to one of the trees or poles (Figure 5.4). The object is for a participant to use the rope for support while traversing as far down the cable as possible. Meanwhile, the rest of the group acts as spotters.

Another version of the Tension Traverse involves three cables, attached to trees in the form of a triangle. In this case, two ropes are attached to the same tree or pole, and two people traverse at the same time, but in opposite directions.

> SAMPLE PROCESSING QUESTIONS FOR
> TENSION TRAVERSE
>
> - How did you use the rope for support? What strategies did you use?
> - What are other supports for you in your life—both internal and external?
> - Did you feel as if your spotters were there for you? How could you tell?
> - How did your spotters help you on this element?

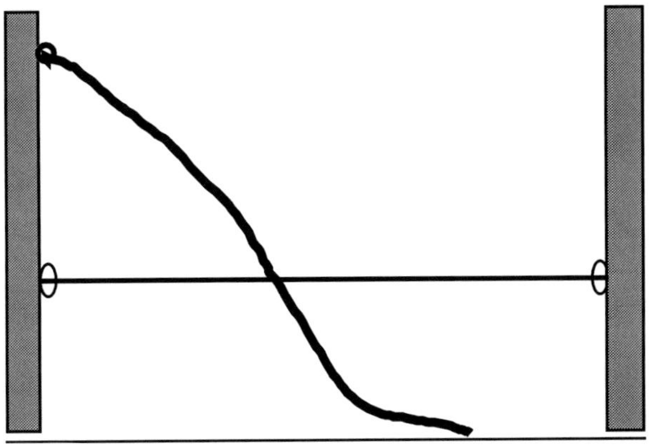

Figure 5.4

Facilitation Notes

As an individual activity, the Tension Traverse allows a participant to challenge him or herself. Ask each person to set a goal, and ask the spotters to support the accomplishment of that goal by offering suggestions and encouragement as needed. Have the student traversing the element state what she or he needs from the spotters. For example, unless the traverser states that she wishes for it to be quiet, the spotters can only guess at what she needs. This might mean that they are offering loud words of encouragement, which is contrary to her particular need.

The rope in a Tension Traverse is very important. How it is used (and there are various ways) can be as important as using it at all. It opens the door to a discussion about different kinds of support—both internal and external. Confidence, for example, can be a powerful internal locus of support for someone. Encouragement from others can be an equally powerful external locus of support. **As with any ropes course activity, do not try the Tension Traverse without proper training.**

> **TRUST FALL FROM HEIGHT**
>
> A fall from height has been a useful and powerful tool for developing trust and support within a group. Some schools have chosen to ban the activity because of a concern that the Trust Fall is more dangerous than other activities. This is a prudent course of action especially when dealing with staff who may have little or no training in Adventure activities.
>
> If, however, the Trust Fall is facilitated by someone with the necessary training, and the group of students is prepared to handle the responsibility of catching their classmates, the Trust Fall from Height can help a class reach new levels of support and empathy. This, in turn, creates an atmosphere where students are willing to take new risks with their learning. The added support allows students to be willing to make mistakes and learn from them.
>
> **As with any ropes course activity, do not try the Trust Fall from Height without proper training.**

SUMMARY: WHEN TO MOVE ON TO PROBLEM SOLVING

Cooperation and Trust are part of group formation. People care about each other and are concerned for everyone's well-being. The Full Value Contract is now well established; the students have a history together that includes trusting each other and taking risks. People understand what it means to make a mistake and how to handle a situation where mistakes occur. Individuals have established personal goals that can continue into the group challenge arena.

Students are now ready to face challenges together. This readiness means that they are willing to struggle with conflict, since solving problems almost always involves differences of opinion and style. These issues will be discussed in greater depth in Chapter 6, Problem Solving: Branching Out.

◊ MOVING TO PROBLEM SOLVING: SOME OBSERVATIONS

	Class Can Move On	**Class Should Stay with Trust**
Making mistakes	• The class has explored and discussed the concept of making mistakes. • Students begin to acknowledge mistakes they make rather than attempting to hide them. • Students begin to articulate what they have learned from a mistake. • When a mistake is made, other students refrain from teasing or put-downs. • Both in individual and group situations, students are willing to try something new—even if it may not be perfect, or falls below expectations.	• Students laugh at each other when someone makes a mistake. • When a mistake is made, students tease or use put-downs. • Students hide mistakes for fear of being put-down. • Students blame others or external factors for mistakes they make. • Students balk at trying something until they can do it "perfectly."
Empathy	• Students perform simple random acts of kindness for each other without prompting (helping to pick up dropped items, for example). • Students show concern for each other's physical and emotional safety. • When engaged in conflict, students can express understanding for another's feelings. • During class meetings, students acknowledge each other's ideas even if they do not agree.	• Students actively do things to harm others—physically and/or emotionally. • Students do not recognize when others are at risk—physically or emotionally. • Students are passive when others are at risk—they do nothing to prevent harm.
Trustworthiness	• Students can identify what it means to be trustworthy. • When engaged in trust activities, students take their responsibility seriously. • Students show through repeated practice that they know how to keep others safe from physical harm. • Students can articulate how to support others through words and actions.	• Students accuse each other of trying to harm them, either physically or emotionally. • Students seem to be reticent about sharing ideas for fear of reprisal from others (this is common if there is someone known as a bully in the class). • Students must be closely monitored during trust activities due to inconsistent follow-through on safety directions. • Students cannot express what it means to be "trustworthy."
Risk taking	• Students support each other's choices about taking risks. • Students can express the difference between a healthy and unhealthy risk. • Students show they understand that risks are different for different people. • Students can set goals about the types of healthy risks they choose to take. • Students have an understanding that there is a difference between encouragement and pressure when supporting others' taking of risks. • Students can articulate how to decrease risk by using thought, resources and education (using a bike helmet and learning the rules of the road before riding a bike, for example).	• Students heckle or tease others into taking risks (e.g., calling someone "chicken"). • Students think that all risk taking is either good or bad—cannot differentiate. • Students do not feel free to try new things for fear of being put-down. • Students engage in impulsive risk taking—without examining consequences.
Physical/ Emotional trust	• Students can explain the differences and similarities between physical and emotional trust. • Students show an ability to spot others during increasingly more demanding activities. • Students agree to and practice confidentiality when asked. • Students can talk about why it is helpful, and how to take care of, others' feelings.	• Students have little or no regard for others' feelings or physical well-being. • Students cannot articulate the difference between emotional and physical safety.

References

[1] Goleman, Daniel. *Emotional Intelligence.* (p. 43)

Chapter 6

PROBLEM SOLVING: BRANCHING OUT

When a class arrives at the Problem Solving stage, it is an indication that they are ready to branch out into more complex tasks and interactions. As the teacher, you offer them group challenges to solve together. You also act as a process observer to help them make sense of how they are working together as a class.

Conflict is a hallmark of problem solving, because people are now comfortable asserting themselves by sharing opinions and taking on leadership roles. Sometimes the conflict is between individual students. Other times the source of the conflict rests with you, the teacher, as people attempt to make sense of their roles within the class. Since you have been seen as the expert up to this point, it is not uncommon for students to challenge your authority. This is a sure sign that the class is entering the storming stage, and searching for ways to have influence in the class. It is time to quietly celebrate that the process is moving along and that relationships are growing to meet the additional challenges that await.

PROBLEM SOLVING
- Decision making
- Group goals
- Taking turns
- Leadership
- Conflict resolution

Activities
Problem-solving initiatives
Team low ropes elements
Conflict resolution
Academic content

You can offer students strategies for dealing with conflict without actually solving their conflicts for them. Through activities that focus on conflict-resolution skills, students can learn how to work through the rough spots and begin to develop class norms in challenging situations.

Many operating norms for the class are developed during Problem Solving. A common scenario is this: During the first problem-solving initiative, very little planning occurs. The class appears disorganized, forming into many small groups—all of whom are attempting to come up with a solution to the challenge. A small argument breaks out between members of the mini-groups about which solution to attempt. Meanwhile, a third group begins a solution. People stop arguing and join in.

After the activity is over, the students discuss what happened. You ask if everyone felt included in the decision. Some say yes, others say no. They discuss why they felt included or not, and what they think caused this to happen. If no one brings it up, you offer the observation that you saw many small groups discussing solutions, and you wonder how that influenced the planning process.

The discussion continues for awhile until someone suggests that the class stand in a circle to strategize solutions to the challenges, thus making sure that everyone is part of the planning process. The students agree to try it during the next challenge. As they gain more experience, students begin to monitor class planning, calling people together to form a circle in order to keep everyone involved. A norm has been born.

As long as issues are dealt with, the class continues through the process of norming. They learn more about how this group works, as well as particular strengths of each student. Leadership begins to ebb and flow with the strengths of individuals, and students become more interdependent when working together. This class has come of age.

PROBLEM-SOLVING ISSUES AND SKILLS

◊ DECISION MAKING

Every group must consciously decide how to decide. There are various ways to make decisions. Without discussion, it can become autocratic, where the person seen with the highest status charges ahead and everyone else follows. At other times the "rule of loud" comes into effect. This happens when many people talk at once, and the loudest person gets heard. Another strategy involves the "arbitrator approach," where students ask the teacher to choose between conflicting sides. None of these methods is very useful to an inclusive community.

Many groups choose to use a majority vote method because students are used to this type of decision making. As a rule, majority vote is exclusive because only 51 percent of those voting need to agree. Those who "lose" the vote may either go along with the decision, choose not to participate, or hide their agendas and even sabotage the group process.

Consensus is an inclusive—albeit sometimes time-consuming—alternative. One myth of consensus decision making is that it is an either/or situation. A strategy that can easily be taught is "five-finger consensus." When a decision is to be made, it should be articulated so that everyone understands what they are deciding. Then everyone holds up the appropriate number of fingers to show agreement:

- Five fingers = This is the best thing since sliced bread.
- Four fingers = It's really great.
- Three fingers = It's an OK thing to do.
- Two fingers = I'll go along with it.
- One finger = I won't block it.
- A fist = Block.

Using this method, there are five ways to agree with a decision and one way to block it. If even one person blocks it, the students must discuss alternatives in order to meet the objections of that one person.

It is important to learn why a decision is being blocked, because it cannot be resolved otherwise. Part of the Full Value Contract is that people will work toward class goals. If someone is blocking a decision for a self-serving reason that cannot be addressed by the students no matter how hard they try, then a block can be overruled. If, however, the blocker articulates principled, well-thought-out objections, the block stays in place, and the class must find another way to meet their challenge together.

Five-finger consensus can also be used to determine the quality of a decision. If everyone holds up only one finger, then it is probably best to re-evaluate the decision. (If everyone holds up their middle finger, you have another issue to deal with.)

Deciding how to decide can be accomplished through the normative process by working through challenges and gaining experience together. As different types of decision making occur, help the class sort through what is going on and how it is working for them. Help them develop decision-making strategies that work for them, and offer skills that will help them be as inclusive as possible.

◊ GROUP GOALS

One way to practice the art of consensus is to embark on a process for arriving at group goals. Since people are working together to solve problems, you need to focus on group goal setting. This can be an arduous process or it can be totally painless, depending on the goal to be set. It is sometimes difficult for people to compromise on an opinion, but it is a necessary skill when working with others. It is important to notice if the same people are "giving in" all of the time, while others are forever "getting their way." This is an issue of influence that needs to be addressed.

> **LOOKING FOR THE WIN-WIN SOLUTION**
> Take some time to discuss the concept of win-win solutions. It is not always enough to compromise; a compromise can mean arriving at a solution where one—or all—parties feel as if they have lost or have given in to keep the process moving. Help your students recognize that win-win solutions are better long-term responses to problems or conflicts that arise.

You can help students practice group goal setting by asking them to start with a small goal. Many Problem-Solving initiatives are uniquely suited for group goal setting, especially if the activities are being timed. Once a base time has been set, ask the class to set a goal about what time they would like to achieve during the next round. Observe how they arrive at the decision, and help them scrutinize their decision-making process during the discussion following the activity.

As they gain experience with group goal setting and decision making, students will set norms around how to arrive at group goals. Depending on the goal to be determined, they might need you to mediate a discussion; at other times students will take on that role. It is important to ask the students if they want your assistance before diving in to mediate.

◊ TAKING TURNS

The subject of taking turns can be an issue of influence, outright enthusiasm, or a trust issue disguised as enthusiasm. During the Cooperation and Trust activities, everyone got a chance to do everything. While solving problems together, however, people must take on roles depending on the needs of the class in relation to the task at hand. Some parts of the task are glamorous, like being the first one to try something or being the one to bring over the imaginary "serum" to save the world. Other tasks are more commonplace, like being one of the middle people to get to the other side.

According to the age and maturity level of the class, taking turns can be quite an issue. There can be physical fights between people who are pushing to be the first to attempt an activity. Feelings can get hurt when people argue over who gets to carry the "serum."

The first step is to sort out the underlying reason for the conflict. It could simply be that a few people are overflowing with enthusiasm. In this case, it is only a matter of slowing people down to make a more conscious decision, including how to share the more attractive tasks over time. If the issue is one of influence, then the students need to discuss how decisions are to be made. On the other hand, it could be a trust issue, because someone may feel that the only way to do the task right is to do it him or herself. This issue needs to be addressed during processing time in order to revisit emotional trust issues.

Whatever the motive, the issue of taking turns is common in the beginning stages of Problem Solving. If it is not resolved, it will return in force time and again until a solution is worked out.

◊ LEADERSHIP

It is difficult to find a word that carries more baggage than *leadership*. In our society, being in the lead is almost always seen as positive, while following is negative. But in a community, leadership must be shared. By definition, communities are places where people arrive at the table as equals, able to collaborate to accomplish mutual goals.

Historically, leadership has variously been defined as autocratic, democratic or *laissez faire*. These definitions all see leadership as a static role, where someone is considered a leader if he or she is in a position of authority. Increasingly, though, people are asked to take on leadership roles as members of small groups or communities. These roles take place *within* the group, rather than *above* or *separate from* the group.

Given this change in focus, it is vital that young people learn how to work as group members, taking initiative when necessary and stepping back to help others when appropriate. This type of collaborative leadership means that students learn how to develop relationships with those around them. They take turns sharing leader and follower roles, according to the strengths of those in the group.

Camp Manito-wish YMCA in northern Wisconsin has developed Seven Qualities of a Collaborative Leader. These qualities were articulated from the staffs' 75 years of combined experience working with teenagers and young adults.

A Manito-Wish Collaborative Leader:

- **Builds a shared vision:** Works with others to create group goals so that everyone can head in the same direction.
- **Shares a common space with others:** Gets together in a circle, around a table, in a classroom—wherever. Students must sit down together at some point in order to open lines of communication for true collaboration.
- **Builds a model—tries it...changes it...tries it again:** Has the ability to try something, learn from his or her mistakes, and then improve the next time. Sometimes groups get into "analysis paralysis" because members are trying to perfect an idea even before they try it. At other times, groups get into a rut by trying something over and over without changing it.
- **Lets others amplify her/his abilities:** Recognizes that the combined strengths of everyone allows people in a class to accomplish more than anyone could alone. This is known as synergy—where 1 + 1 = 3.
- **Remembers that followership and leadership go hand-in-hand:** Leadership "percolates" in a class depending on the strengths of individuals. It is an act of leadership to consciously take a step back to allow someone else to move ahead.
- **Doesn't collaborate to turn out the lights:** Collaboration is not always useful, as in the case of an emergency (such as a fire), or when a task is so simple that it can be done by someone taking the initiative.
- **Celebrates successful collaborations:** It is important to acknowledge and celebrate collaborations, as well as individual effort. Sometimes, when a class has come through a particularly grueling process, it is even more important to celebrate.[1]

These qualities can be explored while students work together to accomplish tasks. They offer some direction when examining the concept of collaborative leadership.

◊ CONFLICT RESOLUTION

My partner, Bert, is an elementary school counselor. One day he came home from a meeting with a new insight. His group had been discussing conflict resolution, and another counselor shared the belief that conflict resolution can only take place in the context of community. Without community, there is no reason to resolve the conflict. Why should anyone care?

Given that conflict is an inevitable part of problem solving, this is a perfect time to teach conflict-resolution skills. There is usually much opportunity for practice. A wonderful resource is *Adventures in Peacemaking*, by William Kreidler and Lisa Furlong. This book, a joint venture between Educators for Social Responsibility and Project Adventure, is an Adventure-based approach to teaching conflict resolution. Even though the book is geared toward children ages 5–12, its concepts are universal. It contains many activities that give participants a chance to learn about how conflict escalates and to practice conflict-resolution skills.

In general, being able to resolve conflict involves building cooperation and trust, along with becoming more emotionally aware. These attributes are the focus of the Cooperation and Trust levels in this community-building sequence. Once students have reached a certain degree of cohesion, they can tackle an ABCD conflict-resolution process*:

- **A**sking: What's the problem?
- **B**rainstorming possible solutions
- **C**hoosing the best solution
- **D**oing it

Conflict-resolution skills are invaluable both in and out of class. The only way to practice them is to be involved in conflict—a thought that makes many of us shiver. It is the community that allows conflict to take place in a safe environment, where people are committed to resolution rather than perpetuation.

PROBLEM-SOLVING ACTIVITIES

◊ ROLE OF THE TEACHER

When you see students struggling to come up with solutions to a challenge, it is essential that you back off. As much as you might want to jump in, with your many years of experience, to help the class through a frustrating moment, it does not help them learn how to deal with frustration. Unless they are considering an unsafe solution to the challenge or are close to an outright fight, they must be allowed to struggle.

As a **mentor,** you can act as a process observer. Sometimes a well-placed time-out for an observation from you is all your students need in order to refocus. For example, maybe students have been using the "rule of loud" to make decisions, and then during the processing session they have decided to use a stick as a prop to show who is talking. During the next activity, the stick is forgotten; the class reverts to the "rule of loud." If no one in the class points this out, you can stop the class in order to hold up an imaginary mirror. Ask them what they see in regard to

> **S**ymptoms of frustration: checking out, blaming, taking control, saying "this is stupid *or* boring," etc.
> **Causes of frustration:** Disparity between expectations and outcome, exclusion from the process, task is too difficult, decision making gets bogged down (conflicting opinions, power struggles, class is in a rut), etc.
> **Solutions:** Look at causes instead of symptoms, take time out to reassess, go to another activity with option of coming back later if students feel it is necessary, etc.

---

* Thanks to the Mediation Center, Asheville, NC, for this concept.

decision making. Most of the time, people will see that they have not been following their own resolution. If not, you can point it out.

A mentor offers feedback by sharing observations and suggestions with the people who are being mentored. These can help make students aware of strategies that they may not have known about before.

Problem-Solving Initiatives

Initiative implies ingenuity, motivation and taking the first step. Therefore, the rules for the following activities are kept to a minimum to allow for creativity. Most of these activities have open-ended solutions. In fact, I have learned that as soon as I think I have seen everything, someone comes up with another way to solve a problem. These activities require few or no props, and many can take place right in the classroom.

53. Warp Speed

Focus: Group goal setting, decision making, leadership
Materials: One soft throwable object (fleece ball, Nerf™ ball, wadded-up paper....), stopwatch

Suggested Procedure

1. Clear the desks or tables away. Have students stand in a circle.
2. Ask everyone to raise one hand to show that they have *not* had the object yet.
3. Call someone's name and throw the object to her. She puts her hand down to show she's had the object. Then she calls the name of someone whose hand is up and throws him the object. This continues until everyone has had the object and it is returned to you.
4. Figure out who is the youngest person in the class. Give that person the object.
5. Tell the class that this is a timed activity. They must send the object to the same person they threw it to before. The activity must begin and end with the person who starts it (in this case, the youngest person in the group). Try this, and get a baseline time.
6. Now reiterate the rules. Then give them time to discuss strategies.
7. Try the activity multiple times to arrive at a mutual solution.

THINKING "OUTSIDE OF THE BOX"

Problem-Solving initiatives give us an opportunity to play with solving problems creatively. As teachers/facilitators, we often see students locking themselves into one way of viewing a problem because of the assumptions they make. Even if a rule is not stated, past experience dictates how they will view the activity, and a rule is somehow conjured up in one or more minds.

I once heard, "If a rule is not stated, it does not exist." Encourage your students to think "outside the box" and address their problems with creativity and imagination. The community you have created is a safe place in which to experiment. Many of the ideas will not work, but some will. Future challenges will then be addressed with open minds, making the chances for success that much greater.

SAMPLE PROCESSING QUESTIONS FOR WARP SPEED

- What was your group goal for this? Did you know what you all wanted to accomplish together?
- How did you decide which idea to try?
- How did your solution change each time? Were you willing to learn from each attempt?
- Do you feel you took a leadership role in this activity? How?

Facilitation Notes

It is fair to say that Warp Speed has an almost limitless number of solutions, which is what makes the activity so popular. It can also be accomplished in a relatively short amount of time.

Many groups decide to stand next to each other rather than stay in their original configuration.

Other groups stay put and play with different ways to get the object around without moving themselves. One class was together on an overnight weekend, and they decided that their group goal was to get the object around as slowly as possible. They figured out how long each person would keep the object, then began sending it around during the rest of the three-day experience. Students were setting their alarms in the middle of the night just to pass off "Mr. Corn" to the next person in the sequence.

Adaptations for Students with Disabilities: Warp Speed

Cognitive disabilities	• Use a slower-playing ball such as a Boingo™ ball or Balzak™.
Orthopedic impairment	• Drop a beanbag on one of these students' trays; he or she would then have to drop the beanbag on someone else's tray. This should work for OI students with reasonable hand control.
	• Use a slower-playing ball such as a Boingo™ ball or Balzak™.
	• Use a larger item to throw.
Hearing impairment	• The thrower must make eye contact before throwing the ball.
	• The leader should stand behind the hearing-impaired participant and give a physical cue when his or her name is called.
Visual impairment	• Group members could hand off a beanbag to this participant; he or she would then hand the beanbag off to the next participant.
	• Use brightly colored/larger objects for improved tracking.
GENERAL NOTES	• Do not require a crisscross pattern; allow students to hand the ball to the person next to them if necessary.
	• Have participants roll the ball instead of throwing it.
	• Use larger balls.
	• De-emphasize the ball drops.

MPS: Group Juggle

54. Moonball

Focus: Group goal setting, leadership, taking turns
Materials: A beachball

<u>Suggested Procedure</u>

1. Clear the desks or tables away. Have students stand in a circle.
2. Tell the students that the object is to hit the beachball into the air. Each time the ball is hit, it counts as a point. The ball cannot be hit by the same person twice in a row. If the ball stops or touches the ground, they must start over. Throw the ball in the air for them to start.
3. After students have tried some rounds, adjusted their strategies and had some success with this, add a new rule: *Everyone* must hit the beachball once before anyone can hit it a second time.

SAMPLE PROCESSING QUESTIONS FOR MOONBALL

- What goals did you set for yourselves? Did it help to set goals? Why or why not?
- If you did not set goals, what goal were you personally striving for? Were people's individual goals compatible?
- What were some strategies you used to achieve your goals? How did these strategies change over time?
- Did you feel you were included in this activity? Why or why not?

Facilitation Notes

Moonball is a great activity to try every once in awhile because it offers the class an opportunity to assess their progress. How they approach this activity will be different after experience working together on other initiatives.

The rules to Moonball are vague by design. This allows the class to discuss a variety of strategies and interpretations. Generally they will begin with the "chaos method." Sometimes this actually works once, but replicating the results is another issue altogether. Finally, students will begin to arrive at an agreed-upon scheme to become more consistent.

A common influence issue that must be addressed is one of ownership—making sure that everyone has the chance to be involved, rather than a few people hitting the ball while others stand around and watch. Encourage your class to set some goals. If they do, they might find that a goal gives them a place to go, rather than hitting a beachball for no other apparent reason.

> **MOONBALL-A-THON**
> The middle-school class of Gus Pausz, retired art teacher and Adventure educator in Skokie, Illinois, decided to use the Moonball initiative as a fundraiser for Play for Peace (whose mission is to "bring children of conflicting cultures together through play..."). The students got pledges of a penny a hit. By the time they were done, they had collected hundreds of dollars for the organization.

Adaptations for Students with Disabilities: Moonball

Cognitive disabilities	• Use balloons instead of balls to slow the activity down and help participants remain focused.
Orthopedic impairment	• Use Balzak™ (a cloth fabric that covers a balloon) or a balloon. They will float in the air more slowly, benefiting participants with slower reaction times.
Hearing impairment	• No major modifications necessary.
Visual impairment	• This activity may not be an appropriate choice for someone with a severe visual impairment.
	• Try this in smaller groups with brightly colored balloons. Everyone in the small group could hold hands to keep the balloon up.
GENERAL NOTES	• Have students who are less mobile form the center part of the circle and students who are more mobile form the outside of the circle.
	• All students could be limited in their movement by standing on a poly-spot or other identified spot.

MPS: Moon Ball

55. Balloon Frantic

Focus: Group goal setting, decision making, leadership
Materials: Two balloons per person, stopwatch

Suggested Procedure

1. Clear the desks or tables away. Have students stand in a circle.
2. Give everyone two balloons to blow up and tie off, including yourself. Each person keeps one balloon; the others are put in a pile near you.
3. Tell the class that this is a timed activity. On a signal, they are to hit their balloons into the air (they *must* be hit in the air—not held or stuck anywhere with static electricity!). **Every five seconds, you will add another balloon from the pile.**

4. The time starts when the signal is given. Time stops when the group has amassed six penalties. A penalty is called when a balloon touches the ground (desk, table, etc.) or is stopped. Students have five seconds to get the balloon back in play, or another penalty is called on the same balloon.
5. Upon the sixth penalty, the time stops and the round is over. Students get 5 rounds to get their "best" time (however they define it).
6. They can strategize between rounds for the next round.

SAMPLE PROCESSING QUESTIONS FOR BALLOON FRANTIC

- Did you discuss a group goal for this activity? What were your goals?
- Describe how you feel you improved (or did not improve) your strategies for solving this problem.
- How were decisions made? Did you feel you had input into the decisions?
- What leadership roles were taken, and by whom?

<u>Facilitation Notes</u>

This is one of my favorite indoor initiatives. There are so many elements to consider that it is impossible to predict how it will go. Some people focus on the time element, others on the reduction of mistakes. Some believe that the class should split up and handle the balloons individually, while others think they should join hands, pile them up, and keep the balloons moving like a popcorn popper.

Without a stated goal, students will generally head in a variety of directions, causing greater conflict and frustration. Deciding on a group goal can help them along. Many times a group goal is related to time or mistakes. Some classes, however, have decided that their goal should have nothing to do with time or mistakes; they all want to try hitting the balloons as creatively as possible. They have had fun and learned much about goal setting in the process. We have already said that different types of goals are appropriate for different situations. For example, a creativity goal would work for a computer software designer, but not be as effective for someone working on the line creating the computers.

With younger students, modify the initiative; have them work in smaller groups to see how long they can bounce a balloon without it hitting the ground. Give them each a stopwatch to monitor themselves. Once they are proficient, have them add just one more balloon. It makes a huge difference.

Adaptations for Students with Disabilities: Balloon Frantic

Cognitive disabilities	• Start with each person having one balloon, then add one or two more to make it challenging. Work up to more balloons over time.
Orthopedic impairment	• Students should work in pairs to keep one or two balloons going. Add more balloons very sparingly to increase the challenge.
Hearing impairment	• Agree on visual cues in advance to enhance communication.
Visual impairment	• This activity may not be an appropriate choice for someone with a severe visual impairment.
	• Students should work in pairs to keep one or two balloons going.

56. Pathfinder

Focus: Taking turns, asking for help

Materials: A large tarp with a 10 × 10 grid drawn on it with permanent marker (a grid taped to the floor works just as well, though is obviously less portable), drawn map of the "correct" path for your eyes only

Suggested Procedure

1. Clear the desks or tables away. Have students stand around the laid-out tarp on the floor.
2. Tell the class that their task is to get everyone from one side to the other. The problem is that there is only one solid path, and it is invisible (see Figure 6.1). The other parts are quicksand.
3. To get across, only one person can be on a horizontal row at any given time (this means that there can only be, at most, 10 people on the tarp at a time—if it is a 10 × 10 grid). No one may skip a row or column; students must move only to a square directly in front, front diagonal or side positions (no backward moves).
4. They may not place any markers (other than their own bodies) on the tarp.
5. If someone steps on a solid point in the path, she or he will be signaled a "thumbs up" (by you). If someone steps in a quicksand section, she or he will be signaled a "thumbs down" and must return to the starting side.
6. No one may offer help to anyone unless that person asks for it. To do so, he or she asks someone directly for help, and by name.

One possible path: START

Figure 6.1

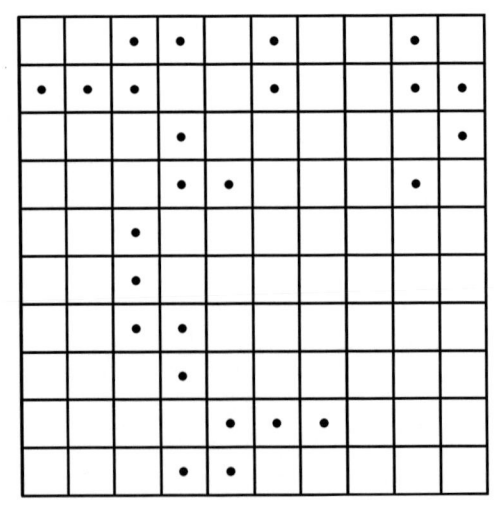

FINISH

SAMPLE PROCESSING QUESTIONS FOR PATHFINDER

- How easy or difficult was it for you to watch people on the path and not be able to help?
- Did you find it necessary to ask for help? Was that an easy decision for you, or did you find it difficult to ask for help?
- When are appropriate times to ask for help?
- Are there times when you ask for help but don't really need it? When?
- Do you feel that people waited their turns and were helping each other through the path?

Facilitation Notes

Pathfinder is a slow yet engaging activity that takes thought and focus. If students rush through this, it can become quite an exercise in frustration. Another difficult aspect for some students is not being able to give help spontaneously to someone in the middle of the path. This condition alone can evoke many metaphors about giving and receiving help.

Sometimes a group discovers the path quickly but runs through it, thereby stranding a few people at the beginning. Although these people have gotten through it, they have forgotten that they were responsible for helping others.

With a larger class, try having two or more tarps, or have half the class do the activity while the other half watches (the fishbowl technique), then have them switch. Younger students can do this with a smaller grid, working up to a larger one. For an easier challenge, allow them to use place markers.

Adaptations for Students with Disabilities: Pathfinder

Cognitive disabilities	• Use a smaller grid (4 × 4 at first), working up to larger ones.
	• Allow students to use markers for their path.
	• Start out with easier paths and work up to more challenging ones.
Orthopedic impairment	• Create a grid on the floor that is large enough to accommodate a wheelchair.
Hearing impairment	• Have interpreters available to facilitate communication if necessary.
Visual impairment	• Create a 3-D grid by using ropes.
	• Have a hand-held grid that is raised so these students can follow along.

57. All Aboard

Focus: Decision making, leadership
Materials: A tarp

Suggested Procedure

1. Clear the desks or tables away. Have students stand in a circle around an open tarp.
2. Tell them that they are scientists who are stuck in a huge pit. Their only hope is to get everyone onto the "growth machine pad" together *(although it's still in its testing phase)*. Once they have enough weight (the weight of the entire team) on the pad for five seconds, they will grow one size bigger. This must be done over and over again, until they are big enough to get out of the pit.
3. Start with the tarp open wide. When students get the entire group on the tarp, count to five. Then ask them to step off.
4. Fold the tarp by a third. Try this again.
5. Continue folding and having them stand on the tarp until it is a bit of a struggle. Then fold it one more time—just a bit.

> **SAMPLE PROCESSING QUESTIONS FOR ALL ABOARD**
>
> - How did your strategy change during this activity? Why did it change?
> - What did you do to listen to each other so that you could make a group decision? Did it work?
> - Were you a listener, a talker or both during this activity? How do these enter into being a leader?

Facilitation Notes

As the tarp gets smaller and smaller, the solution to the problem changes. At first, students can simply step on the tarp. As the space tightens, they need to coordinate their efforts. Make sure that you are spotting this activity. Warn students to step off the tarp slowly, rather than in a large, uncontrolled clump.

Adaptations for Students with Disabilities: All Aboard

Cognitive disabilities	• Work more gradually to a smaller-size tarp.
Orthopedic impairment	• Start with a very large tarp to accommodate a wheelchair.
	• Add extra spotters for balance issues.
Hearing impairment	• Have interpreters available to facilitate communication if necessary.
Visual impairment	• Agree on verbal cues so that these students know when and where to go.

58. Turn Over a New Leaf

Focus: Decision making, leadership, taking turns
Materials: A tarp for every 8–12 people

Suggested Procedure

1. Clear the desks or tables away. Break the class into smaller groups of 8–12.
2. Have each small group stand on an open tarp.
3. Tell them that the object is to turn the entire tarp over without anyone stepping off the tarp.

> **SAMPLE PROCESSING QUESTIONS FOR TURN OVER A NEW LEAF**
>
> - How did you decide who was going to move and when? Was this important?
> - Why did you choose to do the task in that way? Are there other ways?
> - Did you find this task easier or harder than you first thought? What made it easier or harder?

Facilitation Notes

This activity is more difficult than it seems. At first, students think they can simply step to one side and turn the tarp over. Quickly, they realize that it is more complicated than that, necessitating the movement of people from one place to another and possibly back again. Not everyone can be moving at once. Some groups fold the tarp diagonally, others twist it. Still others roll and shuffle. No one way is the best way. The smaller the tarp, the more difficult the task. Once students have accomplished it one way, challenge them to find an alternate solution.

Adaptations for Students with Disabilities: Turn Over a New Leaf

Cognitive disabilities	• Use a larger tarp; work gradually to a smaller one.
	• Try this in smaller groups first.
Orthopedic impairment	• Use larger tarps.
Hearing impairment	• Have interpreters available to facilitate communication if necessary.
Visual impairment	• No major modifications necessary.

59. Setting the Table*

Focus: Decision making, leadership, group goals
Materials: A tarp

<u>Suggested Procedure</u>

1. Clear the desks or tables away. Have students stand in a circle around an open tarp.
2. Ask students to think about what they "bring to the table" when working with others in a group. What are their strengths and skills? Have each person say a strength/skill out loud and step onto the tarp ("table").
3. Tell them that once they are on the tarp, even when everything is pulled out from under them, their strengths and skills keep them standing.
4. To test this, they are to choose two "magicians" from the group. These two should step off the tarp.
5. The rest can rearrange themselves on the tarp in preparation for the "magicians" to pull the "tablecloth" out from under them. Their task is to end up in the same place in which they are standing, but with the "tablecloth" gone. This means that they cannot jump away from the tarp while it is being pulled.

SAMPLE PROCESSING QUESTIONS FOR SETTING THE TABLE

- How did you decide who would be the magicians? Do you think this was a fair way to decide?
- Did this activity turn out to be easier or more difficult than you had thought?
- What strategies did you use to accomplish this task? How did you decide on which strategy to use?

<u>Facilitation Notes</u>

Setting the Table has a higher perceived risk than actual risk; therefore, people tend to over-analyze the situation. Generally, the group will decide to jump at the same time, while the "magicians" pull quickly. Sometimes they will choose to have everyone jump continuously while the tarp is pulled slowly.

---

* Thanks to Jim Dunn and Candace Peterson for inventing this activity.

Adaptations for Students with Disabilities: Setting the Table

Cognitive disabilities	• Work in small groups—4–5 students per tarp.
Orthopedic impairment	• This activity may not be appropriate for individuals with orthopedic impairments.
	• Offer to help pull the tarp.
Hearing impairment	• Have interpreters available to facilitate communication if necessary.
	• Agree on a visual cue for students to jump.
Visual impairment	• Provide extra spotters for these students.

60. Marshmallows

Focus: Taking turns, decision making, leadership

Materials: Two boundary markers (ropes work well) set about 20 feet apart, 8–10 "marshmallows" (carpet squares, poly-spots, or bathmats cut up into squares)

<u>Suggested Procedure</u>

1. Clear the desks or tables away. Set up the boundary markers. Have everyone stand on one side of the markers.
2. Tell students that they are standing on one side of a very large vat of hot chocolate. It is so hot that, if they were to step in, it would scald their legs badly. The trouble is, they are being chased by a pack of wild boars, and they must get to the other side.
3. Luckily, they have some "marshmallows" with them. They can use these to float in the hot chocolate, but there are a few rules:
    - If students lose contact with a marshmallow, they lose that marshmallow. (Model this by throwing a marshmallow to someone—tell her that she would lose the use of this marshmallow because no one is touching it while it is in the air.)
    - They must get as many of the marshmallows to the other side as possible when they are done.
4. If anyone should touch the hot chocolate during the traverse, everybody must all start over.

SAMPLE PROCESSING QUESTIONS FOR MARSHMALLOWS

- Were you happy with your role in this activity? How were the people chosen to be first and last?
- How did you make sure that people stayed in contact with the marshmallows and that no one fell in?
- What happened when a marshmallow was lost? Was it OK to make a mistake?
- What leadership roles did you take during this activity—what did you do to help complete this task?

<u>Facilitation Notes</u>

Marshmallows is a wonderful initiative for people of all ages. Even adults can struggle with getting across the vat of hot chocolate. There are many details that cannot be overlooked, like making sure that someone is always stepping on a marshmallow, or supporting each other so that no one falls in. If someone steps off a marshmallow, then the idea of making mistakes is brought into focus.

Usually, a group will choose to set up a path of marshmallows, with everyone following. Of course, the tendency to rush causes mistakes to be made, and frequently marshmallows are lost along the way, especially the closer people get to the other side. This allows for a discussion about how, if one focuses too much on the goal, sometimes we lose sight of the process.

For younger students, try doing this without the rule of having to touch the marshmallows all the time. You can also insert a rule that people must be connected at all times. For a bigger challenge, place the two halves of the group on each side of the boundary markers, each with half the marshmallows. Their task, then, is to end up on the opposite sides.

NOTE: Make sure you include the rule that the marshmallows cannot be slid across the hot chocolate (they melt…).

Adaptations for Students with Disabilities: Marshmallows

Cognitive disabilities	• Allow some flexibility in not letting the marshmallows be in the hot chocolate without contact.
Orthopedic impairment	• One of the front wheels of any wheelchair must be touching a spot. As the student's wheelchair passes over to the next spot, the rear tire should touch the previous spot (one wheel on a spot at all times).
	• Allow students in a wheelchair to have a stick or extension to use to stay on the marshmallows.
Hearing impairment	• Use a visual signal to let hearing-impaired students know when the group is going to move to the next spot.
Visual impairment	• Participants who are visually impaired can be paired with other students who can help guide them through the marshmallows.
	• Use poly-spots or other flat objects as the stones.

MPS: Stepping Stones

61. All Toss

Focus: Taking turns, group goals, decision making
Materials: A soft throwable object for each person

Suggested Procedure

1. Clear the desks or tables away. Have students stand in a circle.
2. Give each person an object. Ask students to put their objects at their feet.
3. Tell students that the object of this activity is to see how many items can be thrown and caught all at the same time. All objects must be thrown at the same time. They cannot be thrown to oneself or to the person on either side of the thrower.
4. Start with one object. Count to three, and throw your object into the air. If no one catches it, then try again until someone does.
5. Ask someone else to pick up his or her object. Now there are two items in play. Then count to three and both people should throw their objects *simultaneously*. If both objects are caught, have a third person pick up an object to throw along with the other two.
6. Whenever an object is dropped, it is taken out for the next round. Whatever is caught is thrown again. For example, if five objects are thrown and two dropped, the next round involves the three that remained in play. If those are caught, then a fourth one is picked up for the round after that.
7. As the task becomes more difficult, allow time for the students to create strategies.
8. If time is running low, or if frustration or boredom begin to set in, ask the class to set a goal for how many attempts they have to throw all of the items at the same time.

> **SAMPLE PROCESSING QUESTIONS FOR ALL TOSS**
>
> - When did you decide to really begin to communicate? What made you decide to do that?
> - Why did your strategies change?
> - What did you need to do to make this work?

<u>Facilitation Notes</u>

At first, most groups do little planning when attempting this task. As more items are added, however, and items begin to hit each other, the need arises to communicate and collaborate more closely. Although this is unstated, many groups decide to stay in a circle to complete the task. Some groups, though, decide to get into two lines and throw across from each other, especially when items begin to hit each other in the middle of the circle.

Some of the more interesting conversations after this activity surround goal-related issues: Is it more important to be organized or to have fun? Can one be organized and still have fun?

With a large class, try dividing into two groups for this activity. Once both groups have had a chance to try, then combine the two into one large group for more challenge. For an even bigger challenge, add the rule that every time an item hits the floor, students must totally start over.

Adaptations for Students with Disabilities: All Toss

Cognitive disabilities	• Use one item for every two people.
	• Use larger throwing objects.
	• Use throwing objects that are slower to fall (beachball, Balzak™).
Orthopedic impairment	• Allow a certain number of people to pass their object to the person next to them.
	• Use larger throwing objects.
	• Use throwing objects that are slower to fall (beachball, Balzak™).
Hearing impairment	• Have interpreters available to facilitate communication if necessary.
	• Agree on a visual cue to use when throwing items.
Visual impairment	• This activity may not be appropriate for students with visual impairments.
	• Use larger, brightly colored objects to throw.
	• Allow some students to pass their object to the person next to them.
	• Use beeping balls.

62. Basic Group Juggle and Variations on a Theme

Focus: Decision making, leadership, taking turns, group goals
Materials: Many soft throwable objects

<u>Suggested Procedure: Basic Juggle</u>

1. Clear the desks or tables away. Have students stand in a circle.
2. Tell students they need to know the name of the person on their right. Give them time to see who that is.

3. Take one item and throw it around the circle to the right. Each person calls the name of the person to his or her right before throwing the object. Go around a couple of times.
4. Place the objects on the ground and say, "This is *A*, as in apple." Have everyone line up in alphabetical order starting there. They should re-form the circle in this order.
5. Check out if everyone is in the new order by having them call out their names.
6. Ask each student to identify where the person who used to be on his or her right is now. He or she should continue to throw to that person.
7. Pick up an object and begin this pattern by calling the name of the person who used to be on your right and throwing your object to that person.
8. Now tell students that, as a group, they will juggle all of the objects. Everyone must always throw to the original throwing partner. Then throw the objects one after the other and watch chaos reign.

Group Juggle Variation 1: You're In or You're Out*

1. Do a Basic Juggle to teach the activity, then divide the class into groups of 4–6.
2. Give each group an object, and have them set their own juggle pattern in their small groups.
3. Each time they complete a full pattern without dropping the object, they should take a step back.
4. If an item is dropped during the pattern, they should take a step in.
5. After they have tried this for awhile, give each group more items to juggle.

Facilitation Notes

This variation of Group Juggle is particularly well-suited for younger students. It allows them to assess how they are doing by seeing how far back they are standing after a given amount of time. For older students, ask them to choose how many items they think they can handle. This is a good way to deal with the issue of realistic versus unrealistic goals.

This variation needs more room, so using the gym or going outside are the best options.

Group Juggle Variation 2: Low Drop Juggle

1. Do a Basic Juggle. After setting the pattern, but before going through the first round with all the items, tell the students that each person must count his or her own misses.
2. Demonstrate what a miss looks like: Throw your item toward your catching partner, but deliberately throw it on the floor. Even if it is your fault, the catcher must count it as a miss. Then throw it to someone who is not your catcher. Your catcher must count it as a miss, too, because she didn't catch it—someone else did. Any miss is counted and added up for a group total of misses.
3. Try the activity with everyone throwing to their original catching partners. Make sure to throw the items quickly, one after the other. Remember, we want some chaos here.
4. If someone finds an item on the floor nearby, he or she must pick it up and throw it to the usual catching partner.
5. Either the items will all return to you or they won't, and you will have to stop the action. Go around and ask each person for her or his total misses. Add them up. This number is generally quite high.
6. After announcing the total, ask the class how they can reduce the number of misses. Get specific strategies.
7. Try the activity again.

---

* Thanks to Carla Hacker for creating this variation.

Facilitation Notes

The results of this activity are generally quite impressive. All it takes is adding a group goal, thus changing from an individual point of view to a group orientation.

For older students, ask them what kind of a goal they would like to set for themselves, rather than stating the goal for them. This could be anything from fewer misses to a fixed number of misses to a goal unrelated to the number of misses. Help them settle on one goal; then ask them for strategies to achieve it.

Adaptations for Students with Disabilities: Group Juggle

Cognitive disabilities	• Speed/time should not be an issue.
	• Use a slower playing ball such as a Boingo™ ball or Balzak™.
Orthopedic impairment	• Drop a beanbag on the tray of these students; they would then have to drop the beanbag on someone else's tray. This should work for OI students with reasonable hand control.
	• Use a slower playing ball such as a Boingo™ ball or Balzak™.
Hearing impairment	• Throwers need to make eye contact with these students before the ball is thrown.
	• The leader should stand behind any hearing-impaired student and give a physical cue when his or her name is called.
Visual impairment	• Group members could hand off a beanbag to these participants. They would then hand the beanbag off to their "catching" partners.
	• Use brightly colored/larger objects for improved tracking.
GENERAL NOTES	• Do not require a crisscross pattern; allow participants to hand the ball to the people next to them if necessary.
	• Have participants roll the ball instead of throwing it from participant to participant.
	• Use larger balls.
	• De-emphasize the ball drops.

MPS: Group Juggle

Group Juggle Variation 3: Juggling for Our Lives

1. Do the Basic Juggle (see page 124) through step 7.
2. Divide your throwable objects into two piles—one to go through the pattern forward, the other pile to go through the pattern backward. Put all the stuffed animals in one pile (for example) and all the fleece balls in another pile.
3. In addition to the two piles, have two wadded-up pieces of paper and a cup of water handy.
4. Take one pile. Tell students that these objects represent their lives—what they do every day, their roles, their responsibilities. Ask them to call out some of the things they do every day (e.g., homework, sports teams, baby-sitting...).
5. Take four or five of these items and go through the regular pattern, with everyone still throwing to the same person.
6. Next, take the other pile. Tell students that these objects represent all of those curve balls in our lives—the unexpected. Have them label these (illness, car accidents...).
7. Try sending four or five of these items through the pattern backwards. With these, everyone throws to the person who was just throwing to them.
8. Take out the two wadded-up pieces of paper. Tell them that these are rumors, which can go anywhere. When in play, students can throw these to whomever they wish.

9. Finally, take out the cup of water. Tell students that this represents their school responsibilities. You will be passing it around the circle, hand to hand.
10. Then start the Juggle—sending items out in all the various directions. Either they will all come back to you, or you will need to stop the action.
11. Ask students how they felt about this round. Generally, you will get answers like "crazy," "overwhelming," "exciting."
12. Now ask them for strategies to bring their "life" into a semblance of order. The two uncontrollables are needing to use the same items and needing to stand in the same place. What can they control?
13. After eliciting strategies—like slowing down, communicating better by making eye contact, or waiting until someone is ready before loading more objects on—try it again. The results can be impressive.

> **CONTROLLING CHAOS**
>
> In order to make sense out of chaos, one must experience it. Group Juggles are a unique and safe way to get at the issue about controlling what one can, while letting go of the parts that cannot be controlled. Most of these juggles require us to go a little crazy, trying to juggle everything even when it is impossible (which is why the objects must be soft). This "controlled" chaos allows us to look at the situation and manage the parts that are controllable—our speed and communication, for example. The uncontrollables—number of objects or where we are standing—can be left alone.

Facilitation Notes

This variation works well for high-school students. The metaphor resonates with many of them, creating an avenue to issues about leadership, decision making and goal setting in their lives. It is also striking to focus on the behaviors in life that can be controlled, as opposed to pointing fingers at others who are outside one's sphere of influence. It is truly amazing how much people can effect change if their focus is strong enough.

SAMPLE PROCESSING QUESTIONS FOR GROUP JUGGLE

- What skills/qualities did you need in order to juggle all of the objects successfully?
- How did setting group goals affect the activity?
- What made the difference between the first and second attempts?
- What parts of this were you able to control? What was outside of your sphere of influence?
- What parts of your life are you able to control? What parts are outside your sphere of influence?

---

63. Puzzles

Focus: Taking turns, group goals, decision making, leadership
Materials: Legos™, blindfolds (optional)

Suggested Procedure

1. Divide the class into groups of 4–5. Have each group sit around a table.
2. Give each group a handful of Legos™. Student groups are to create a sculpture using no fewer than 15 pieces and no more than 20 pieces. Give them 10–15 minutes to create their sculpture.
3. When everyone is done, tell them that they will have 5–10 minutes to create a plan to put the sculpture back together **with their eyes closed** (or wearing blindfolds). During the planning session, they may not take the sculpture apart.
4. When the time is up, groups should take their sculptures apart, mix up the pieces, then close (or blindfold) their eyes.

5. Give them 10–15 minutes to put their sculptures back together.
6. When done, give each group an opportunity to share their sculpture with the class. They should talk about some of the successes and challenges they had with the task.

SAMPLE PROCESSING QUESTIONS FOR PUZZLES

- What plan did your group come up with to re-create your sculpture? Did it work for you? Why or why not?
- What roles did you take on? Were you in there putting things together, or did you wait until your pieces were needed?
- How did you communicate when your eyes were closed? What strategies did you use?
- Which was easier for you: creating the sculpture or re-creating it? What made it easier or harder for you?

Facilitation Notes

This is a nice activity to use when exploring the idea of creating a common vision or group goals. People often think that re-creating the sculpture will be easy, then quickly learn otherwise. Your discussion can transition to the idea that creating a goal or vision is really the easy part; making it happen is where people usually get bogged down.

Adaptations for Students with Disabilities: Puzzles

Cognitive disabilities	• Use large Legos™ with fewer pieces.
Orthopedic impairment	• Use large Legos™.
	• People can pair up with these students to help them place puzzle pieces.
Hearing impairment	• Allow these students to keep their eyes open, but they cannot touch the puzzle pieces. They can offer help through physical touching (*not* of Legos™), sounds and yes/no signs.
Visual impairment	• No major modifications necessary.

64. Blind Polygon

Focus: Taking turns, group goals, decision making, leadership
Materials: A large rope for every 6–8 people (cotton clothesline works well), blindfolds (optional), cards with the words of different shapes on them (*square, triangle,* etc.)

Suggested Procedure

1. Clear the desks or tables away. Break the class into smaller groups of 6–8.
2. Give each group a rope tied in a circle. Have everyone stand around their rope, holding on with at least one hand.
3. Ask them to either close their eyes or put on blindfolds.
4. The task is to create different shapes with the ropes. Everyone must keep at least one hand on the rope at all times. When a group thinks they have it, they can look.
5. Start with a circle for everybody, just to get the idea. Then hand out cards to each group. Groups are to create the shapes, one at a time, at their own pace.

> **SAMPLE PROCESSING QUESTIONS FOR BLIND POLYGON**
>
> - How did you communicate while doing this? What worked?
> - Did anyone stand silent and just do as instructed? Was this a useful strategy? Why or why not?
> - With people talking and not being able to see, how did you make decisions? How did you take turns talking?
> - What kind of leadership qualities helped in this activity?

Facilitation Notes

The creation of these shapes vary in difficulty depending on the number in the group and how picky the small group members are about the correctness of the shape. For example, a square is easy to make with a group of four, but difficult with a group of five. If students want to make an exact rhombus, then each side must be the same length. Some groups struggle with one shape, while some groups speed through them all.

Have younger students try this without the rope, simply holding hands.

Adaptations for Students with Disabilities: Blind Polygon

Cognitive disabilities	• Have group members (helpers) with eyes open help to direct members with eyes closed.
Orthopedic impairment	• Students in power wheelchairs should not be blindfolded.
	• Students in wheelchairs may need assistance, but no major modifications should be necessary.
Hearing impairment	• Use sign language to inform these students which shapes will be made.
Visual impairment	• No major modifications necessary.

MPS: Blind Polygon

65. Numbers

Focus: Group goals, collaboration
Materials: A number sheet for each person (see Figure 6.2)

Sample Number Sheet

```
   58   4      28      41 49 16
10         23       12            35
    17 54      52       40  7
34           29     27         18
    48 13      2           60      1
 6                    43  8 44
       39 24 53              22 57
    33             14 36
21      3  46                 26    32
    55         25 51       5
42      15 56          37      19
       59      9            45    50
47 11         30     20 38    31
```

Figure 6.2

Suggested Procedure

1. Give each person a number sheet. Tell students to turn the sheets face down. They may not write on or tear them.
2. Tell students that when you give the signal, they are to turn their papers over and touch the numbers in order from lowest to highest. They will have 60 seconds to get to the highest number possible.
3. After the minute is up, they are to turn their papers face down again.

4. Try this a few times.
5. Now tell students they may work with as many people as they wish, but they cannot work alone.
6. Together, using one number sheet, they are to do the same task—on a signal, turn the paper over and touch as many numbers as possible, in 60 seconds, in order from lowest to highest.
7. After one round with the groups, give them a minute to create a strategy.
8. Try this a few times.
9. Give the groups a few minutes to compare results between working alone and working in groups.

> **SAMPLE PROCESSING QUESTIONS FOR NUMBERS**
>
> - Did you prefer working alone or working with at least one other person? What made it preferable for you?
> - How were your results? Were they the same or different when working alone versus with a group? If different, what do you think made the difference?
> - What tasks work best for you when collaborating? What tasks work best for you when working alone?

Facilitation Notes

This is a great activity that takes very little time and has a big message: On certain tasks, working together creates synergy—a cooperative effort where the group result is greater than the individual parts. Generally, the groups get much further than the individuals on this task—especially if the small groups work out a strategy where each person is responsible for a smaller section of the whole paper of numbers. This focus allows each person to be more efficient. Many groups choose to fold the paper to delineate between the areas of focus for each individual.

By the way, experience shows that having four people in the small group generally produces the best results.

Adaptations for Students with Disabilities: Numbers

Cognitive disabilities	• Have a paper with fewer and larger numbers on it.
	• Do not time this at first to let students find all the numbers.
Orthopedic impairment	• Have these students work in pairs so that partners can help point to numbers.
	• Allow for more time, or do not time the activity.
	• Time this to see how long it takes, then have students try to reduce the time.
Hearing impairment	• No major modifications necessary.
Visual impairment	• Have some number sheets available in Braille or in raised letters.
	• Allow more time, or time the activity to see how long it takes.
	• Have fewer numbers on the sheet.

66. Don't Touch Me

Focus: Group goals, decision making, leadership
Materials: A Hula Hoop™ or short rope, stopwatch

<u>Suggested Procedure</u>

1. Clear the desks or tables away. Have students stand in a circle. Place the Hula Hoop™ on the floor in the middle of the circle.
2. Ask everyone to identify a partner across the circle. Have students point to the feet of their partners; they should be pointing at each other's feet.
3. The object of this initiative is to trade places with partners without touching anyone else. At some point in the switch, each person must put his or her foot in the Hula Hoop™. This can be done simultaneously or alone; it is up to the students.
4. This is a timed activity. The time will start when the first person moves from his or her spot. The time will stop when the last person has assumed his or her place on the other side of the circle.
5. Students should have "bumpers up" (hands out with fingers pointing to the ceiling) when moving across the circle.
6. Try this a number of times, allowing for some strategizing between attempts.

SAMPLE PROCESSING QUESTIONS FOR DON'T TOUCH ME

- Did you set a group goal for this activity? What was it?
- How did you arrive at this goal?
- Can you think of other solutions for this task?

IT'S ALL IN THE DOING

Remember, it's not just *what* a group does to solve a problem, it's also *how* they solve it. Our own biases as teachers/facilitators come out loud and clear when we observe a class in action. Many times our brains tell as that students are going about this all wrong, when in fact they are just doing it another way. Before intervening, take a step back to survey the scene and examine your own biases about how things should be done. Step in only when safety is an issue or the frustration level surpasses the students' ability to deal with it.

Processing the experience, too, is more about how things were handled rather than what was done. It may start with the *what*, but the group should continue to look for connections with the bigger issues of *how* and *why*. Otherwise, our students leave with an understanding of what to do if they happen to stumble upon some throwable objects or a beachball, but with little understanding of the general principles of leadership, decision making, conflict resolution and the like.

<u>Facilitation Notes</u>

As with many of these initiatives, there are a variety of ways to accomplish the task. Some groups remain in the circle formation, while others rearrange themselves to improve their efficiency. Most groups will choose to set a goal to lower their time, but a few have chosen to see how many different solutions they can find.

Adaptations for Students with Disabilities: Don't Touch Me

Cognitive disabilities	• Start this with two lines of students facing each other. See how long it takes to just switch with a partner.
Orthopedic impairment	• Allow people to stand next to their partners, if it is difficult to move quickly across the circle.
Hearing impairment	• Agree on a visual cue to signal to these students when it is time to move.
Visual impairment	• Have partners help guide these students to their spots.

67. Channels

Focus: Taking turns, goal setting, decision making, leadership

Materials: Purchased set of materials (Pipeline, available from Project Adventure 1-800-796-9917) or Channels made with 1/2 inch PVC pipe, cut lengthwise with a band saw, in 12"–18" sections, ball bearing to fit in channel (or use paper towel tubes cut lengthwise, or use corner molding found in supply stores and cut into 12 18" sections), tin can

Suggested Procedure

1. Clear the desks or tables away so that there is an aisle through the classroom at least five feet wide.
2. Every student is given a channel. The task is to move the ball bearing across a predetermined area and into the can. The area needs to be longer than the length of the group standing next to each other. (This means that you may have to create a route that starts at one end of the room, heads into a corner and goes back to the other end of the room).
3. Explain all the rules to the students:
   - No one may touch the ball bearing with their skin or clothing.
   - The ball bearing may not touch the floor.
   - If either of the above happens, the group must start over.
   - When an individual has the ball bearing in his or her channel, they may not walk.
   - Channels may not be made into tunnels by putting two channels on top of the other.
   - Each person must remain in possession of his or her own channel.
4. Once the students have gotten the ball bearing in once, try increasing the challenge by adding more ball bearings. Ask them to set a goal for how many they think they will get into the can. If a ball bearing hits the floor or touches a person, then that one is taken out of play.
5. Try other items such as marbles, ping pong balls, golf balls, and even raw eggs.

SAMPLE PROCESSING QUESTIONS FOR CHANNELS

- How did you decide to organize your group in order to accomplish this task? Why not spread out more?
- Given the nature of the task, could this have been accomplished alone?
- How were you able to accomplish this task in a group, when you could not have done this easily alone?
- How was each person a leader and a follower in this activity?
- What strategies worked for you? What did not work?

Facilitation notes

This task is harder than it appears, and a group must have the capacity for patience. It is common for the ball bearing to fall more than once, with the group having to start over many times. The frustration level can get high. That is usually when communication breaks down and people stop working together. If this happens, it provides good fodder for discussion with a focus on how to recognize the need for, and provide structure for, a group when facing a difficult problem.

If you choose to "raise the stakes" by introducing raw eggs (best done outside), the processing can turn into a discussion about how students reacted to the increased challenge. Did people find themselves focusing more, or less? When have the stakes been raised for them at school? How have they reacted?

Sometimes it is helpful to try this activity in small groups first; then combine the groups for a "grand finale" attempt when everyone has had an opportunity to practice.

Adaptations for Students with Disabilities: Channels

Cognitive disabilities	• Work in pairs first for practice. Then try it in groups of three, and then groups of four, etc.
	• Use paper towel centers and ping pong balls to slow down the pace.
	• At first, just practice moving the ball from one place to another. Work up to having a specific goal.
Orthopedic impairment	• Pair students up with one channel so that they can help each other.
	• Use paper towel centers and ping pong balls to slow down the pace.
	• If students are unable to hold the channel steady, allow them to pass the ball by hand.
Hearing impairment	• Agree on communication signals for when the action speeds up.
Visual impairment	• Have partners help guide these students to the end of the line when it is necessary to move.

Low Challenge Ropes Course Activities

A challenge course has many activities that require more specific equipment. These courses are generally stationary, and teachers/facilitators need formal training to run the activities safely. **It is necessary to have the proper training before doing any ropes course elements. If you do not have the necessary training, contract with a reputable provider of ropes course services.** (See Questions to Ask Ropes/Challenge Course Providers in the Appendices.)

The following activities offer a representative sample of low ropes course elements.

68. Islands

Focus: Decision making, taking turns, leadership

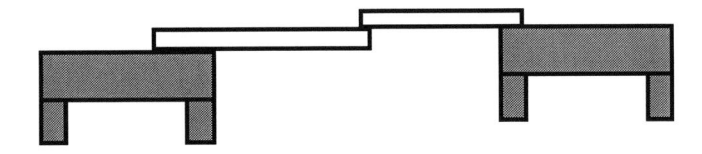

Figure 6.3

This element consists of three separated platforms ("islands"), either forming a line or forming an L shape (see Figure 6.3). Everyone is asked to stand on an end platform and is given one or two boards to use as tools. (Each board, by the way, does not span the entire space between platforms.)

The object is to get the entire group to the farthest "island" without touching the ground. Students are not allowed to jump.

SAMPLE PROCESSING QUESTIONS FOR ISLANDS

- Since there is only one way to solve this problem, how did you decide to use this method?
- What did you do when you were not physically involved in getting someone over to another island? Did you feel you were still part of the process?
- What did you take into consideration when choosing who should go first/next/last?
- What roles did you assume during this activity? Did your role change at all?

<u>Facilitation Notes</u>

Unlike most problem-solving initiatives, there is a single answer for Islands—using the boards to build a bridge between platforms. How this is done depends on the decisions made by the students. At first they will devise a diving board-like structure, where some people stand on one end, and have a smaller person go out to place the second board on top of the first, thus creating a bridge. Since students are not allowed to jump, once the bridge is built, they must make choices about the order in which people go across. Eventually, the bridge must be moved between the second and third islands.

Some of these considerations, of course, are made due to body size and type, which can be uncomfortable for some people. Body type, though, is not the only consideration. Much depends on how many people are standing on the end of the board, and where the person crossing places his or her weight. Leverage is a key component, which can be discussed during the debriefing time—especially in relation to how, when working together, people can accomplish different (and often more) things than when acting alone.

Another issue that can arise during this element is that there is down time for people. Only a handful of people can be actively involved in the solution at any given time. The rest must watch and wait. How does one stay engaged in the process, even when not physically active in it? How can the solution be constructed to maximize involvement of all participants? The discussion can then move to the "real world," as when people work together in cooperative groups, or work on a project with others. How can the way they work together keep everyone involved so that a few people are neither doing all of the work nor being excluded from the task?

Adaptations for Students with Disabilities: Islands

Cognitive disabilities	• Allow boards to touch the ground.
	• Help students figure out how to set up the boards to maximize safety.
Orthopedic impairment	• There is a version of Islands that can be built as a universal element and can accommodate wheelchairs.
Hearing impairment	• No major modifications necessary.
Visual impairment	• Have extra spotters to make sure these students do not step off an island, but get across without falling.

69. Nitro Crossing

Focus: Decision making, leadership, taking turns

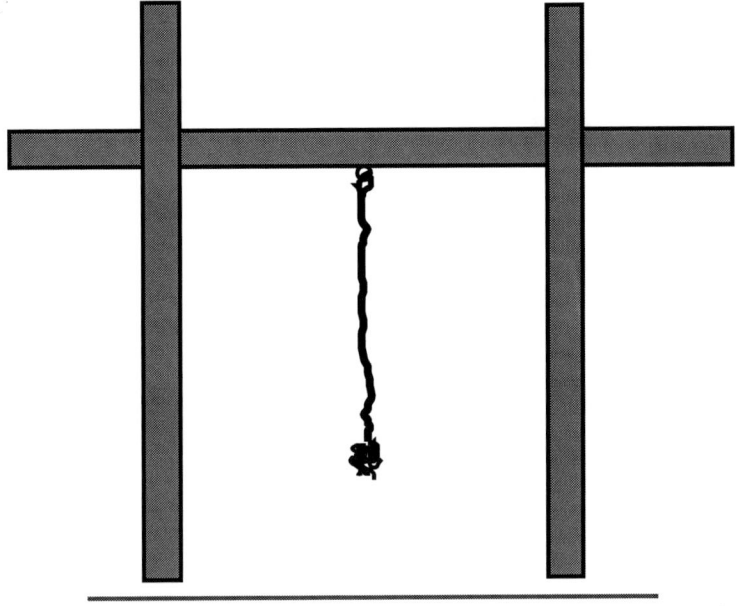

Figure 6.4

Nitro Crossing consists of a rope hung from a cable or beam (see Figure 6.4). Boundaries are set, with the rope hanging between the boundaries. The class should stand behind one of the boundaries. Their task is to get over to the other side without touching the ground between the boundaries (usually described as a chasm at least a mile straight down…). They also are given a bucket of water (commonly called *nitro, serum,* or *magic potion*), which must be transported to the other side without spilling a drop. Sometimes a platform (or an area marked with Hula Hoops™) is set up on the other side, where everyone must end up together.

SAMPLE PROCESSING QUESTIONS FOR NITRO CROSSING

- How did you choose who would take certain roles? Why were these people chosen?
- Do you feel you were listened to during this activity? Why or why not?
- How did you support each person who was going to the other side? Did some people need more support than others? How did you know?
- Name at least one thing you did to help accomplish this task. How might what you did be described as a leadership role?

Facilitation Notes

Nitro Crossing is really a series of problems to solve. It begins with having to get the rope, which is just hanging there. Since students cannot jump for the rope, they must find an alternate way to get it. Sometimes they are told that they can only use what they have on them to get it; at other times they are given more leeway.

Other problems include getting the people over, getting the "serum" over, and even having everyone fit onto a platform or into Hula Hoops™. Consequences for spilling the serum or stepping off the platform range from just getting back on the platform to having the whole group come back and start over.

Taking turns can become a big issue, especially with elementary and middle-school students. It can become a competition about who gets to go first, or who gets to take the "serum." Some students may get hurt feelings, check out, or even sabotage the situation if they feel excluded. Sometimes it helps to stop the process for a moment to discuss the immediate issues. Focus on what is working and what is not, and develop some quick strategies. Then start the process going again. Later, during the debriefing session, a wider-angle view can be used to see how that incident fit in with the whole activity.

It is also common for smaller groups to form, each discussing their own solution to a problem, but neglecting to communicate between the groups. Conflict can arise when different groups or individuals spar about which idea to try and when. This scenario can expand into a discussion about cliques, playground disputes, etc.

As with any ropes course activity, do not try Nitro Crossing without proper training.

Adaptations for Students with Disabilities: Nitro Crossing

Cognitive disabilities	• Allow these students to have the rope at the beginning (save that challenge for another time).
	• Do not include the bucket of water as an added challenge.
Orthopedic impairment	• There is a universal version of this element called the Nitro Trolley.
Hearing impairment	• Agree on a visual cue so that these students know when they should come over and when other people are on their way.
Visual impairment	• Have extra spotters to make sure these students do not fall off the element.

70. Spider Web

Focus: Decision making, taking turns, leadership

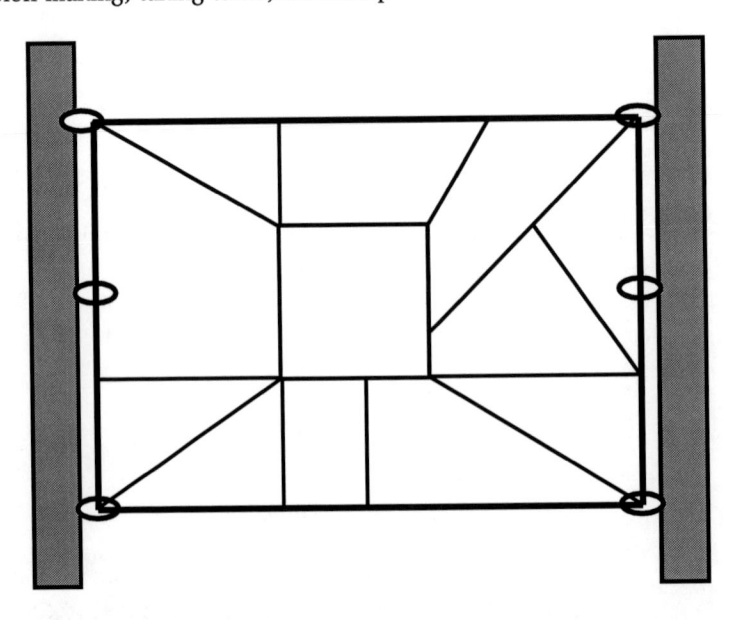

Figure 6.5

The Spider Web stands about 6 feet high and can be either stationary or portable. It looks like a giant web, with a rectangular frame that is attached to trees, poles or movable supports (see Figure 6.5). The inner frame is strung with small Bungee™ cords or string, with a variety of openings in different sizes and shapes. The object is to pass everyone through these holes without touching any part of the web. Usually a hole can be used only once or twice. This requires that some people must be picked up and passed through the upper holes, while others will step or crawl through the lower holes.

Consequences for touching the web vary from having the group count the number of touches to having everyone go back and start over—for only one touch.

Here are a couple of variations:

Jim Dunn of the Madison (Wisconsin) Public Schools has younger students use only one bottom hole. However, they must all get through it without touching the web, while maintaining contact with at least one other person.

Karl Rohnke introduced a variation that Project Adventure has used with their portable game frame, at the TEAM Conference in Chicago. Students take a 50-foot piece of rope and weave it through the entire web without touching the web. My experience with this is that it gives the brain a great workout and everyone wishes they had at least one more arm each.

SAMPLE PROCESSING QUESTIONS FOR SPIDER WEB

- What role(s) did you take on during this activity? Were there other roles you could have assumed? Why or why not?
- Why did you choose the order that you did? Did you have a rationale?
- Did you feel that you had a choice about what hole you would go through and how you would go through it?
- What did you do to keep each other safe when going through the web?
- If you could do this activity over again, what would you do in the same way? What would you change?

Facilitation Notes

The Spider Web takes a great deal of planning in order to get everyone through. Body size and type are emphasized, which can be uncomfortable for some people. It is also necessary to ascertain how comfortable individual students are with being picked up and passed through the web. Past experience with trust activities and discussion will help in determining how willing people are. As the teacher, you can model asking if someone is willing to be lifted, especially if the other students are making the assumption that it is OK.

It is common to see the "rule of loud" come into play during this activity. Since there is so much planning involved, many ideas begin to flow. Sometimes many people talk at once, and only the loudest are heard. It is helpful in these situations to call a time-out, mention your observation that many people seem to be talking at once, and let students process that piece of information.

There is no one right way to do this activity. Almost every challenge course has a Spider Web, and it is a nice element to revisit. Sometimes a person is the smallest in the group, while the next time he or she happens to be one of the largest. It gives people a chance to take on different roles.

Due to the size considerations, many students assume that the "big" people must do all the lifting, while the "smaller" people should be lifted. This is a good time to show that size is not the only consideration, and that people working together can lift more than anyone working alone.

As with any ropes course activity, do not try the Spider Web without proper training.

Adaptations for Students with Disabilities: Spider Web

Cognitive disabilities	• Have fewer holes to choose from.
	• Be lenient about touches.
Orthopedic impairment	• There is a universal version of this element called the Universal Spider Web, which is attached under the ground. There are holes that a wheelchair can fit through.
	• If these students are willing, they can be lifted out of their wheelchairs to go through a hole.
Hearing impairment	• Agree on visual cues so that these students know when people are going through the Spider Web.
Visual impairment	• Have an assistant available to help these students know where to be to help with spotting.

71. The Wall

Focus: Decision making, taking turns, leadership

The Wall stands 10–12 feet high (see Figure 6.6). The object is to get everyone over the sheer face to the other side. When people are not helping on top, or going over, they are part of the spotting team.

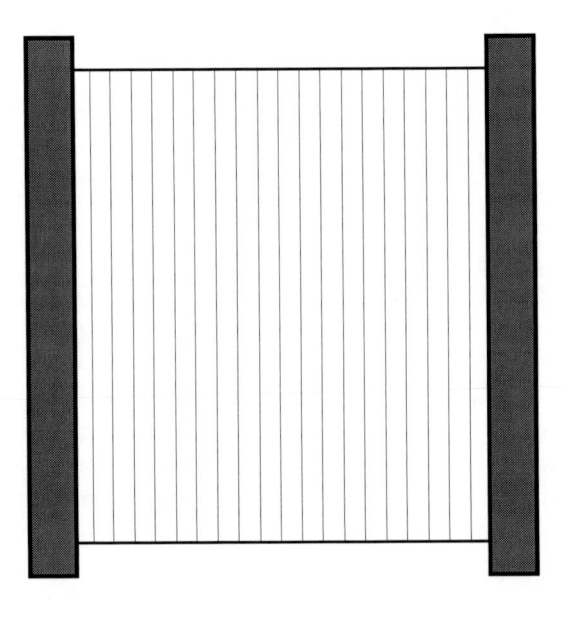

Figure 6.6

SAMPLE PROCESSING QUESTIONS FOR THE WALL

- What role(s) did you take on during this activity? Were there other roles you could have assumed? Why or why not?
- Why did you choose the order that you did? Did you have a rationale?
- Did you feel you had a choice about what role you took in this activity?
- Did you feel you had a choice about going over or not?
- What did you do to keep each other safe?
- If you could do this activity over again, what would you do in the same way? What would you change?

Facilitation Notes

Although The Wall is a simple problem, the solution is far from easy. This is a high-level activity that requires a large amount of cooperation and trust between students. Proper spotting is critical in this activity. Many emotions, questions and skill requirements arise when doing the Wall, and it is important to revisit the concept of Challenge by Choice. Make sure that each person is acutely aware that he or she has a variety of choices about how to participate in this activity.

A challenge such as this, when a group is ready to meet the challenge, can be both taxing and rewarding. It is physical. People are required to physically support each other by lifting, pulling and spotting. It can also be quite an emotional challenge. The anxiety level for some can be quite high, especially if they are dealing with a fear of heights, or a fear of trusting others with their safety. When finished, people feel they have accomplished something that has challenged them to a fuller degree than most of the other elements.

Body size, again, can be an issue here. Watch for people objectifying each other by talking about "getting the small person over," or "getting the big person over first...." When this happens, it is important to call attention to it right away, as this type of objectification can be hurtful. Stopping the process for a quick discussion can help students refocus their intent. Encourage them to call each other by name. Later, during the debriefing session, the idea of objectifying or stereotyping others can be addressed using this experience as an example.

As with any ropes course activity, do not try The Wall without proper training.

Adaptations for Students with Disabilities: The Wall

Cognitive disabilities	• Allow everybody to help anyone going over the wall.
	• Place two people at the top from beginning to end to assist.
Orthopedic impairment	• This activity may not be appropriate for people with orthopedic impairments.
Hearing impairment	• Agree on visual cues so that these students know when to spot and when to go over the wall.
Visual impairment	• Provide assistants to help these people when they are spotting so that they do not get kicked by anyone going over the wall and they know where to be.
GENERAL NOTES	• This is a high-level activity. It is best attempted when a group has shown high levels of trust and a high ability to spot each other. Groups of mixed abilities can do this activity, but they must be ready for it.
	• Provide extra spotters whenever attempting this element with groups of mixed abilities.

Conflict-Resolution Activities

When people come together to solve problems, conflict is inevitable. It can arise from miscommunication, unwillingness to compromise or an intolerance for diversity. It can also arise simply because people have differing ideas or have little practice working with others. The one sure bet is that there will be conflict. Resolving it is another matter, of course. Activities can be used to teach specific conflict-resolution strategies and concepts. *Adventures in Peacemaking* by Kreidler and Furlong contains many such activities, which have provided the spark to create these that follow.

72. **Butter Battle Escalator**

Focus: Conflict resolution: Awareness about how conflict can escalate [2]
Materials: *The Butter Battle Book* by Dr. Seuss, escalator graphic (see Figure 6.7)

Conflict Escalator

Conflict: _____

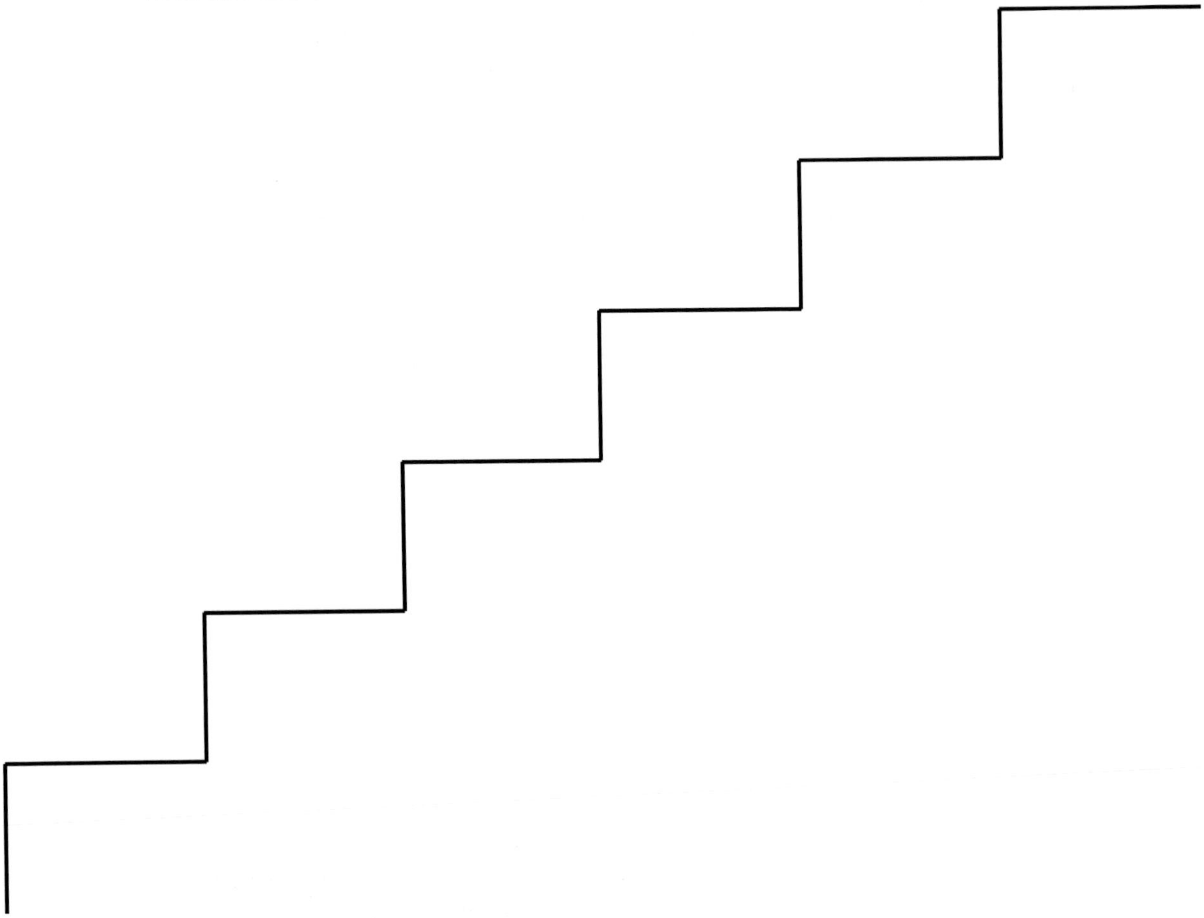

How was the conflict resolved/How could it have been resolved? _____
_____

De-escalators for you: _____

Figure 6.7

Suggested Procedure

1. Read *The Butter Battle Book* by Dr. Seuss out loud to the group. Pay attention to how a conflict escalates between the Yooks and the Zooks. On a large sheet of paper or on the board, chart six steps of the escalation following the model in Figure 6.7.
2. Discuss the following questions:
   - What was the original conflict?
   - What do you think caused the conflict to escalate?

- Read the last page again. Brainstorm at least five possible ways to resolve the conflict.
- What could the Yooks and Zooks have done to de-escalate so that they did not end up as they did?

3. Ask students to each think of a conflict they have had with at least one other person. Then have them chart how it escalated using their own escalator sheets. With partners, they should discuss the conflicts they have charted. Ask the following questions:
   - If the conflict was resolved, how was it resolved?
   - If the conflict was not resolved, how could it have been resolved?
   - When you become angry or upset, what are some de-escalators that help you calm down so that you can deal with the conflict? Write each one on a sticky note (*example:* Listen to music).
4. Post your de-escalators (sticky notes) on a sheet of paper. Create and label categories so that similar ideas are together.

SAMPLE PROCESSING QUESTIONS FOR BUTTER BATTLE ESCALATOR

- What are some causes of conflict?
- Why do you think conflicts tend to escalate?
- What are some strategies we can use in this class to de-escalate conflicts?
- Once a conflict is de-escalated, what are some strategies to resolve the conflict?
- How can we help each other de-escalate a conflict so that it can be resolved?

Facilitation Notes

The Butter Battle Book can be used with students of all ages. It is a perfect allegory for the idea of escalating conflicts. There are many other ways to use children's literature to teach conflict-resolution concepts. This is just one example.

It is important to give students an opportunity to explore how to deal with conflicts at a time when they are *not involved in* a conflict. Later, when a conflict inevitably occurs, they will have heightened skills to deal with it. De-escalation is important, because conflicts cannot be resolved when people are thinking and acting in an enraged state.

As the teacher, it is helpful for you to float between the pairs or small groups to help guide discussion about de-escalators. Some students may have difficulty identifying personal de-escalators because they have little experience with even trying to de-escalate a conflict.

Adaptations for Students with Disabilities: Butter Battle

Cognitive disabilities	• Provide examples of conflicts for the students to consider (maybe ones that occur in class).
Orthopedic impairment	• No major modifications necessary.
Hearing impairment	• Provide an interpreter if necessary.
Visual impairment	• Provide materials in Braille, and graphics that are textured so that these students understand the concept of the conflict escalator.

73. Brainstorming

Focus: Conflict resolution: brainstorming solutions
Materials: An ordinary household or classroom item for each group, paper and pencil

Suggested Procedure

1. Divide the class into groups of 4–5.
2. Tell them that you are going to do a brainstorming activity. The following rules are in place when brainstorming:
   - Every idea is accepted. No matter how outlandish the idea, it is written down.
   - Ideas are not evaluated. Even if you think an idea won't work, it is written down.
   - Go for as many ideas as possible—quantity is important. Choosing the appropriate ideas comes later.
3. Give each group an ordinary item. Have them brainstorm as many uses for it as possible in three minutes.
4. Ask each group to circle the following categories from their list:
   - the three most likely uses of the object
   - the three most unusual uses of the object
5. Have groups share their objects and circled words with the class.
6. Present the class with the following conflict to test their brainstorming skills:

   > Tirana was unhappy with the look of her backyard. She had been looking at those bushes for way too long, and they needed to be cut. Although the bushes were in the neighbor's yard, they were hanging over into hers. One day she went out and started cutting off the top three feet of the bushes. When she was about half done, the neighbor on the other side of the yard came running out the door yelling, "What are you doing? We need our privacy here!"
   >
   > Tirana replied, "What do you care? This isn't even on your side of the yard?" This was Tirana's first meeting with this neighbor, and it didn't appear to be a pleasant introduction.

7. Have each group brainstorm lists of possible solutions to this conflict. Keep the lists handy for further discussion (see box below).

SAMPLE PROCESSING QUESTIONS FOR BRAINSTORMING

- How does brainstorming solutions help in a conflict situation?
- If two people are arguing about who gets to use a ball at recess, what are some solutions to this conflict?
- How might you choose a solution from the list for this conflict?
- Why do you think it is important to accept all ideas when brainstorming? What difference does it make?

Facilitation Notes

Brainstorming is an important skill when working through conflicts. If people are to look for possible solutions, they must be able to arrive at a variety of options. After the list is made, then an appropriate course of action can be chosen.

Adaptations for Students with Disabilities: Brainstorming

Cognitive disabilities	• Try brainstorming as a whole class first.
	• Take an item and pass it around. Have each person say one thing it could be used for and pass it along. If certain students can't think of anything, they can ask for help from the rest of the group.
Orthopedic impairment	• Make sure there is someone in the group who can scribe—either on computer or on paper.
Hearing impairment	• No major modifications necessary.
Visual impairment	• Make sure these students know what their item is before starting the brainstorming.

74. Conflicts—the Real...the Imagined

Focus: Conflict resolution: using a model to resolve conflicts
Materials: ABCD Conflict Resolution Model[2] (see below), 3″ × 5″ notecards

---

ABCD Conflict Resolution Model

A Ask: What is the problem?
B Brainstorm possible solutions.
C Choose one.
D Do it.

Suggested Procedure

1. Have the students get into groups of 4–5.
2. Discuss the concept of *conflict*. What is a conflict? Have people share some examples—they can be major or minor.
3. Give each group some cards. Have students write down a description of a conflict on each card. Collect all the cards.
4. Introduce the ABCD problem-solving model.
5. Get some volunteers to role-play a conflict. First have them pick a card, then role-play how the conflict might go *without* using the ABCD model.
6. Have them replay the conflict using the ABCD model. Make any necessary clarifications about the model to the class.
7. Pass out a card to each group. Have each group role-play without *and* with the ABCD model.

SAMPLE PROCESSING QUESTIONS FOR CONFLICTS—THE REAL...THE IMAGINED

- What was the difference between the two role-plays for your group?
- What are some instances when using this model would be helpful?
- When is it difficult to use this model?
- Does solving a conflict using this model have to take a long time? Why or why not?

Facilitation Notes

Again, this activity provides practice in using a conflict-resolution skill when students are *not* involved in a conflict. The more practice they have with the model, the more they will be able to use it when the need really arises. Keep some of these cards on hand for times when you have a few moments between tasks or classes. Pick one out, and have volunteers role-play the conflict to the class. Then have the class brainstorm some solutions.

Adaptations for Students with Disabilities: Conflicts—the Real...the Imagined

Cognitive disabilities	• Brainstorm conflict scenarios as a large group.
Orthopedic impairment	• No major modifications necessary.
Hearing impairment	• No major modifications necessary.
Visual impairment	• No major modifications necessary.

75. Rearrange the Classroom

Focus: Conflict resolution: reaching win-win solutions and consensus
Materials: 11" × 17" piece of paper for each group of 3–4 students, paper pieces representing room furniture, scissors, glue

Suggested Procedure

1. Divide the class into groups of 3–4.
2. Tell students that you want them to create a way to rearrange the classroom using the following guidelines:
   - Have defined areas for individual quiet space, group work space, and group social space.
   - Make sure that windows, bulletin boards, doors and chalkboards are unblocked.
   - Keep things that go together, together—for example, the teacher's desk and file cabinets should be near each other. If there is a pet in the room, the pet supplies should be near the cage, etc.
   - Add one new thing to the classroom to make it a more comfortable place for learning.
3. Go over the concept of win-win decisions, and revisit the idea of five-finger consensus (see page 110).
4. Give each group a set of materials.
5. When everyone is done, have each group present their concept of the rearranged classroom.

SAMPLE PROCESSING QUESTIONS FOR REARRANGE THE CLASSROOM

- What were the easy parts of this task? What were the more difficult ones?
- Did you disagree on any part of your vision for the room? What was it? How did you resolve any disagreements?
- Did you look for win-win solutions? What were they? How could they have been win-lose, or lose-lose solutions?
- What are some skills you need in order to arrive at win-win solutions?
- Does compromising always mean that everyone wins?

Facilitation Notes

This activity can take some time because the students are basically starting from scratch. Each individual must first have a vision of the room, and then they must find ways to blend their visions into something each can appreciate. It is amazing how tenacious of their own ideas people can be, even when the consequences are imaginary. Practice in looking for win-win solutions can help students learn a skill that is extremely useful when the consequences are real.

For fun, you can actually rearrange the room periodically using students' designs.

Adaptations for Students with Disabilities: Rearrange the Classroom

Cognitive disabilities	• Have each group design just one part of the classroom. They can physically rearrange it right then and there.
Orthopedic impairment	• Have larger, 3-D objects to move around instead of paper.
Hearing impairment	• No major modifications necessary.
Visual impairment	• Have larger, 3-D objects to move around instead of paper.
	• Have these students work in small groups on just one part of the classroom—moving the real furniture.

76. Batten Down the Hatches

Focus: Conflict resolution: reaching win-win solutions and consensus
Materials: A list of household items like the one shown here

List of Supplies

matches
5 gallons of gasoline
tent with stakes and poles
case of dog food
raincoat for each person
10-pound bag of oranges
charcoal grill
charcoal
package of toilet paper

car keys
flashlight with new batteries
suitcase with a change of clothes for each person
winter coat for each person
5 boxes of toaster tarts
1 gallon of milk
matches
weather radio
3 pounds of cheese

family photo album
video game
road atlas of the United States
5 gallons of water
jackknife
box of 10 candles
cell phone
emergency flares

<u>Suggested Procedure</u>

1. Tell the class that they are living in southern Florida, and that there has just been news of a large hurricane heading their way. The evacuation notice has just gone out. They have 15 minutes to gather up everything they need before leaving. Due to limited space, they can only take 15 items with them, not including people and pets. The family consists of two kids, parents, and the family dog, Juno.
2. Give each person a list of supplies. Have students rank-order their top 15 items.
3. Divide students into groups of 4–6.
4. Review the idea of win-win solutions and reaching consensus.
5. Ask each group to reach consensus and to list *at least* their top five items. If they get that far, then have them continue to rank-order the other 10.
6. Have each group report their top 5–15 to the class.

> ### SAMPLE PROCESSING QUESTIONS FOR BATTEN DOWN THE HATCHES
> - Which items were easy to agree on? What were some of your disagreements about?
> - How did you reach a consensus on the items? What strategies did you use?
> - Did you feel that you arrived at win-win solutions? Why or why not?

<u>Facilitation Notes</u>

Consensus activities like this can really be a struggle for some people. It is often relatively easy to choose the 15 items to keep; the interesting part is attempting to rank-order those items. Here are a few hints that might make reaching consensus a little easier:

1. Avoid arguing. Try to present ideas logically.
2. Listen to others. They may just convince you to change your mind.
3. It isn't necessary to win or lose. If agreement stalls, look for the next best alternative.
4. Don't just agree to avoid conflict. Yield only if other sides make sense.
5. Avoid conflict-avoiding tactics. Don't flip a coin to decide. Look for the win-win through compromise.
6. Disagreements are healthy. Everyone has a different opinion. Work through disagreements and, possibly, you'll find a great solution.

Adaptations for Students with Disabilities: Batten Down the Hatches

Cognitive disabilities	• Have fewer items to consider.
	• Do not insist on consensus for all things. Have these students agree on a few and talk about why they picked these items.
Orthopedic impairment	• No major modifications necessary.
Hearing impairment	• No major modifications necessary.
Visual impairment	• Have the list of supplies written in Braille.
	• Have 3-D representations of each item.

Academic Content Activities

In her article "The Virtues of Not Knowing,"[3] Eleanor Duckworth speaks of creating classrooms where the "quick right answer" is not the norm. Instead, students are encouraged to explore realms in which the right answer is unknown. Dr. Duckworth sums it up with the statement: "The virtues involved in not knowing are the ones that really count in the long run. What you do about what you don't know is, in the final analysis, what determines what you will ultimately know."

Although that statement has the ring of a paradox, a closer examination speaks to the *process* involved in real learning. Academic content can be approached much like working through problem-solving initiatives. Giving students an opportunity to explore content without narrowly looking for one "right" answer can be a great gift, especially since there are few simple answers in daily living. Most of our great "life" lessons are not handed to us on a silver platter.

Adventure can be woven right into your existing school curriculum. A community of learners means that students can set academic goals, take risks to push their own cognitive limits, and work with and support others while they struggle with concepts. Here are a few examples of how students can approach academic tasks as a class challenge.

77. The Compass Walk

Focus: Math skills, problem solving, peer teaching and learning, reading directions
Materials: Simple orienteering compasses (enough for half of the class), directions on how to take a bearing (should come with the compasses), blindfolds (optional)

Suggested Procedure

Set the stage with a blindfold compass walk. You will need to do this in a large field.
1. Have students get into pairs. They can get blindfolds if they wish.
2. Standing at one end of the field, point out an object at the other end—a tree, pole, home plate of a ball field.... That is everybody's goal.
3. One of the students in each pair volunteers to go first. His or her task is to get as close to that goal as possible *without using the sense of sight.* With either closed eyes or a blindfold, this person has two minutes to see how close he or she can get.
4. The sighted partner's job is to keep the other partner safe. Caution students not to help guide their partners, only to stop them from running or falling into anything. Suggest that sighted partners walk a little behind their other partners, so as not to influence them in any way. Finding the goal is a task only for the sightless partners. Helping takes the sense of exploration away. If any students happen to get to the goal, ask them to remain quiet until the time is up so that the others do not use their noise as a homing signal.
5. After the two minutes, give a signal to stop. Let the sightless partners see how close they are to the goal. They can then talk with their partners about the route they took.
6. Have everyone return to the beginning and switch roles.
7. Discuss what it was like to be blindly searching for something. What strategies did students use? What might it be like to be lost in the woods without one's bearings?
8. Now give each pair a compass and the directions (below) on how to take a bearing. Give everyone time to explore what it means to take a bearing. Applying any previous knowledge, using the written directions, and asking questions of you, let them play with the concept for awhile.

How to Take a Bearing

A **bearing** is a horizontal angle fixing a direction in respect to **north.** You would use a bearing if you were lost and needed to walk in a straight line.
A. Hold the compass so that the "Read Bearing Here" arrow points away from you.
B. Turn the dial toward the arrow so that it points to north (360°).
C. Place the compass baseplate against your belly button so that the arrow is pointing away from you. The "Read Bearing Here" arrow should be pointing forward.
D. Holding the compass tightly, **turn your whole body** until the magnetic needle housing is lined up with the magnetic needle (put the dog in the dog house).

You are now facing due north (or 360°).

E. Look up. Find a stationary **landmark that is close by** where your compass is pointing. That is the direction in which you can walk. You can put down your compass and walk there.
F. Reorient your bearing by repeating steps B–D. Look up again for another landmark. Walk to it.
G. **You are now sure that you are walking in a straight line due north.**
H. Take another bearing using a different direction. Try 60°, for example.

9. Float around to check up on each pair. Answer questions, and guide them to use the directions to get their questions answered.
10. Try the Real Compass Walk activity below with students.

> **A Real Compass Walk**
>
> A. Place a marker on the ground between your feet.
> B. Set your compass for a direction between 0° and 120°.
> C. Face this bearing as outlined in the directions you have just learned.
> D. Walk this bearing for 20 paces and stop.
> E. Add 120° to your last setting. Reset your compass.
> F. Head in this direction for 20 paces and stop.
> G. Again, add 120° to your last setting and walk 20 paces. Your marker should be very nearby.

<u>Facilitation Notes</u>

This lesson can be integrated into a larger unit on geometry, along with activities such as the Blind Polygon and Puzzles. Using the theme of finding one's way, read poetry or stories about being lost. Have students write about a time when they were lost, or felt lost. This can also be folded into a school, neighborhood, town or city search.

78. Books and Quilts*

There are many project-based experiences that provide avenues for students to explore their world without looking for one right answer. Students can research topics, then write and illustrate their own books. These books can be shared with, and even given to, the school library. If the books are written for a younger audience, older students can visit younger classes and read their books out loud.

Quilting is a project that can help students explore their own heritage. Have students research their own backgrounds. If a student is adopted she or he might research the adoptive parent's (or parents') background and traditions, and then make some educated guesses about her or his own background.

Once people have a sense of what their ethnic heritage might be, they can create a class quilt. Have each ethnic group identified by a certain type of fabric. For example, purple might represent South Africa (or Africa in general, if students cannot get that specific), green could be German, floral might be Native American, paisley Cambodian, etc. Each student should be as specific as possible about what percentage he or she is of each of these ethnic backgrounds and create a quilt square depicting this. When they are done with their squares, students can sew them together into a quilt depicting the ethnic heritage of the entire class. This quilt could, in turn, be donated to an organization or raffled off to raise money for a nonprofit group of the class's choosing.

---

* Thanks to Leslie Kebbekus and Jane Stimac for the books lesson, and the School Age Parent Program in Madison, WI, for the quilts project.

SUMMARY: WHEN TO MOVE ON TO CHALLENGE

The class is now a full-fledged community. People are interdependent, taking care of their own needs, and working through conflict when it arises. It is a safe place where ideas are shared freely, and people know what it means to collaborate. When a problem comes up, students turn to each other to solve it rather than running to you. Risk taking is part of the everyday scene, where one person who struggles with reading might risk reading out loud to the class, and another who is testing her math skills might ask another for help.

People feel comfortable challenging themselves within this community. The next step is for them to take on personal challenges with community support.

◊ WHEN TO MOVE ON TO CHALLENGE: SOME OBSERVATIONS

	Class Can Move On	Class Should Stay with Problem Solving
Decision making	• Students consciously work at making decisions. • Students have discussed and tried a variety of decision-making strategies. • When decisions are made, students check in with each other to see if they agree with the decision.	• Students do not seem to be aware of, and make no conscious effort to make group decisions. • The "rule of loud" is frequently used to discuss problems. • A small group of students continually make decisions for the whole group, while others passively wait for decisions to be made.
Group goals	• Students understand that group goals help everyone work together. • Students consciously try to arrive at group goals while working through problems with little prompting. • When group goals are established, students are willing to work toward them. • Everyone's input is sought when attempting to establish group goals.	• Students make little or no effort to establish group goals. • When group goals are established, they are generally ignored or sabotaged. • Individuals assume that their personal goal is the group goal.
Taking turns	• Students take turns doing the difficult and/or mundane tasks. • When one student has already tried something in the past, she or he stands back to let others have a turn. • Everyone is given a chance to participate in activities and/or discussions, even if some people exercise the right to pass. • When an attractive task is to be done, students create a win-win situation, or a fair way to choose the person for the task.	• Students argue or fight over whose turn it is to go next. • The same person or persons are always first or last. • The more assertive or aggressive students are constantly deferred to by the more passive students. • During discussions, the same people do most of the talking.
Leadership	• Students show that they can take the role of both leader and follower, based on what is required of them. • Students can articulate a basic definition of what it means to be a leader. • Students can identify when they have taken a leadership role. • Students can express that there are different styles of leadership and different leadership roles. • Students show that they can collaborate when working in small groups, thus sharing the leadership roles.	• Students cannot articulate a basic personal definition of leadership. • Students accept the notion without question that being a leader is "good" while being a follower is "bad." • Students refuse to share leadership roles, even when it runs counter to solving the problem. • Students cannot identify when they have taken leadership positions.
Conflict resolution	• Students have practiced specific conflict-resolution skills when not involved in a conflict. • Students can identify that conflict does not need to be "bad," but can be a powerful learning experience. • When in a conflict situation, students begin to use conflict-resolution skills. • Students can identify and use de-escalating strategies so that they can be ready to resolve conflicts. • Students can work toward win-win solutions.	• Students do not use conflict-resolution skills, even when prompted. • Students are unable to de-escalate in order to resolve conflicts. • Students work only toward win-lose solutions to conflicts. • Students refuse to work at resolving conflicts.

References
[1] Camp Manito-wish YMCA (Wisconsin) manual. (p. 31)
[2] Kreidler and Furlong. *Adventures in Peacemaking.* (p. 241)
[3] Duckworth. *The Having of Wonderful Ideas and Other Essays About Teaching.* (p. 68)

Chapter 7

CHALLENGE: STEPPING OUT ON ONE'S OWN

The community that has formed through the sequence of Cooperation, Trust and Problem Solving is comfortable. People understand the norms and what to expect from each other. This community, though, is not a mobile entity that can follow its members around for the rest of their lives. Although it can be duplicated, it must stay in this place and time. How, then, do people take necessary risks as individuals outside this community?

Challenge is the time to look inward and outward. With the support of the community, individual students look deep into themselves to explore what risk taking means to them. It is also a time when individuals and small groups leave the smaller community to venture out into the larger one, through community service projects, urban experiences or public presentations. If they run into rough spots, the community is there for support and encouragement.

CHALLENGE
- Individual goals
- Stating needs
- Encouragement/Support
- Fear/Anxiety
- Success/Failure

Activities

High ropes course

Outdoor pursuits

Urban experience

Presentations/Projects

Interdependence takes on new meaning as students learn about being independent. The community is still there; there are people with whom one can consult for information, ideas, encouragement and the like. Now, though, the accountability rests with the individual. If, for example, a small group decides to plan a fund drive to raise money for a local food pantry, the end result is theirs, not the whole community's. In an urban experience, where students may be asked to design and execute a survey, individual students must take the risk of approaching people to ask questions. The whole community is not physically there to do it with them.

Along with this new independence and accountability comes a whole new meaning to success and failure. The stakes are higher now. If someone drops the ball in a group juggle activity, it hits the floor, gets picked up and is thrown back into the game. If, however, someone "drops the ball" when planning the fundraiser, the fundraising goal is not met. A sense of reality is now in place.

Another issue at this stage is the "us" and "them" mentality that can occur when a group of people has formed specific class norms and has had an opportunity to bond. From the beginning, this class has explored diversity as it relates to the people in its own community. It is important to explore issues of diversity outside as well, and appreciate the wonderful variety of race, culture, customs, religion, size, age, and so on. It would be a mistake to create a "caring" place in which those on the inside are suspicious of those outside the community.

Throughout this process, you have had the opportunity to watch a group of nervous students grow into more caring, confident community members. The life cycle of this group is almost complete. Watching them struggle toward independence is a final phase of this journey.

CHALLENGE ISSUES AND SKILLS

◊ INDIVIDUAL GOALS

Up to this point, students have been asked to set behavioral goals and group goals. Now it is time to focus on individual goals. In the beginning, these goals can be more behavior-oriented—such as how far one might climb on a high ropes course element. Later, task-oriented goals are added—like how much time it will take to get a community service project completed.

One tool to help structure this type of goal setting is action planning. When taking action, it is important to consider many variables. Questions to ask are:

- How would you describe your vision for the project?
- What are three to five goals to meet along the way?
- What is your time line?
- What resources will you need? (Consider people, time, money, etc. Be specific!)
- What might be some barriers to getting this project accomplished? Describe how you might deal with each barrier should it come up. How will you address unforeseen barriers?
- How will you evaluate your project?
- How will you celebrate when the project is complete?

Ideas flow with relative ease compared with getting down to the task at hand. Taking action is one of the hardest parts of any project. One of the most valuable experiences a student can have is to see a project through from beginning to end. The sense of accomplishment is priceless, and the fact that it has been done once means it can be done again.

When engaging in action planning, it may be useful to have students begin with something they are already involved in, rather than inventing new projects to undertake. In this way, they can integrate this action orientation into their existing lives.

◊ STATING NEEDS

Part of being independent in an interdependent community is to be able to assess one's own needs and communicate them to others. It may mean asking for help, which can be difficult for some people, but necessary when striking out into new territory. It could take the form of telling someone to stop talking because it distracts from work. It could be asking for advice or encouragement, or telling a joke to cheer somebody up.

Needs are often stated in a demanding or angry way. This can occur when people have kept silent until the need is too strong to hold in any longer. It can happen when people are unaware that a need exists until it is at a crisis point. It can also happen when people are not used to having their needs acknowledged by others. A classic example is when someone is up on a high ropes course element and is scared. People are encouraging that person by yelling up to her. Suddenly she yells back, "Shut up!" Under the circumstances, this is a natural reaction—she is scared, and the yelling is only making it worse. Had she been able to anticipate this by reflecting on what she needed in advance based on her prior experience, she could have stated on the ground, "When I get scared, I need it to be quiet. Yelling encouragement only makes me more scared." In a caring community, students will try to offer what they think the individual needs, unless it is communicated differently by the individual.

People must spend time engaged in self-reflection to become more attuned to their needs. They need to set time aside for thinking, drawing or writing, especially if a challenge situation is just around the corner. They can write individual goals to help put their thoughts into action.

◊ ENCOURAGEMENT/SUPPORT

People naturally want to offer encouragement and support to those they care about. So far, it has been a highlight of this community-building process. The students have gone from focusing on put-ups and put-downs to becoming interdependent when solving problems together. There have been times of celebration and times of frustration. Through it all, they have been encouraging and supportive.

When people begin the process of taking individual risks and stepping outside the community, they tend to become so focused on themselves that class support and encouragement wanes. This is one reason why assessing and stating needs becomes more important, since others aren't always around to ask what individual needs exist. It is important, though, for the community to take time to come together to communicate needs, celebrate successes and provide support for those who are struggling.

◊ FEAR/ANXIETY

We began the process with fear and anxiety, and we end with it as well. This is just one cycle in the unending spiral. As we come full circle, it is apparent that we are at a different place then when we began. Individuals are no longer approaching anxiety alone; they have a supportive community to help them through it. As they become better at stating needs and setting goals, they develop strategies with which to deal with the fear. Fear is no longer an enemy, but a signal that something is happening—a moment of risk taking that, if ridden through, creates a potential for growth.

The challenges are more personal and real now, and the connections to one's life become more apparent. If someone can jump off a pole to hit a bell 30 feet in the air (see page 158), with a pounding heart and maybe a scream of—relief? delight?—then certainly that same person can write the essay that has been put off again and again, or take that driver's test, or give that speech. Calling merchants to ask for donations for a fundraiser is intimidating, but the risk is worth the momentary discomfort to reach a stated goal.

Fear and anxiety are not seen as barriers anymore, but as necessary parts of a process. If learning involves risk, then it involves fear. It is all part of the cycle.

◊ SUCCESS/FAILURE

Much of the risk, fear and anxiety we face is tied into the concepts of success and failure. Fear of failure can be debilitating. If a task seems overwhelming, it is easier for some people to not even start rather than finish with what they consider an inferior product. Frozen in place, goals are left unmet. When it comes right down to it, though, this is a very personal issue, tied to the experience of a lifetime.

Goal setting, action planning, and stating needs are all strategies to help deal with issues of success and failure. People must have ways to assess whether they have been successful or not, which is where goal setting comes in. Action planning helps to break a larger vision down into more manageable tasks. Stating needs in order to get expertise and support from the community gives people a sense that they are not alone. All of these strategies offer a structure to help people manage success and failure.

CHALLENGE ACTIVITIES

◊ ROLE OF THE TEACHER

You are now a consultant. You are part of the community and are seen as having a certain expertise, but you are no longer the sole expert. You provide group members with a connection to the larger arena and offer suggestions that may be helpful. They can choose to take your advice or not. It is their agenda, not yours, that is the primary focus now.

At this point, it is most important to encourage independence. If students approach you for advice that is readily available to them through other means, help them find those sources. They may be other students, written materials, people outside the community, or even the individual students themselves.

Challenge by Choice makes an overt resurgence now because people are, again, in a place of taking risks. The risks of the past seem minor in comparison to the new challenges ahead. Failure may mean public humiliation, or letting oneself down. You can help people determine what types of challenges are appropriate for them by asking pertinent questions and helping them create meaningful goals. You can also provide time for the community to get together in order to meet individual and group needs.

High Ropes Course

A high ropes course is an invaluable tool at the beginning of the Challenge sequence. It is a place where the community can be self-contained while individuals choose their level of risk taking from a variety of elements. These elements are 20–40 feet off the ground (or even higher in some cases). Trained personnel provide special equipment (climbing harnesses, ropes and helmets) in order to ensure a safe experience. When someone is ready to climb, one end of the rope is attached to the climber. The rope goes up through a "shear reduction" system that looks like a pulley, while the other end is fed through a friction device and is held by a "belayer." The belayer is a person who is specially trained to take the slack out of the rope as the participant climbs. If the climber slips, the belayer holds the rope in the friction device to brake the fall. The climber then decides either to continue on the element or to come down. Climbers are always on belay during these elements which eliminates the risk of anyone taking a significant fall.

Some high ropes course elements require balance, others strength, others just plain guts. As you can imagine, all of them induce anxiety and fear. This is by design. A high ropes course is the perfect place to examine these issues. The safety equipment is state-of-the-art, and training is available to make the experience safe and exciting.

High ropes courses can either be indoors in a gym, or outdoors in trees or on poles. Before contracting with an organization for a ropes course experience, it is prudent to research their history. Make sure they have had a safety inspection within the past year, and determine if their

> **HIGH ROPES ELEMENTS AND PEOPLE WITH DISABILITIES**
> In the early years (about 30 years ago), ropes courses were only built for the able-bodied. Any modifications were invented on the spot. Since then, many professionals in the field have focused on changing this. Today elements can be built that are universal—useable by a variety of people, both able- and non-able-bodied. Ask your local ropes course providers if they have universal elements. If not, maybe it's time they had some built.

course was built to ACCT (Association for Challenge Course Technology) standards. Ask what kind of training is required for their staff, who provided it, and what qualifications the trainers have. Ask for references from organizations that are similar to yours. For information on ropes courses near your area, contact the Association for Experiential Education, Project Adventure, or ACCT (see Appendices).

Following is a representative sample of high ropes course elements. **This book is not a substitute for proper training and does not give you enough information to safely run these activities. If you do not have the proper training, contract with a reputable provider of ropes course services.**

The Centipede

This element consists of a series of 4′ × 4′ boards, attached end to end (see Figure 7.1). There are attachments for the climber (who is on belay) to use in order to climb as high as she or he chooses. Since the Centipede is only attached at the top, the element swings as the student climbs, making it more difficult. Some people scamper to the top, while others struggle to make it partway. It is helpful to encourage students to set personal goals for themselves. Later, as they reflect on their climbs, they can assess whether their goals were realistic, if they met their goals, and what motivated them to choose their particular goals. The motivations behind their choices on high ropes course elements tend to mirror their motivations with other challenges in their lives—which can give them insight into how they deal with real-life challenges.

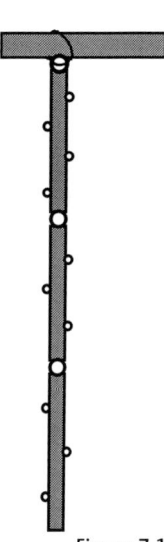

Figure 7.1

Two Line Bridge

The Two Line Bridge (see Figure 7.2), also called the Postman's Walk, is less physically strenuous than the Centipede. Participants are on belay and can climb up to the two bottom cables via a ladder or staples in the poles or trees. The task, then, is to traverse the cables, walking on the bottom one and hanging onto the next one above. The top cable holds the belay system, which is attached to the climber for safety. Since the climber has something to hang onto, this element is a good first try for many.

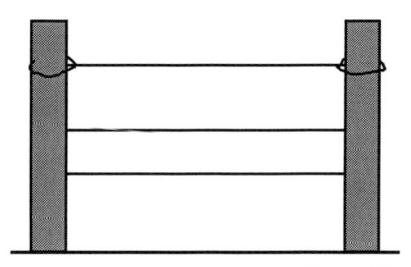

Figure 7.2

The Catwalk

The Catwalk is simply a log attached between two trees or poles (see Figure 7.3). Sometimes it is set at an angle and is called the High Inclined Log. Most of us have tiptoed along a log on the forest floor. There is a huge difference, however, when that same log is 20 or more feet in the air. The climber goes on belay and gets up to the log via a ladder, staples or a rope ladder. The seemingly simple task of walking across the log takes on a whole new meaning when one is faced with little to hang onto. Many a decision has been made on the

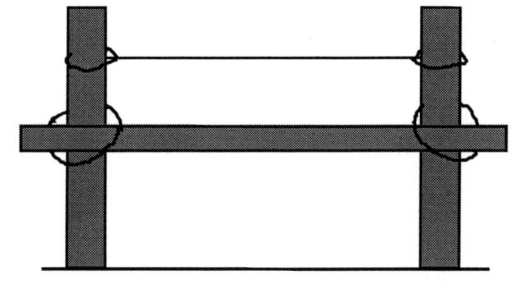

Figure 7.3

Catwalk to push one's limits. These limits are very personal. One person may attempt to cross without touching the belay rope. Others inch out with a firm grip on the rope. Some people dance, do jumping jacks, or walk backwards with their eyes closed. Other people muster up the courage to climb back down.

It is said that there can be no courage with the absence of fear. The Catwalk embodies this concept. Standing up on the Catwalk gives people much to ponder, philosophically and otherwise.

This element can be designed for two people to share the experience. Together, they help each other across the log, offering advice, encouragement and a shared sense of accomplishment.

Pamper Pole

The Pamper Pole consists of a utility pole stuck in the ground. Participants clip into a belay system, climb the pole, stand on top, and then attempt to dive for something hanging six or more feet away. The object can be a trapeze bar, a bell or ball to hit, or even a bandanna for the taking (see Figure 7.4).

> **THE FEAR OCCURS BEFORE THE ACTION**
>
> High ropes course activities engender fear and anxiety. Since these activities are designed to offer safe places for people to challenge themselves, this element of fear must be acknowledged. Although each person will deal with it in a different way, there seems to be a universal reaction to fear in the sweaty palms, dry mouth and butterflies we all experience. Once action is taken, the fear ebbs. The moment of truth for us all is at that decision point.
>
> This phenomenon is clearly seen at the top of the Pamper Pole and on the Zip Line platform. The individual must choose a course of action—to jump or not. For most, the moment passes quickly. A decision is made, and action is taken in a moment or two. For some, it is all but debilitating. Frozen in indecision, they can wait 15 minutes or more before acting.
>
> When someone becomes stuck in indecision, it can tax the patience of both students and teacher. Patience, though, is the key. A decision must be made, because it is the only way for the student to get down. The student is given options: climb down or jump. No matter what the decision is, a powerful lesson has been learned.

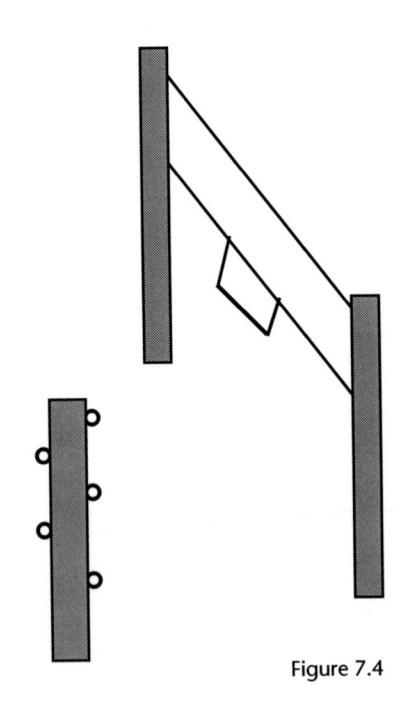

Figure 7.4

Many people describe doing the Pamper Pole as "a rush." It is another place where people make very personal decisions about what they will and will not do. The first choice, of course, is whether or not to even attempt the element. Once made, that choice leads the student to climb the pole. Another decisive moment is reached at the *top* of the pole. Many people describe this point as the most difficult—how does one get on top of the pole? There is nothing to grab but air at the top. (Climbers are asked not to grab their belay rope.) The climber must now rely on his or her sense of balance, the ability to stay calm and centered, and a willingness to push through the fear.

Getting on top of the pole can be quite a feat, yet the climber is not done yet. Hanging in front of the climber is a goal (trapeze, bell, etc.). Ask students to name that goal, either out loud or silently. They should name it something that has meaning for them, and which may seem out of reach to them at this point in their lives. When they do jump from the pole, they may or may not reach it. They may not even try to reach it. This metaphor can give people the opportunity to reflect upon those goals in life that may be difficult to achieve. Sometimes we push hard and still do not achieve our goal. At other times we do not even give it our best shot.

The Pamper Pole is a wonderful activity to use toward the end of a ropes course experience. After people have struggled through a myriad of challenges, the class can come together to cheer on each individual as she or he attempts the challenge.

Zip Line

Since the ride down the cable is so exciting, the Zip Line is an element that many will try even if they have chosen to observe for the rest of the day. Once a student climbs up to the platform, he or she is clipped into a pulley that is attached to the cable (Figure 7.5). When ready, this person communicates with a team of people who are prepared to help him or her off the cable and disembarks from the platform. The resulting ride can be quite exhilarating.

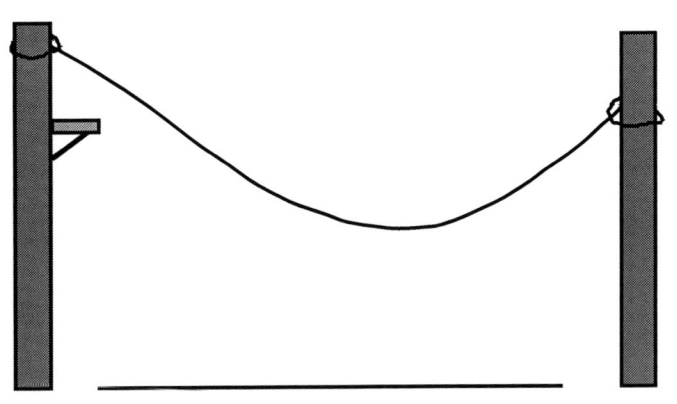

Figure 7.5

◊ LESSONS TO BE LEARNED

As with much of this process, the high ropes course gives students opportunities. What each individual student does with those opportunities is a significant part of the process. A ropes course experience is a safe and powerful metaphor for how one travels through life. It gives people the chance to explore their hearts, minds and spirits. The lessons they learn and the insights they gain can help each person travel her or his path with a bit more focus and direction. It encourages students to make choices which, in turn, helps them to embrace and trust their decision-making abilities. The result is an increased sense of confidence.

Outdoor Pursuits

Another way to begin the Challenge sequence is through outdoor pursuits like snowshoeing, cross-country skiing, rock climbing, canoeing, kayaking, caving or hiking. Given the time and resources, these endeavors can even be turned into extended trips in the back country.

In general, most people have not spent much time engaged in these types of activities. The novelty of the experience, along with the focus on getting basic needs met, can be the cause for much excitement and anxiety. Questions about where to go to the bathroom, how much effort it takes to get from one place to another, and what to do about insects or the cold inevitably come up. This is part of the

> Any time we take students into the great outdoors, it is our responsibility to teach stewardship. In this way we do not perpetuate the notion that the natural world is just another resource to be used. The following are revised Leave No Trace Principles developed by the Leave No Trace organization.*
>
> 1. Plan ahead and prepare.
> 2. Travel and camp on durable surfaces.
> 3. Dispose of waste properly.
> 4. Leave what you find.
> 5. Minimize campfire impacts.
> 6. Respect wildlife.
> 7. Be considerate of other visitors.

---

* Leave No Trace can be contacted at (800) 332-4100 for more information as well as educational materials.

> **WHAT ARE WE TEACHING?**
>
> Climbing down into the earth is a unique experience. Caves are amazing places that are home to bats, long-lived rock formations, tunnels, and absolute darkness. If one really wants to know what it feels like to be alone, sit in the dark in a cave.
>
> There is a cave in Wisconsin that has been used by groups for almost two decades. At first, a few groups would enter it every year, exploring its nooks and crannies and sharing the sparks of wintergreen lifesavers in the dark together. Today, literally hundreds of groups make the trek up to the cave every year.
>
> Some of these groups are more prepared than others. I have seen 30 kids run up the hill, widening the trail, trampling flowers, and causing unnecessary erosion. I have seen groups with only a few light sources and no helmets putting themselves at risk for injury in an unfamiliar place. I have seen bats knocked from the ceiling during hibernation and left to die.
>
> I have also witnessed small groups carefully winding their way up the path, taking the switchback so that the erosion stays with the path. I have seen groups prepared with a helmet and a light source for every person—and extra supplies in a backpack, which also contains the first-aid kit. I have listened to guides instruct students to feel free to look at the bats and rock formations without touching them, to leave them in their natural state. I have watched as people haul trash from the cave.
>
> Before we head out to the wilderness, we must ask ourselves what it is that we are teaching. Running through a cave with no respect or concern for the habitat, or even for personal safety, is a dangerous lesson. It runs counter to everything that the word *community* stands for. Part of learning about community means learning about connections to the larger communities of which we are all part, whether the larger environment, a neighborhood or the world.
>
> If you are looking for a place that is exciting, where people can run around at will without regard to noise, and where people are hired to clean up the mess, you may be looking for an amusement park.

adventure—to not know what is going to happen next. A class must be ready to undertake a trek into the wilderness, even if the "wilderness" is the county park. Everyone must deal with different levels of anxiety, set individual goals, receive support and offer support to other students.

Along with outdoor experiences comes the notion of stewardship. This is a perfect time to connect the experience of community to the larger realm of the environment. When people are out on the trail, they can learn about minimum-impact camping, keeping the area clean by picking up trash, observing plants and animals in their natural environment without molesting them, learning how to use water wisely, and how to dispose of (or carry out) waste to keep the environment clean. Being in the wilderness allows students to learn about the connections among all types of communities.

When choosing the level of outdoor experience, you must take into account your own level of expertise. If necessary, contract with an organization that specializes in the particular outdoor pursuit your class is interested in undertaking. Organizations that run ropes courses also often offer outdoor pursuit activities, or they can offer suggestions in your area. Check with the nearest outdoor equipment store; look in magazines that specialize in your area of interest. The world is out there, and the expertise is available. It is your responsibility to make sure that your outdoor experience is undertaken in a safe manner, which means involving people with the necessary equipment and qualifications.

Urban Experience

Many times there is no need to take a trek into the wild; it is only a matter of opening the front door. The city wilderness can be as exciting, challenging and novel as a whitewater rafting trip. Even a small town has much to offer a class that is willing to explore.

An urban experience can be designed to meet the age and maturity level of any class. Even very young children can go out in small groups with an adult chaperone to explore parts of the neighborhoods where they have never been. Searches are explorations of one's community. They can begin in the school itself, then branch out to the larger community. Some look like scavenger hunts, with lists of things to find, while others are more open-ended. Depending on the age of the students and the targeted skills, any number of searches can be devised. Once students understand the concept, they can create their own questions to be answered about their school, neighborhood or larger community.

Here are two examples of searches for the City of Madison, Wisconsin. One is meant for younger students, while the other is geared toward older students.

City-County Building

Students in grades 2–6 get on a city bus. Each group of 3–4 students, along with an adult who is there just for safety, get off the bus at a designated stop. From there, they are given a sheet of paper with a series of questions. How they find the answers is up to them.

1. Find the City-County Building. Write down the address.
2. Find the mayor's office. Get her signature if she's there, or get her secretary's signature.
3. Find the Common Council Office.
4. Get the signature of one of the secretaries.
5. Who is the alderperson for your school?
6. What is an alderperson?
7. On what floor is the jail located?
8. Who is the County Executive? Where does she work? What is her job?
9. Find the Department of Public Works.
10. Get Marilyn's signature at the Department of Public Works. What is her job?
11. What do the people in the Department of Public Works do?
12. Find the Municipal Building. There is a statue in front of this building. Who is it?
13. Find the Transportation Department.
14. In the Transportation Department, you will find the Bike Safety Coordinator for the City of Madison. What is his name? What does he do? Get his business card to prove you were there.
15. Ask 10 people what they think is the best thing about Madison.
16. What is located at 107 State Street?
17. Perform an act of kindness. Your group must decide what it should be. Describe what you did.
18. Find the Memorial Union by 1:15. Meet in the lobby.

NOTE: If you finish early and have eaten lunch, brainstorm with your group members about a fun thing to do, and then do it. Report what you did to the class later.

Make sure to collect things as you go along. They may come in handy when you're trying to explain how your day went!

Facilitation Notes

After a city search, students return with brochures and other items they have collected along the way. Many of the people they visit give them magnets, business cards, pencils, stickers and buttons. The students prepare a presentation to the class and write about their experiences. This experience can be built into larger units on government and social studies.

Each group has an adult along who watches out for safety and helps them sort through conflicts and frustration. Many times parents go along and have as much fun as the students. It is important to emphasize to the adults that the process is as important as the product. Encourage them to intervene only when necessary, being careful not to supply answers.

I once accompanied a group of fifth-graders on an urban experience in Madison. Our task was to visit the South Union at the university, Camp Randall Stadium, and the geology museum on campus. After they found the union, and we explored that for a bit, we stepped outside. In front of us was the tallest building around—the meteorology building. Two of the students had never been in a building that had more than two floors, so they said, "Let's go to the top!"

That's exactly where we went. As we entered the building, they spent some time pushing the buttons on the computer in the lobby and looking at the different satellite pictures. Then we hopped in the elevator. This was the first time these two had ever been in an elevator, and it was wonderful to relive this experience through their eyes.

The doors opened on the top floor, and we stepped out into a hallway with a bunch of offices. They were looking for a door to the roof, and they stopped at an office where someone was working. They knocked politely and asked the man inside if he could show them the way to the roof. Surprisingly, this man dropped everything and took us straight to the roof. He showed us the views and then offered to give us a tour of the building. What a treat. It turned out he was he chair of the meteorology department, and we all learned more about weather in that hour than many learn in a lifetime.

We never did make it to the geology museum. It didn't matter. The exploration by these students turned the day into a great adventure, and the learning was invaluable on many levels. It was a day we would never forget.

These city searches do take a fair amount of preparation. Although these are public places, it is necessary to visit every site and talk to the people who will be approached by the students. Usually these folks are very willing to chat with the small groups that come to visit, especially since each class has about 6–8 groups going to different places, so that each official is dealing with only one small group. It is good practice to check in with them in advance so that they know groups of students will be coming around during the next week or two. If they do not wish to meet with the students, then they can voice that, and the students can go somewhere else.

Once the search is set, it can be reused every year, with only a small amount of follow-up. Every town has its share of history and interesting sites, yet it is surprising how little many of us know about the communities in which we live. Some other searches used in Madison are: state historical museum, the state capitol (including the supreme court, governor's office and state legislature), public library, civic center, city convention center, senior center, many sites on the university campus (geology museum, student union, athletic facilities, dairy sciences) and the school district administration building.

Preparation with the students is essential. Discussions and role plays about whom to approach for help, and how, are necessary. Help students identify who is safe to approach for directions. Teach young students how to ask for help from someone they do not know. Here is a six-step process:

1. Say "excuse me" to get the person's attention.
2. Tell this person what you are doing. Say something like, "We're on a field trip for school."
3. Ask your question.
4. Wait and listen for the answer.
5. Repeat the answer to make sure you have heard correctly.
6. Say "Thank you."

Many times young students run up to someone, ask the question, and leave without hearing the response. Much of this is due to anxiety, so role-play practice can be quite helpful.

Community Exploration

This exploration was designed for high-school students. The main focus was an extension of the community-building and problem solving that they had done as a class. Give your students instructions like those that follow.

> **You and your base team are to go into the community. You have a variety of tasks:**
> 1. **Create a challenge** for yourselves. (e.g., talk to someone for 10 minutes, go to a place you normally wouldn't go and interview people—like a government building or a senior center).
> 2. Discover an **unknown resource**—something that will be of use to you.
> 3. Perform an **act of kindness.**
> 4. **Interview 20 people** re: What do they think are the biggest problems facing our schools, and how would they propose solving them?
> 5. **Create a skit** depicting your day. Present it to the whole group during the next class session.
>
> **What do you want to get out of this experience?**
> A. Write down a personal goal for each person in the group.
> B. Develop a group goal for the community exploration. What do you, as a group, wish to get out of this?
> C. What is your challenge?
>
> **Debrief. To be done at the end of the experience.**
>
> **What?** Discuss what happened during the experience. What was the hardest thing you did? The most scary? The most rewarding? What did you do together that made the tasks easier/harder? Describe any surprises or anecdotes about the day. Review your goals. Did you accomplish them?
>
> **So what?** What does this mean? Why might some things have happened the way they did? How did you handle difficult situations as a team (or *not* handle them)? Why was this? What caused you to accomplish/not accomplish your goals?
>
> **Now what?** What can we take from this experience? Did you learn anything about yourself and/or your partners? Do you have any new goals that grew from this experience?

<u>Facilitation Notes</u>

A community exploration can take many forms and have many focuses. If students have been studying government, for example, the search can be geared toward finding resources within the town or city that use town, city, state or federal funding. How might one register a vehicle? To whom does one report a stolen bike? Students can generate a list of questions, then search for the answers in their own communities.

Public Presentations and Projects

Small groups can be assembled within the class to design projects that are connected to academics or community service.* The object is to plan and carry out the project so that it has some benefit outside the classroom community. Examples include:
- Fundraising for a community organization
- Organizing snow shoveling and raking for elderly neighborhood residents
- Designing an orientation program for newcomers to the school
- Testing a nearby water source for pollution and reporting the results to the city council
- Cleaning up a nearby park
- Researching and designing new playground equipment for the neighborhood
- Compiling oral histories from long-time neighborhood residents
- Mapping the area to include highlights and things for visitors to do

In exploring issues of diversity, consider projects like:
- Taping and sharing stories from relatives about family traditions
- Interviewing a variety of people from the neighborhood and compiling these stories into a book
- Visiting various places of worship
- Exchanges with others in the school—go to dinner at their houses, invite them to yours
- E-mail and penpals with people farther away
- Researching and arranging for local speakers on topics of interest that have to do with equal opportunities, civil rights, or cultural awareness
- etc.

> There is a fourth-grade class at Lincoln Elementary School in Madison, Wisconsin, that goes on an expedition every year. Since Wisconsin history is part of the curriculum, Dave Spitzer helps the students design a trek through Wisconsin. They research Wisconsin history, make contacts with people, and create their own textbooks. Then they're off for a week on a bus, visiting small towns, historical sites, and other schools. They sleep on gym floors and are welcomed into the homes of gracious hosts. One year, the city kids from Madison visited a veal farm in Brillion, a Menominee tribal school in Keshena, and the Green Bay Packer Hall of Fame as part of their trip.

The list is endless; it is only limited by the imaginations of your students. Resources, of course, also play a role in what can actually be done.

SUMMARY: WHERE TO GO FROM HERE?

This class of individuals has gone from being dependent on you to becoming independent. They understand interdependence and collaboration because they *do* it. They have ownership in their community because each of them is a vital part of it. If even one of them leaves, the community is changed. They have arrived at this place over a winding path that has included some tears, joy, frustration, laughter and struggle. No matter where these individuals go, the experience of community stays with them. They carry along a feelings vocabulary and conflict-resolution skills. They have experienced empathy and trust. Because they have experienced it, they can now duplicate it in other parts of their lives. This is one step in a very long journey, but it creates hope and optimism. It is one leg of a *journey into the caring classroom.*

---

* See *The Kid's Guide to Service Projects* by Barbara A. Lewis for over 500 service ideas.

Chapter 8

FACILITATING THE PROCESS

Your equipment bag now contains a compass and a map. These may get you where you want to go, but not in one piece. Your pack still needs the provisions to take care of daily needs. This section addresses how to structure Adventure activities to create community.

SHAPING AN ADVENTURE PROGRAM

How activities are presented is usually more important than the activity itself. Clifford Knapp shares that "direct experience is not enough. If such experiences are to be meaningful and applied to life situations, teachers must help students learn from carefully planned and guided reflection sessions."[1] A discussion about formulating an Adventure program means that we must revisit the Experiential Learning Cycle (Figure 8.1).

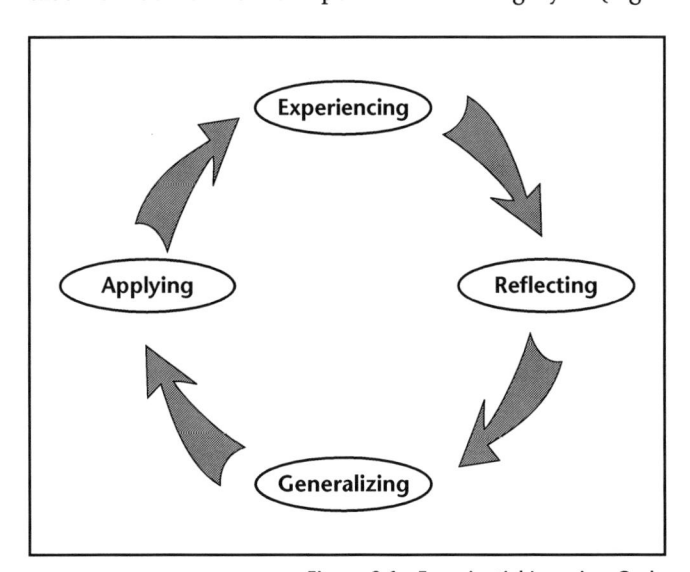

Figure 8.1: Experiential Learning Cycle

As discussed earlier, the Experiential Learning Cycle is an integral part of experiential education. Kolb created this basic model in the mid 1980s to represent an innate process where people learn from experience. Without it, learning would consist of one activity after another with nothing to hold the experiences together. People may or may not gain insight from the experiences, and they may or may not find them useful.

The cycle begins with an experience. This can be one occurring naturally in the environment, or in the case of formal education, it can be a contrived experience chosen to meet certain goals or address certain issues. For example, when a group gets together for the first time, an Icebreaker activity is chosen because the goals of the group include meeting each other. If left to chance, people may or may not get to know each other (witness many college level classes, where, even after months together, it is possible to know nobody's name in the entire class).

After an experience, people are given an opportunity to reflect upon the experience. This can be verbal, written, thinking time, drawing or working with clay, to name just a few strategies. People look back on what they did, thought, saw, and how they behaved. At this point, the process has turned into experiential learning.

The experience, however, is still one in isolation unless people take time to generalize how this experience relates to others. They should look at prior experiences and see how this one measures up. Are there patterns in their behavior or in how they approach risk-taking situations, for example? This is the search for meaning.

Finally, people are asked to look for insights that are applicable to their real life, or that make sense when working with this particular group on the next activity. While the other parts of the cycle are concerned with the present and past, this one brings the future into the picture. Participants are asked to consider how learning from this experience, in combination with past experiences, can impact their lives in the future. In this way, learning is incorporated into a whole mural, rather than being one painting hanging on an otherwise empty wall.

The group now will put to use the learning of the last experience into a new experience, thus starting the next spiral in the cycle.

The Experiential Learning Cycle in action might look something like this:

◊ ACTIVITY

A group of sixth-graders have been working on issues around problem-solving. They have just completed the problem-solving initiative Marshmallows, where they have had to get the group across a 20-foot span using only small boards. No one was allowed to touch the ground. The group members argued about strategy; some people talked loudly, while others were silent. After having to start over five times because someone stepped off a board, the group finally started holding hands to steady each other and complete the task.

◊ REFLECTION

The group members are asked to think of one word or perform one action that describes how they felt during the activity. Everyone is given time to think. They hold up a thumb to indicate they are ready. When everyone is ready, students go around the group to see or hear what people have come up with. Words are thrown out: *frustrated, confident, left out, stressed, confused*. One boy shows what he felt by putting his hands over his face, and a few people pass.

Next, students are asked to share why they chose that word or action. One person shares that he was confused because everyone was talking at once, and he felt that he was not part of the decision. "I wasn't really sure about what to do, which is why I kept messing up. I felt kind of stupid." "Yeah," says another, I said 'left out' because I couldn't get a word in at all. I just went along so that we could finish the job."

◊ GENERALIZING

After time to share feelings and thoughts around this activity, the group is asked to look back at other activities to see how they handled this one in comparison. One student notices that they are still having trouble communicating: "We keep yelling instead of talking, and it seems like the same people are making the decisions." Others agree, even those who have occupied most of the air-time during the activities. They, too, are tired of the inefficiency.

◊ APPLICATION/TRANSFER

Finally, the group members are asked to glean gems of knowledge or insight from what has just occurred. One person says, "I think we should take time to plan as a whole group before we start doing something." Another chimes in, "Let's stand in a circle so we can see everyone." One of the louder group members says, "I'm not going to be the first person to talk next time, and let others have a chance."

◊ EXPERIENCE

Given the previous discussion, the facilitator chooses to do the activity Balloon Frantic, because it requires planning and discussion. The learning from the previous activities is blended into the next in the continuing spiral of the Experiential Learning Cycle.

PROCESSING

Processing *is* a process. It refers to an "activity that is structured to encourage individuals to plan, reflect, describe, analyze, and communicate about experiences."[2] Processing can occur at any time before, during or after the experience. We do not do these activities just so that people will know what to do if they are walking around in the woods and happen to find an oversized Spider Web hanging there. The Experiential Learning Cycle provides for the application, or transfer, of learning to participants' lives. Processing is the vehicle with which to accomplish the transfer.

Michael Gass discusses three theories of transfer in Adventure education: specific, nonspecific and metaphoric. Specific transfer is directly related to learning skills, such as climbing in a ropes course helping someone to learn rock-climbing skills, or the connection between learning how to belay and learning how to rappel. Nonspecific transfer is connected more with attitudes or beliefs. An example would be when someone explores leadership skills during a group problem-solving initiative, then transfers those leadership skills back to the school setting. Metaphoric transfer is the most abstract; people glean the essential principles from a learning situation, then transfer them to a seemingly unrelated environment—thus using the specific learning situation as a metaphor for more general learning. After working together to get across the cable event called Walk of Life, and learning that it cannot be done alone, participants are able to ask for help in other parts of their lives.[3]

All of these types of transfer can occur in Adventure education. It is processing that helps participants make the connections. Sometimes the participants themselves will share these moments of insight. At other times, the facilitator creates this fertile ground by introducing activities with ready-made metaphors. This is known as *framing*, or frontloading, the metaphors.

One way to structure activities is to use a model called the Adventure Wave (see Figure 8.2). The Adventure Wave is the core structure of Adventure Based Counseling as described in *Islands of Healing*.[4]

◊ BRIEFING

- Describe the activity (this is the time to frontload a story or metaphor to go with the activity, if you have one to share).
- State any rules.

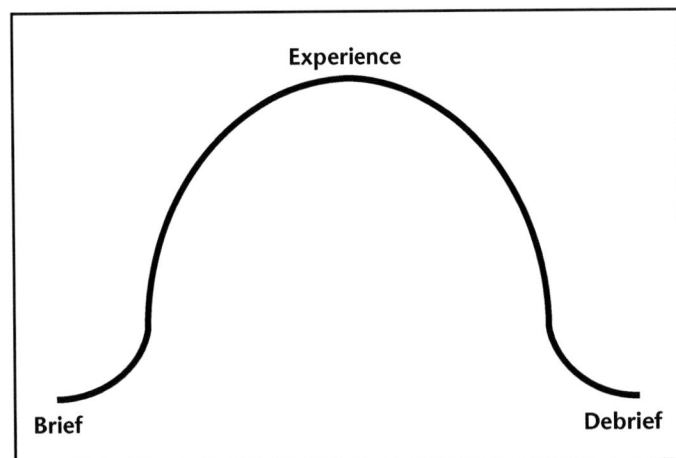

Figure 8.2: The Adventure Wave

- Cover all safety considerations.
- Answer questions.

If you forget something, it will become obvious in a very short time. When this occurs, you have two choices:

1. Stop the activity and clarify.
2. Go with it.

Just remember that if you choose to change the rules in the middle of an activity, you may have a mutiny on your hands. If your omission has made the activity easy for the group, you can let it go. When students have finished, ask them to do the activity again with the additional rules.

Although uncomfortable, this mutinous situation offers grist for the debriefing mill. It may allow both you and the group members to understand more clearly the power structure in the group. It may provoke changes that benefit everyone. Of course, if there is a safety issue, *always* stop and clarify.

◊ EXPERIENCE

Where the group is in the group cycle dictates your role as facilitator. If you are just starting out, your role may be more assertive and directive. As things progress and students can assume more control, your role may be more of an observer, mediator, clarifier. A guideline is to try to give the group as much control over their destiny as possible. If they end up in a situation they cannot handle, it is time to process and analyze what is (or what is not) going on. These are the moments of insight that allow people to make choices about their behavior. Once awareness is raised, people are operating from a vantage point of understanding.

◊ DEBRIEFING

After an activity is a time to reflect upon or debrief the what, why and how of things. It is a time for asking questions, and maybe answering some of them. Many times we leave a debriefing session with more questions to ponder. It is the stuff of growth. Here is one model for structuring a debriefing session:

What?
So what?
Now what?[5]

What? So what? Now what? comes from Terry Borton as quoted in Clifford Knapp's book, *The Art and Science of Processing Experience*, pp. 6–7. It is utilized for "sequence" debriefing—that is, to lead gradually into the ultimate lessons of the debrief first; description, second; and prescription, third. *Islands of Healing* and *Exploring Islands of Healing* (working title), its sequel, both utilize this structure as a method of exploring the debriefing experience.

What?

What happened? Everyone in the class will have a different perspective. Some heard put-downs, others heard only put-ups. Some were left out, others were too busy to notice. Some were active participants, others observers. Every perspective is valid. The "what" gives everyone a chance to state a perspective. Some people naturally skip this step because they are already generalizing the experience, or even looking at how it transfers. However, it is important to maintain this part of the debrief in order to allow those who need the reflection time the opportunity to have their needs met.

This is the beginning of reflecting on the experience. Since the class contains a variety of people with a variety of processing styles, it is important to offer differing strategies in which to reflect. Holding an outright discussion is great for the verbal folks, but what about those who process best through artwork, are kinesthetic by nature, or would rather write? Mix it up. Here are a variety of reflection methods.

"What" Strategies

- **The Round Robin/Whip/Go Around:** Give everyone a chance to say one thing by "whipping" around the circle. For example, you can say, "Say one thing that you saw or did during that activity" or "Say one word about how you felt during that activity." Everyone has a chance to say something or pass.
- **The Snapshot:** Tell the group to imagine a whole stack of photos laid out in front of them that were taken during the activity. If they were each allowed to take only one picture home to put on the wall or refrigerator, what would it be? Do a round robin or ask for volunteers.
- **Crumpled Paper:** Give everyone an identical piece of paper and a pen (no pencils—they smear). Ask them to write how they think the activity went, or how they feel, or how they think things are going. It can also be totally open-ended: "Write anything you want about the group." Students then crumple their papers up, throw them in a can/hat/bowl and mix them up. Everyone takes one and reads it aloud to the group. This is done anonymously. If someone gets his or her own, it is read anyway.

    Make sure to offer this method of reflection when you have adequate time to address issues that may come up. Since the activity is anonymous, people may feel freer to "let it out." If you have five minutes at the end of the day, and someone "drops a bomb," it does not give the group members time to deal with it. Another strategy is to structure your questions with the caution about keeping the thoughts positive, or making sure that no one is being put down in the process.

- **The Bouncing Ball:** The group stands in a circle. A ball is used to bounce around the circle at random. It can be bounced to anyone. If they have something to say (either in general or to a specific question) they say it or say "pass."
- **Creation:** Bring out clay/paper/scissors/pipe cleaners, etc. Give everyone a chance to sculpt/draw/paste together something that represents how he or she thinks the group did, or how she or he felt during an activity. Students should then have an opportunity to describe their work to the group.
- **Balloons:** Give everyone a balloon and an indelible marker. Students should draw a face on the balloon showing how they think things went, how they felt, and so on.

> **A Talking Circle*** is a way to offer everyone an opportunity to share. The group sits in a circle, and an item is chosen to designate the speaker. If the item has meaning, all the better. People are asked to speak from the heart and listen from the heart. When a person holds the item, she or he can choose to sit silently, speak or simply pass the item on. Everyone else is silent and listens to the speaker. Based on the amount of time, the item can go around more than once.
>
> Talking circles can be used with a specific question or can be open-ended. It is also invaluable if a group is having difficulty and no one seems to know why. Maybe there's a white elephant in the room that nobody wants to talk about. Convene a talking circle. Many times, the issues will come out.
>
> Dan Creely uses a Talking Circle extensively in his work. He says, "This is the most powerful tool I use. A very, very powerful processing tool." He has some suggestions:
> - Use a special object that has meaning to you. Tell the story of the object, and it will receive respect by the students.
> - After each student has finished talking, he or she says "thank you," then the group says "thank you." It is a chance to honor what has been shared.
> - Add a candle to the circle. Students know that when the candle is lit, what we talk about is important (from *Calling the Circle* by Christina Brown).

---

* Thanks to Dorothy Davids for teaching me about Talking Circles.

> **Journals** are great tools for processing. It is helpful to have three different journals: (1) One that is public, where every student knows that what is written will be shared with the group; (2) One that is between student and teacher only, where students can communicate with the teacher in private; (3) One that is absolutely private. The writing only gets shared if the author so chooses.
>
> Have the students create/decorate their journals. Offer books of quotes so that people can embellish their journals with words of wisdom from those who have gone before them. Whenever there is formal journal-writing time, allow students to choose which journal to write in. Store the private journals in a locked cabinet to ensure privacy, but have the public ones out for people to read at their leisure.

Paper plates can also be used. Students then present their faces to the group.

- **The Magic Circle:** Everyone gets close together in a circle. Have students shuffle to the right; when someone says "stop," he or she says one quick thing about how things went. Then shuffle to the left until someone says "stop" and has a chance to say something that happened. Keep going until people run out of things to say, or you run out of time.
- **Feelings Marketplace Cards™:** This is a large set of cards with emotion words on them. They can be used in a variety of ways. Spread them out on the floor, and have people choose one or more cards describing their emotions during an activity. Do a round robin, or have people volunteer to show and tell. Another strategy is to pass out three cards to every person. Then give students a few moments to trade cards before they share their cards with the group. It's also fun to play emotion charades with these cards.
- **Postcards:** Collect a variety of postcards that students can choose to represent how they felt, what they thought about, or how they experienced the activity.
- **Boxes:** Cut out the fronts of boxed foodstuffs like cereal. They contain a wide variety of pictures and adjectives that can help describe an experience.*
- **Partner "chats":** Everyone gets a partner. Students are given one to two minutes of uninterrupted time to talk to their partners about whatever the subject is (the facilitator either poses a question or has partners talk about how a particular activity went). One partner says absolutely nothing—she or he just listens. If the talker finishes before the allotted time, partners sit silently until the time is up. Then the other partner is given the same amount of time. After both partners have talked, they are given some conversation time to compare notes and prepare a synopsis of their feelings to the larger group.
- **Anticipation/Result:** Before a particularly difficult challenge or task, have each member of the group write down on a card what he or she anticipates the activity will be like. After the activity, have them write on the other side of their cards what it was really like. They can share, compare and discuss their cards.

So What?

Once the "what" has been established, it is time to search for patterns. These areas of discussion come from the "what." If someone saw something particularly good, it is time to explore that. For example, if someone said in a round robin, "We were all included," you might ask, "What caused us to be included?" It may sound like an odd question, but there is a reason for it; it usually means that everyone felt the activity was important and did something to make it happen. You might also ask, "Do all of you always feel included?" Where/how do students feel included or not included? Explore it, mess with it, bat it around.

Another example of using the "what" to lead to the "so what" would be when using the balloon strategy. After observing all of the balloon faces, you might say, "I see that there are quite a few sad faces. What do you think caused so many people to draw sad faces?" The students can come up with reasons and explore why people may have felt sad. It may be that

---

* Thanks to Floyd Asonwha for this idea.

people were being put down, or one person took over and wouldn't listen to any other ideas. Maybe the task was frustrating. A follow-up question might be, "How could we have done this activity differently so that people could feel better about it?" All of these "so whats" lead to the next stage, described below.

Now What?

After the class has reflected and spent time putting this activity into context with other experiences, it is helpful to bring some sort of closure to the discussion by exploring ways to put the "so what" into action in real life. For example, a "now what" response to the balloon situation could be, "What can we do to make people feel included in our group when we're doing something else—like math or recess or physical education?" Students can then brainstorm ways to include people. This moves them much closer to putting their ideas into action. Once articulated, thoughts become real possibilities. In the case of the sad balloons, the "now what" could be, "How can we make sure everyone's ideas are heard from now on?" or "How can we handle frustration without putting ourselves or other people down?" In this way, people can transfer the learning from this experience to the rest of their lives.

It is the act of processing that allows students to learn from their actions—and from each other. It is what differentiates the community-building process from pure recreation. When engaged in recreational activities, individuals have the opportunity to learn from their experiences. When participating in a community-building process, individuals consciously try to learn from their experiences, and then apply their new learning to the next activity—hence the wave. When joined together, these waves facilitate the continuation of learning from one activity to another (Figure 8.3).

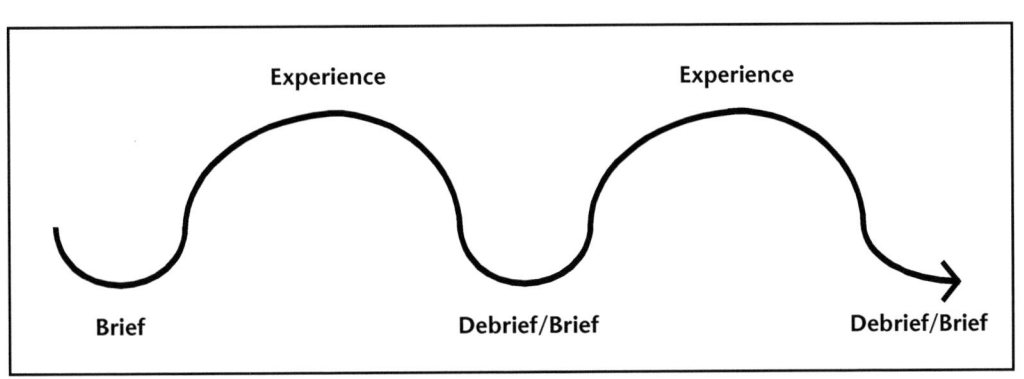

Figure 8.3

The Adventure Wave, then, fits into the Experiential Learning Cycle as shown in Figure 8.4.

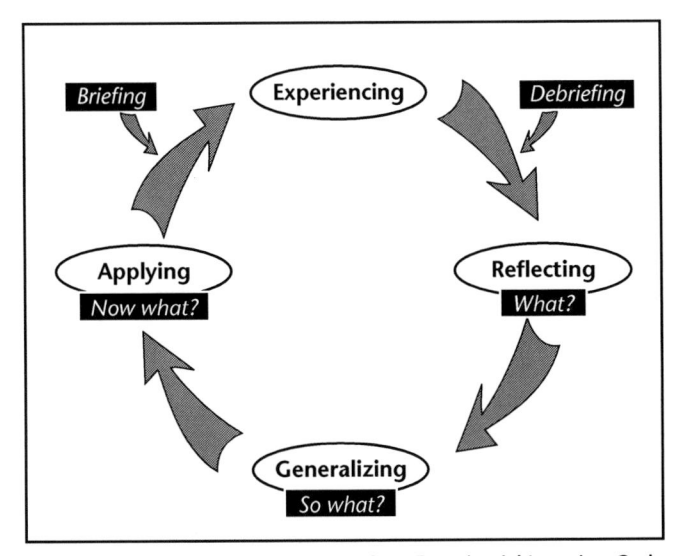

Figure 8.4: Experiential Learning Cycle

DEBRIEFING STRATEGIES

Debriefing is a process where one idea leads to another. There is no one right way to go through a debriefing session. Facilitators must consider their own style, the reason the group was formed, developmental level of the group, time available, and experience level. Given these factors, here are a few guidelines:

- **If an issue is not dealt with, it will come back.** Sometimes there are too many issues to address. Which one should be considered first? Maybe one just jumps right out at you. The others will still be around later. Participants often remind you of these issues later, by bringing them to your attention either verbally or through acting-out behavior.

  Sometimes an issue is right in front of everyone, but people are choosing to avoid it. That usually means that they are not ready to deal with it. Maybe it is too threatening or brings up too many bad memories. Yet, the issue will not go away. There will be other opportunities to address it. Maybe working on trust issues will allow the participants to become more comfortable with each other and, thus, be more willing to open up to each other.

- **Try to work on one issue at a time.** Sometimes issues are intertwined. If it is possible to sort them out into individual issues, they are easier to resolve. For example, you are told that Robyn hit Chris. On examination, here is what actually happened: Stacy bumped into a desk, which hit Robyn. Robyn thought Chris hit her. She hit back. There are a few issues here. First, Stacy bumped a desk. Was it an accident or intentional? This is important; if Stacy meant to set up Chris, then we are dealing with a hidden agenda. If not, then we are dealing with Robyn's quick and erroneous judgment and reaction. Chris ends up being a victim either way. Maybe Chris is regularly scapegoated. Maybe Robyn has trouble controlling her temper. The bottom line is that things can get very complicated very fast. Try to focus on one issue at a time, then build one on another.

- **The facilitator's responsibility is to provide opportunity.** As facilitators, we can only open doors. The participants choose whether or not to walk through them. A safe environment is the key to these doors.

- **Engage in active listening.** Make eye contact with speakers. Acknowledge the person speaking. Clarify what he or she might be trying to say. It is very disconcerting for a person to say something and get no reaction.

- **Encourage "I" statements and talking to each other.** Early on, group members will focus on you as the leader. They will talk to you, answer your questions, and speak in generalities. As the process continues, encourage them to talk directly to each other, especially when trying to make decisions. It may even be necessary to remove yourself physically from the group for this to happen. Also encourage participants to say how they feel, such as, "I felt angry when the group voted for Anita's idea because I think people were voting for their friend," rather than "People were just voting for their friend."

- **Have participants refrain from personal attacks.** No problem is unique. Certain issues permeate our lives; they are part of the human condition. If someone hears a put-down, or if someone is excluded, encourage students to avoid "pointing the finger" at specific people, unless the people involved are active in the discussion. Also, talking about people in the third person—as if they were not in the room—is hurtful. Referring to specific students by name causes blame to be cast, and defensiveness is not far behind. The issue then becomes a power struggle, and the real issue gets lost. If this happens, you need to stop the argument and try to return to the original issue. Once this is addressed, the argument is usually moot.

- **Be prepared to be challenged.** There comes a time in the development of every group when issues of influence arise. Sometimes this means that students will challenge your authority as the leader. When this happens, it is time to cheer. The message is very clear: "We want to control our own destiny." It is then time to renegotiate the power structure in the group. New limits must be established, and new norms incorporated. The facilitator's role is to provide enough structure to allow the students to debate their issues in a safe environment. (Some things are non-negotiable: safety, respect for each other and one's self.) In the beginning, your role is more central. Later you become more of an active observer than an active participant.

- **Try to keep your ego in your pocket and not on your sleeve.** This is difficult, especially if the class is challenging your authority. Although it may sound and feel personal, it is not. Every individual strives for power and control over his or her own life. Sometimes this means that it is necessary to challenge the closest authority figure. If the goal is for students to have as much control and responsibility as possible, a power struggle is counterproductive. Try to stand back from the personal attacks and address the issue as a participant, not as the authority figure. You have the right to voice your feelings and thoughts, too.

- **Listen to what people are saying.** Try to keep your agenda in the back of your mind. Hear what the students are saying to you and to each other. It may mesh with your agenda, or it may not. Try to go with the class's agenda except in cases of safety or confusion. For example, I know that gender issues are common to many groups, so I am always on the lookout. If the group I am working with is dealing with something else entirely, and I push my agenda about gender roles, it is at best unproductive. At worst, it can cause conflict where none existed. Tune in.

- **Debrief with yourself or a colleague.** Check up on yourself. Keep a journal. Ask yourself "what, so what, now what" after a session. Share your experiences with colleagues to see how they might have handled different situations, or how they think you handled it. Keep the process of growth going.

- **Be true to yourself.** If a discussion feels superficial and fake, it probably is. Follow your instincts, be sincere, and you will be on the right track. Remember, your facilitation style is unique.

- **If all else fails—punt.** There will be moments when the following will probably float through your head: "What am I doing here?" "I have no idea what's going on!" "What happens next?" Then it might be time to take a deep breath, see where the discussion is going and let it flow. Or, maybe it's time to finish up and move on to another activity. Maybe you can even share with the group, "I'm confused. Can someone tell me what we're talking about?" As a last resort, stop everything and bring out a bag of candy to share. Be careful about taking things too seriously. Have fun!

◊ COMMON THEMES

Whether or not you are aware of them, there are some themes that tend to be present in most groups, regardless of age or maturity level. I have seen these in groups of third-graders and in groups of high-functioning adults. The package may be different, but underneath the issues are the same. Here are some of the most common themes to look for. (Please remember, however, that there are many issues that are unique to your particular group. Those listed here are not the only ones!)

- **Doers vs. Reflectors.** I can safely say that every group I have ever worked with has had to deal with the issue of balancing time between doing and reflecting. During activities, it is possible to see the same people run to the front, get the equipment and start the process rolling. Meanwhile, others continually stand back and watch. Are they just shy? Are the others just overbearing? Generally not. Usually the people who are action-oriented make quick decisions and start things going. The reflectors need time to consider options and talk the decisions through. This difference in style is grist for the processing mill, which the reflectors are happy to engage in. The doers, at this point, become antsy and can't wait to get back to the activity.

It is possible to attain a balance if the students recognize what is going on. You will need to make many attempts to find the balance point as the pendulum swings between overprocessing and too much activity.

- **Gender issues.** As much as I would like to believe that gender is not an issue, it keeps cropping up. Young children show signs of gender distinction, and it continues through adulthood. In general, it shows itself when students begin group challenges together. At a place like the Spider Web, for example, the girls step back when it is time to do the lifting, and the boys step in to lift. This is not a case where the boys barge their way in; it is a two-way street. There may be times when a bigger, stronger person may be chosen to lift because she or he may be one of two people left, and is the one better able to take on that task. In general, though, when there is a team of people working together, it is unnecessary to differentiate based on gender.

    With some classes this is a big issue; with others, it is a non-issue. Encourage students to make decisions based on their combined attributes rather than on assumed individual strengths or weaknesses. This issue offers an opportunity to discuss how people get pigeonholed based on stereotypes, reputation or cultural norms.

- **Objectification.** One of the main goals of community-building is to humanize rather than objectify people. This is usually accomplished at the beginning stages of group work. Later, however, objectification can reappear when the class is solving problems together. It can be seen during lifting activities, or if someone has been asked to take on a particular role, such as being blindfolded during an activity. Early on, group members may begin to refer to certain people by labels such as "the blind guy," or "the small one." You hear things like, "Let's get the big person over first." As you can imagine, this objectification can be harmful to a person's self-image. It is worth putting on the table for discussion. It can also lead to a bigger discussion about stereotyping and labeling.

- **Body Image.** Many activities require decisions based on size. Depending on how cohesive the class is and how much trust has built up, this can be cause for grave embarrassment, with people opting out of activities. If this occurs, it is imperative to be sensitive to what is going on and work with the individual to explore how he or she might choose to be involved in the activity. At the Spider Web (an activity that deals directly with body size), that person my choose to go under the web, or walk around and help spot. Bringing this issue up for the group to process is very delicate for the individuals involved. Body image can be dealt with on a more general level in regard to the Spider Web, as it is an issue for everyone. You can open a door for discussion by asking if people felt included in the activity. If the person who exercised a choice to not go through the web chooses to respond to the question, then it can be discussed directly. This issue can lead to the more global topic of body image in our society.

- **Your reputation precedes you.** There is a constant dilemma about students who have a history of behavioral problems in school and their participation in community-building. On the one hand, we want everything to go smoothly, and they just "mess it up." On the other hand, we know that these students need community-building the most, and we don't want to exclude them. What to do? Consistency demands that we include students as much as possible. Often, behavior turns out to be a non-issue. As a matter of fact, many times these students surprise us and become leaders in the community. At other times, safety concerns are paramount, with students exhibiting behavior that could put themselves or others at risk. In these cases, it might be beneficial to search for adults who can act as mentors. Ask a parent, counselor, social worker, educational assistant or friend of the family to be present whenever possible. Make sure this person is available for field trips. This adult can discuss with the student problems that arise that are outside the scope of the community. This adult can also intervene, if necessary, when a safety situation occurs. In this way, your focus can be on the community as a whole, while this student can have more individual needs met. Although it may be difficult to find someone who can give the time and energy to one student, it is well worth the effort.

- **"We act different in here..."** Sometimes students develop situational relationships, in which they are trusting and trustworthy in the class, but harass each other outside the room. If this issue is not addressed in the community, it will not change. Talk about what makes students different outside the group, and how their outside behavior toward each other affects relationships in the room. Generally it has more to do with peer groups than with their individual perceptions of each other.

There is a time for doing and a time for reflecting. Deciding when to do an activity and when to process is one of the more difficult tasks for a facilitator. There will be times when you do one activity after another and no issues arise—it is enough to do and have fun. At other times it is impossible to do anything because there are too many unresolved issues floating around—whatever you do has no spark. Then it is time to talk. There are days when all we do is talk, but it provides the space to get back to business when the air is clear. As we all know, it is difficult to go very far with a ton of baggage on one's back.

Please remember that this is a process. It is never completely smooth and rarely easy. Some groups go far; others seem to stay in the same rut day in and day out. You have helped to open some doors, and they have chosen to walk through or stay put. That, more than anything, is what this process is all about: making educated, responsible choices in the context of the whole. As Tom Smith would say, "If you can't see the big picture, you think you are the big picture."*

SEQUENCE AND FLOW

If the world were a static place, with everything predictable and orderly, a group would proceed from Cooperation to Trust, then into issues of Problem Solving, and finally wind up at Challenge as neatly and tidily as it is described in this book. **IF** the world were a static place....

Thus we are back to the question of sequence and flow. The *sequence,* again, is the set of concrete activities outlined by the facilitator who is planning a program according to the theoretical development of a group. The *flow* is how that sequence plays out according to the *real* development of the group. The reality of group work is that it is quite tidal—it ebbs and flows depending on individual personalities, backgrounds, age, maturity level and the like. As soon as you think the group is on firm ground with trust, someone new joins the class and you're back to the beginning. After a long history of problem solving, one student refuses to spot another on an element because she thinks he has spread a rumor about her. Back we go to trust issues.

We must also deal with external pressures such as time and scheduling. Every time a class gets together, it is necessary to back up a bit to help ease back into the group process.

---

* Tom, a long-time Adventure educator from Cazenovia, WI, attributes this quote as a collaborative insight between himself and Keith King, also a weathered experiential educator from Alton Bay, NH.

This means starting a session with an activity from an earlier step in the sequence. In a 45-minute class three times a week, this is a slower process. It is less conducive to community-building than a class that is together every day.

If you have contracted with an outside agency to go to their ropes course on, say, April 14, chances are that there are few options when April rolls around and you are wondering if your class is ready for the experience. You can decide to cancel the trip, or you can head out anyway to help students progress from where they are in the process at that moment. It is important to remember this: *It is not the activity that dictates what is accomplished, but the level at which the group is operating.* If the class is still working with trust issues, and you decide to do a problem-solving initiative, they will work together on the initiative like a group that is still dealing with issues of trust.

In an ideal world, flow and sequence blend. In the world in which we live, they sometimes trip over each other. You can help facilitate students' issues rather than push them into places where they are not ready to go. This is the value of understanding the life cycle of a group.

How you handle these situations as a facilitator depends on these factors:
- The purpose for the group
- Your personality and style
- Where the group is in its life cycle

◊ GROUP PURPOSE

There are many reasons for groups to undertake an Adventure-based community-building process. A continuum (shown below in Figure 8.5) depicts one way of looking at the different types of groups and their purposes.

Adventure-Based Groups in Schools

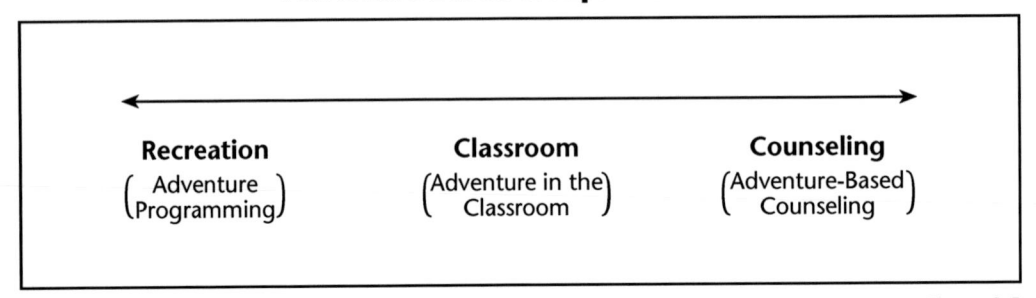

Recreation	Classroom	Counseling
(Adventure Programming)	(Adventure in the Classroom)	(Adventure-Based Counseling)

Figure 8.5

Each of these three approaches has a different focus: one is physical, one cognitive, one emotional. (Of course, all of these approaches incorporate the other focuses to a lesser degree.) Their one shared focus is social. The social nature of community helps every group achieve its goals.

The chosen approach leads the teacher to choose activities in a sequence to help further the group's goals. A physical education teacher, for example, may choose activities that require the members to be more physical—running tag games, doing physical trust activities, and taking risks in the context of climbing. A classroom teacher, on the other hand, might choose more sedate activities that get group members thinking through problems, and might bring academic content into the activities. A counselor could focus activities on emotional trust and taking emotional risks with friends and family.

The depth of processing also reflects the group's mission. A counseling group, for example, might spend more time processing than actually engaging in activities. On the other end of the continuum, the physical education class will spend more time in activity than processing. The classroom group will be somewhere in between.

Although the focus, the selected activities and the discussion time may look different from group to group, the process is the same. There is a profusion of activities to choose from, variations on the activities, and metaphors that can be drawn from each activity to make it useful to a group.

◊ FACILITATOR PERSONALITY AND STYLE

I love to process; I could sit for hours and chew a problem to death. This is how I make sense of the world. There are other people who would rather spit the problem out and get to work on it. They want to yell at people like me, "Quit sitting around and get on with it!" They make sense of their world by testing problems.

As a facilitator, you have choices about sequence flow as well as how to deal with issues as they come up during activities. One of the most difficult hurdles a facilitator must face is balancing the group's need to sit and process with the need to be active. As a processor by nature, I have had to subdue my need in order to provide space for other styles. I remind myself that, although I learn an enormous amount from the actions and insights of the participants, that is not the main reason I am there. I am there to facilitate the learning of the students in this developing community. Their needs are paramount. As Steve Butler says in *QuickSilver*, facilitating means "helping [group members] learn from each other."[6]

In reflecting on my own facilitation, there are many times when I reach the conclusion that we processed too much. That is the side I err on as a facilitator. There are other times when (in an effort to correct for my propensity to overprocess) I don't give the students *enough* time to process; we run from one activity to another without even taking a breath. As the pendulum swings back and forth, I search for balance. It is a never-ending process. The important thing is to think about it. Be aware of your style, your personality and your habits. The better you know yourself, the better you can step out of your own head and make decisions based on what is right for your group.

> **THE GIFT**
>
> It was a crisp day in October at the SPRITE ropes course near Oregon, Wisconsin. The sixth-graders were in the middle of a full day. After a morning of low ropes, we were preparing to try a high element or two. I was still fairly new at facilitating, having been practicing for a couple of years. I felt good about my skills—maybe too good.
>
> My belaying post was at the Pamper Pole, where students were being asked to climb to the top of a 25-foot pole, dive off and try to hit a bell. One of the smaller girls in the class was suited up in the harness and ready to go. Then she got cold feet. In my great "wisdom," I knew that she would feel wonderful if she could get up there and jump toward that bell. So, I proceeded to talk her into climbing, talk her up the pole and talk her into jumping. She did it all, and I felt great!
>
> What happened next is what I now consider a great gift. She came down, walked over to me and said, "I wish you hadn't done that. I didn't need to do that."
>
> I came to the quick realization that *I* needed her to climb that pole. It was *my* agenda, not hers. My ego was at stake, and she paid the price for it. Given the power differential between us (me, the facilitator, teacher and adult) and her (the participant, student and child), it took some courage for her to speak her mind. I am grateful, for with that realization I finally began to walk the path of becoming a true facilitator—and not a controller—of experiences.

◊ GROUP DEVELOPMENT CYCLE: IT NEVER GOES AWAY

If a group is struggling with issues of influence, choosing a get-to-know-you name game will seem stale and superficial. People who are ready to get into the meat of an issue need something to sink their teeth into, and playing silly games just doesn't cut it. On the other hand, offering a trust activity to people who are just getting to know each other can elevate the anxiety level—sometimes to the point of panic. People will be bailing out right and left.

Challenge by Choice is more than a concept in this case, it becomes a survival tool.

The closer the activities—and subsequent processing—are aligned with the group cycle, the more likely group members will get their needs met, so the process can forge ahead. As we know, internal and external factors affect this process, so that each group travels as far as it can in the time allotted.

Summary

Facilitating is both a science and an art. It takes some theoretical knowledge about sequencing and flow, the Experiential Learning Cycle, group development and the Adventure Wave. Processing the experience can be enhanced by an awareness of general themes that crop up, as well as by procedural knowledge about effective facilitation. This chapter has offered some guidelines for facilitation along with strategies to get at the "what," "so what" and "now what" of Adventure-based learning.

How one approaches facilitation has much to do with the purpose of the class, one's own personality/style and where the class is in their life cycle. Overall, though, learning to facilitate is a process in itself. Just as taking the first step off the Zip Line platform is generally the hardest, it requires commitment to take that first step and persevere down the path to facilitation. We must be prepared to make mistakes and learn from those mistakes. Inevitably, the students have much to teach us if we are willing to listen.

References
[1] Knapp. *Lasting Lessons.* (pp. 2–3)
[2] Luckner and Nadler. *Processing the Experience.* (p. 8)
[3] Gass. *Theory of Experiential Education.* (p. 33)
[4] Schoel, Prouty and Radcliffe. *Islands of Healing.* (pp. 132–135)
[5] Schoel, Prouty and Radcliffe. *Islands of Healing.* (pp. 170–181)
[6] Rohnke and Butler. *QuickSilver.* (p. 8)

Chapter 9

STARTING AN ADVENTURE PROGRAM

The first step in establishing an Adventure program is to review your own perspectives about the nature of education, the roles of student and teacher, and the most important goals for young people as they become adults in our society.

The Adventure philosophy views learning as a process that includes the ability to take risks. Risk-taking allows students to push their boundaries, make discoveries that may otherwise be out of reach, and be open to new insights and ideas that spring from their own reflections. The consequent opportunities for learning increase exponentially. Learning is transformed from a one-way conduit between teacher and student to a "learning web" where everyone exchanges ideas.

The next step is to review your own situation. If you are a classroom teacher, the place to start is in your classroom. Try a few activities, begin regular class meetings to encourage processing, create a Full Value Contract. Begin to share some decision making with your students. Embark on your own tour through the Experiential Learning Cycle by trying activities, reflecting, looking for patterns, and applying them to your classroom. At first, it might feel painfully slow and arduous. Like any expedition, it takes some time to get the muscles toned and attitudes shifted from the regular routine.

Once you have decided to begin the journey, go to a conference on experiential education, or get some specific training through workshops offered from an organization like Project Adventure. Look for educational conferences that feature people like Alfie Kohn, Howard Gardner, Susan Kovalik or Daniel Goleman as speakers. Ask your administration or professional organization to sponsor workshops and speakers on these subjects. There is much out there if one is willing to do the research.

Another step is to research ropes courses in your area. If you find an appropriate one, take your students. Consider advocating to build such a course in your school or district. Without exception, ropes courses are established in school districts where there is one person—a champion—who sees the project through from beginning to end. Sometimes this is an administrator. More often it is a teacher, social worker, counselor or psychologist. Sometimes it's a parent. Frequently, this person has worked for almost a decade looking for funding, convincing administrators, and persuading colleagues. The end result has been the same: success through tenacity.

Although community-building can be accomplished without a ropes course, it can be a valuable tool to address specific issues around trust, problem solving and challenge. A pitfall, however, is when the ropes course alone is viewed *as* community-building. Using a ropes course as an end in itself reduces it to the level of a playground, and an expensive one at that. Given this pitfall, it is vital to understand the process of community-building so the ropes course can be put into perspective. It is a tool, much as a book is a tool to promote reading.

> **A**s a recovering control freak, it took me years to let go of my iron grip on the classroom. I began the process by taking off my watch. Since the clock in our room was broken, I had to rely on others for the time of day. Since we were in a self-contained class, the other outcome was that the rigid schedule began to bend. It became unnecessary to stop math at 10:52; we moved on when we were ready. The upshot was that we actually accomplished more by removing the invented structure—there were fewer distractions and transitions. This new structure made me more open to the idea of integrated curriculum; it just suddenly made sense.
>
> Libby Roderick wrote a song that helps remind me to let go of artificial structures in my classroom as well as in my life:
> "Lay it all down, when you can't hold it
> Let it all fall, set it all free
> When the night falls and it grows cold in
> The midst of the journey, and you fall to your knees
> Sometimes two legs simply can't hold us
> Sometimes two arms are simply too weak
> Lay it all down when you can't hold it
> Let your life carry you like a boat on the sea..."[1]

Modeling the Community-Building Process

A typical educational scenario goes something like this: Politicians dump on school boards, who dump on administrators, who dump on principals, who dump on teachers, who then dump on students. When students dump on each other, we wonder what's wrong with them.

Try this simple activity with your colleagues: Hold your arms straight out in front of you, one arm above the other, and palms facing each other. Clap your hands together. Then say, "When I say "go," clap your hands." Get everyone into position, then say, "One, two, three..." [clap your hands], "GO!" Most people will clap when you clap your hands, *not* when you say "go." This is but a small example of how powerful modeling can be. Talk *really is* cheap. It is what we do, not what we say, that carries the true power.

If we are to advocate community-building with our students, we must look at the school as a whole. How do decisions get made? Are there opportunities for collaboration? Do people take time to get to know each other, share ideas and discuss educational philosophy?

The reality, of course, is that this is easier in some situations than others. For some, especially if a large grant is available, people will commit to taking the time needed to engage in their own community-building process. If the administration is working in partnership with teachers, and if teachers are willing to examine their own philosophies, the goal of aligning the school environment with the classroom is on solid footing. This is the "whole school" approach that is best for making large-scale changes.

At other times, this holistic approach is not possible due to lack of resources like time, money and just plain energy. Then it is necessary to become a grassroots organizer. Examine your sphere of influence. Talk to people who are open to your ideas, and model the process in your own situation. Create partnerships with others who are like-minded. Whether you are an administrator, teacher or support staff, you can find opportunities to promote a sense of community.

◊ MADISON METROPOLITAN SCHOOL DISTRICT (MMSD) STRESS/CHALLENGE PROGRAM: A GRASSROOTS EFFORT

The MMSD Stress/Challenge program began with the vision of Pete Albert. As an Outward Bound instructor, he had witnessed the power of Experiential and Adventure Education. In 1979, as a social worker, Pete brought these ideas to the Madison school district. It all began with the support of one teacher and a group of at-risk students. Over time, Pete made connections with people in the juvenile justice system and the county. Together, they built the first ropes course in the area that would serve kids from the schools and juvenile corrections facilities.

By 1984, the program had caught the eye of a few administrators and many teachers who were looking for ways to promote community in the classroom. Middle school principals donated one day per week of one teacher's time for someone to focus on the program. Dee Tull, an administrator for students with learning disabilities, donated another 2.5 days per week of a teacher's time. I had received some training at Project Adventure and became the first formal Stress/Challenge facilitator. Eventually, the position became full-time.

This program operated on "soft money" for a decade, risking the chance of being cut at any moment. It was only through the commitment of a few administrators that the funding continued. Stress/Challenge was finally brought to the level of a department in 1994. During that time, I worked with hundreds of teachers and thousands of students. I only went to a class if invited. At first, that meant a dozen or so. Soon, however, I could not keep up. As with any grassroots organization, ours took the route of water: At first, water flows into areas of least resistance. Eventually, as those areas get full, water begins to defy gravity and the whole container begins to fill.

> Verona, Wisconsin calls itself "Hometown USA." Just outside Madison, it has one middle school. Ruth Heffron, longtime and well-known Verona resident, was one of the physical education teachers there. She had a vision to build a ropes course to enhance her students' learning. She maintained this vision for a long time, because there was never the money or the structural will to make it happen.
>
> Joy Pfeffer is a mom and a registered nurse who lives in Verona. Her son, Patrick, died suddenly when he was a sixth-grader at Verona Middle School. From this tragedy came a great gift. Joy wanted something to come of Patrick's death that could benefit all kids in Verona. When Joy's energy met with Ruth's vision, the money was raised in Patrick's name to build an indoor ropes course at Verona Middle School.
>
> The Patrick Pfeffer annual run-walk event continues to support the program. Joy continues to be a moving force in raising money, working with students and offering training to keep this ropes course available to all middle-schoolers in Verona.

People who were the most skeptical of the program became our biggest advocates. And, in 1994, we needed all the advocates we could get. The program had just achieved departmental status, and it was on the chopping block. I sent out a letter to teachers informing them of this development. The evening that our program was slated for discussion at the school board meeting, over 150 students, teachers, parents, administrators and other supporters came. People spoke about what the program had to offer, what it meant to them, and how it had even changed their lives. Stress/Challenge was no longer a mere program; it had taken on a life of its own. The school board let the program stand.

Today, MMSD has ten ropes courses. It has provided hundreds of people with formal training, and has given thousands of students, teachers and administrators the opportunity to learn about being part of a community.

This is how the vision of a single person can make a powerful difference.

Summary

Starting your own Adventure program can take many forms depending upon the resources, interest and collective will of your school community. Because using Adventure to create community requires the belief in a particular philosophy, it may be necessary to start alone, working with other like-minded people in the school and the larger community. As the anecdotes in this chapter demonstrate, one person's commitment can have a large effect over time.

References
[1] Roderick. *Lay It All Down.* 1997

Afterword

> Step by step the longest march
> Can be won, can be won
> Many stones do form an arch
> Singly none, singly none
> And by union what we will
> Can be accomplished still
> Drops of water turn a mill
> Singly none, singly none
> —*United Mine Workers preamble*

Is our society really going down the tubes? Marian Wright Edelman of the Children's Defense Fund recently revealed some stark statistics:

> Every 4 hours, a Black child is murdered; every 4.3 minutes, a Black baby dies; every 6 hours, a Black child dies from a gunshot wound; every 20 hours, a Black or young adult under 25 dies from causes related to AIDS; every 46 seconds, a Black child drops out of school...every 95 seconds, a Black baby is born into poverty; every 104 seconds, a Black teenage girl becomes pregnant...every 11 minutes, a Black child is arrested for a violent crime...every 7 minutes, a Black baby is born to a mother who had late or no prenatal care; and, every 3 minutes, a Black baby is born to a mother who did not graduate from high school.[1]

Although African-American children are not the only youngsters in dire straits, the above statistics offer a barometer for our society. These statistics are further illuminated by our response to problems of crime in our society—in the past decade, the prison space in our country has *doubled*. Even Captain Kangaroo (Bob Keeshen) has charged that "...there is a 'mean-spiritedness' in America's failure to commit itself to the upbringing of young children, particularly those from at-risk backgrounds."[2]

Is there no hope?

We seem to be surrounded by both hand-wringing and cynicism. However, neither attitude will change the world. Hand-wringing denotes powerlessness—people worry, but feel there is nothing to be done. The cynics are *sure* that nothing can be done, and are quick to point blame at everything and everyone for the mess we are in. No, the world cannot change if we adopt these attitudes.

Yet, look around. Look at all of the kids who, against all odds, have stayed *off* drugs, who have *not* committed suicide, who cooperate with others, who can look toward the future as a better place for themselves and their contemporaries. It is the norm; it points to what is possible for every human being.

Yes, circumstances may dictate a person's attitude. Poverty, racism, classism, violence, homophobia, addiction all play a part in a person's outlook on life. These environmental circumstances can wreak havoc on a person's sense of hope and optimism. A Pollyanna is not born from need. As a society, however, we have control over these environmental influences. We can choose to wring our hands in blighted hope, or we can choose to pursue an optimistic course of change. We can, if we so choose, focus on the positive, while doing everything in our power to transform the negative.

To make these changes, we are compelled to examine our own spheres of influence—to determine what we have control over and work with it, while letting go of those areas that are out of reach. As educators, this means we can create a safe environment in our classrooms and in the school community as a whole. This vision does not represent a place without conflict, but a place where people have the skills to resolve conflict without resorting to violence. It is a place where students can take risks, thus maximizing their growth.

Even if one must walk through a metal detector to get inside, a school can be a haven and a place of empowerment. If we can develop a spirit of collaboration, where all students have the opportunity to be leaders, imagine what could eventually happen when they get out into the "real" world as adults. It is one step in a very long process.

Arthur Wellington Conquest III, a longtime Adventure/Experiential Educator, states: "[Adventure] Education is the key ingredient for developing and nurturing our children so they can live productive lives, adapt to today's rapidly changing society and, more importantly, begin to learn how to control the factors which most profoundly affect their destiny...."[3]

The change process exists inside each and every one of us. It begins with an attitude that sees the possible rather than the unobtainable, that sees potential in every human being, and that knows it is necessary to work, and to work hard. It is truly a *journey toward the caring classroom*.

References
[1] *Zip Lines*, Summer 1996
[2] Associated Press, 1996
[3] *Zip Lines*, Summer 1996

Appendices

Educational Standards and Adventure Education

There is much debate these days about the efficacy of educational standards and how they are assessed through standardized tests.* The standards do, however, have redeeming value in that they offer a way for us to focus on student learning. Authentic assessment techniques can then be used to inform our teaching to maximize learning potential.†

In determining outcomes and goals for a program, educational standards offer suggestions that are highly useful. These days there is a recognition that students bring more to school than their heads, and standards have been developed to address thinking and reasoning, self-regulation and working with others, to name a few. The following are examples that, in my opinion, relate to community-building in the classroom and have been developed by McRel‡ as standards and benchmarks.

Standards that deal directly with community-building and the tools discussed in this book:

Self-Regulation

Standard 3: Considers risks

Grades K–12

- Weighs risks in making decisions and solving problems
- Uses common knowledge to avoid hazard or injury
- Applies preventative measures prior to a task to minimize security or safety problems
- Selects an appropriate course of action in an emergency
- Identifies emergency and safety procedures before undertaking hazardous procedures
- Thinks clearly under stress

Standard 4: Demonstrates perseverance

Grades K–12

- Demonstrates perseverance relative to personal goals
- Demonstrates a sense of purpose
- Maintains a high level of energy over a prolonged period of time when engaged in tasks
- Persists in the face of difficulty
- Concentrates mental and physical energies

Standard 5: Maintains a healthy self-concept

Grades K–12

- Has basic belief in ability to succeed
- Uses techniques to remind self of strengths
- Uses techniques to offset the negative effects of mistakes
- Avoids overreacting to criticism

---

* For a comprehensive discussion on these topics, please read *The Schools Our Children Deserve* by Alfie Kohn. This is a must-read for educators and parents alike.

† Beverly Falk, in *The Heart of the Matter*, does a wonderful job of outlining how to go about using standards to inform our teaching and learning, rather than as mechanisms for high-stakes testing that punishes students for not "measuring up."

‡ Used with permission ©1997 Mid-Continent Research for Education & Learning. You can find the McRel Standards on the internet at www.mcrel.com, or purchase a copy. (See Resources in this section under Kendall, John S. and Robert J. Marzano.)

- Uses affirmations to improve sense of self
- Analyzes self-statements for their positive and negative effects
- Examines "shoulds" to determine their negative and positive effects
- Revises "shoulds" to reflect the reality of personal needs
- Understands that everyone makes mistakes
- Understands that mistakes are a natural consequence of living and of limited resources
- Takes criticism in a dispassionate manner
- Analyzes criticisms to determine their accuracy and identifies useful lessons learned
- Uses high-self-esteem body language

Standard 6: Restrains impulsivity

Grades K–12
- Keeps responses open as long as possible
- Remains passive while assessing situations
- Suspends judgment

Working with Others

Standard 1: Contributes to the overall effort of a group

Grades K–12
- Challenges group practices that are not working
- Demonstrates respect for others in the group
- Identifies and uses the strengths of others
- Takes initiative when needed
- Identifies and deals with causes of conflict in a group
- Helps the group establish goals
- Engages in active listening
- Takes the initiative in interacting with others
- Evaluates the overall progress of a group toward a goal
- Keeps requests simple
- Contributes to the development of a supportive climate in groups

Standard 2: Uses conflict-resolution techniques

Grades K–12
- Communicates ideas in a manner that does not irritate others
- Resolves conflicts of interest
- Identifies goals and values important to opponents
- Understands the impact of criticism on psychological state, emotional state, habitual behavior and beliefs
- Understands that three ineffective responses to criticism are (1) being aggressive, (2) being passive, and (3) being both
- Understands that three effective responses to criticism are (1) acknowledgment, (2) token agreement with a critic, and (3) probing clarifications
- Determines the causes of conflicts
- Does not blame
- Identifies an explicit strategy to deal with conflict
- Determines the seriousness of conflicts
- Identifies mutually agreeable times for important conversations with opponents

- Identifies individual versus group or organizational interests in conflicts
- Establishes guidelines and rules for negotiating
- Determines the mini-max position of those in a conflict

Standard 3: Works well with diverse individuals and in diverse situations

Grades K–12
- Works well with the opposite gender
- Works well with different ethnic groups
- Works well with those of different religious orientations

Standard 4: Displays effective interpersonal communication skills

Grades K–12
- Displays empathy with others
- Displays friendliness with others
- Displays politeness with others
- Seeks information nondefensively
- Provides feedback in a constructive manner
- Uses nonverbal communication such as eye contact, body position, voice tone effectively
- Does not react to a speaker's inflammatory deliverance
- Identifies with speaker while maintaining objectivity
- Uses emotions appropriately in personal dialogues
- Makes use of confrontation when appropriate
- Makes eye contact when speaking
- Reacts to ideas rather than to the person presenting the ideas
- Adjusts tone and content of information to accommodate the likes of others
- Communicates in a clear manner during conversations
- Acknowledges the strengths of others

Standard 5: Demonstrates leadership skills

Grades K–12
- Occasionally serves as a leader in groups
- Occasionally serves as a follower in groups
- Enlists others in working toward a shared vision
- Plans small wins
- Celebrates accomplishments
- Recognizes the contributions of others
- Passes on authority when appropriates

These standards and benchmarks can be emphasized while engaged in community-building activities:

Self-Regulation

Standard 1: Sets and manages goals

Grades K–12
- Sets explicit long-term goals
- Identifies and ranks relevant options in terms of accomplishing a goal
- Prepares and follows a schedule for carrying out options

- Understands personal wants versus needs
- Establishes personal milestones
- Identifies resources necessary to complete a goal
- Displays a sense of personal direction and purpose
- Maintains an awareness of proximity to goal
- Makes a cumulative evaluation of goal
- Understands the differences between various types of goals
- Sets routine goals for improving daily life
- Identifies explicit criteria for evaluating goals
- Makes contingency plans

Standard 2: Performs self-appraisal

Grades K–12
- Distributes work according to perceived strengths
- Identifies personal styles
- Identifies personal strengths and weaknesses
- Utilizes techniques for overcoming weaknesses
- Identifies basic values
- Performs analysis of employability
- Understands preferred working environments
- Understands career goals
- Identifies a compensating strength for each weakness
- Develops an inventory of wants versus needs
- Determines explicit behaviors that are used and should be adopted to obtain wants and/or needs
- Identifies personal motivational patterns
- Keeps a log documenting personal improvement
- Summarizes personal educational background
- Summarizes personal work experience
- Identifies key accomplishments and successes in life
- Identifies peak experiences and significant life experiences
- Identifies desired future accomplishments
- Identifies preferred life-style

Thinking and Reasoning

Standard 5: Applies basic troubleshooting and problem-solving techniques

Grades K–2
- Identifies simple problems and possible solutions (e.g., ways to make something work better)

Grades 3–5
- Identifies issues and problems in the school or community that one might help solve
- Studies problems in the community and how they were solved
- Analyzes the problems that have confronted people in the past in terms of the major goals and obstacles to those goals

Grades 6–8
- Identifies alternative courses of action and predicts likely consequences of each
- Selects the most appropriate strategy or alternative for solving a problem

- Examines different alternatives for resolving local problems and compares the possible consequences of each alternative

Grades 9–12
- Applies troubleshooting strategies to complex real-world situations
- Understands that troubleshooting almost anything may require many-step branching logic
- Engages in problem finding and framing for personal situations and situations in the community
- Represents a problem accurately in terms of resources, constraints and objectives
- Provides summation of the effectiveness of problem-solving techniques
- Reframes problems when alternative solutions are exhausted
- Evaluates the feasibility of various solutions to problems; recommends and defends solutions

Standard 6: Applies decision-making techniques

Grades K–2
- Makes and defends decisions about daily activities (e.g., what books to read)

Grades 3–5
- Studies decisions that were made in the community in terms of the alternatives that were considered
- Analyzes important decisions made by people in the past in terms of possible alternatives that were considered

Grades 6–8
- Identifies situations in the community and in one's personal life in which a decision is required
- Secures factual information needed to evaluate alternatives
- Identifies the values underlying the alternatives that are considered and the criteria that will be used to make a selection among the alternatives
- Predicts the consequences of selecting each alternative
- Makes decisions based on the data obtained and the criteria identified
- When appropriate, takes action to implement the decision
- Analyzes personal decisions in terms of the options that were considered

Grades 9–12
- Evaluates major factors that influence personal decisions

Academic content can be presented experientially using the Experiential Learning Cycle.* Content can also be woven into community-building activities. The concepts encompassed in the following standards and benchmarks can easily be addressed during problem-solving activities and then transferred to academic content:

Life Work

Standard 7: Displays reliability and a basic work ethic

Grades 9–12
- Completes tasks on time
- Chooses ethical courses of action

---

* See *Adventure in the Classroom* by Mary Henton for a comprehensive discussion on this topic. Project Adventure teaches a workshop on this topic as well.

- Uses appropriate language in work situations
- Requests clarification when needed

Standard 8: Operates effectively within organizations
Grades 9–12
- Understands the organization's basic goals and values
- Understands the extent to which organizational values are compatible with personal values

Thinking and Reasoning

Standard 1: Understands and applies the basic principles of presenting an argument
Grades K–2
- Understands that people are more likely to believe a person's ideas if that person can give good reasons for them
- Provides coherent (though not necessarily valid or convincing) answers when asked why one believes something to be true or how one knows something
- Asks "how do you know?" in appropriate situations

Grades 3–5
- Understands that reasoning can be distorted by strong feelings
- Raises questions about arguments that are based on the assertion that "everybody knows" or "I just know"
- Seeks reasons for believing things other than the assertion that "everybody agrees"
- Recognizes when a comparison is not fair because important characteristics are not the same

Grades 6–8
- Identifies and questions false analogies
- Identifies and questions arguments in which all members of a group are implied to possess nearly identical characteristics that are considered different from those of another group
- Compares and contrasts the credibility of differing accounts of the same event

Grades 9–12
- Understands that when people try to prove a point, they may at times select only the information that supports it and ignore the information that contradicts it
- Identifies techniques used to slant information in subtle ways
- Identifies or seeks out the critical assumptions behind a line of reasoning and uses that to judge the validity of an argument
- Understands that to be convincing, an argument must have both true statements and valid connections among them
- Evaluates the overall effectiveness of complex arguments

Standard 2: Understands and applies basic principles of logic and reasoning
Grades 6–8
- Understands that some aspects of reasoning have very rigid rules and other aspects do not
- Understands that when people have rules that always hold for a given situation and good information about the situation, then logic can help them figure out what is true about the situation

- Understands that reasoning by similarities can suggest ideas but cannot be used to prove things
- Understands that a single example can never prove that something is true, but a single example can prove that something is not true
- Understands that some people invent a general rule to explain how something works by summarizing observations
- Understands that people overgeneralize by making up rules on the basis of only a few observations
- Understands that personal values influence the types of conclusions people make
- Recognizes situations in which a variety of conclusions can be drawn from the same information

Grade 9–12
- Analyzes the deductive validity of arguments based on implicit or explicit assumptions
- Understands that people sometimes reach false conclusions either by applying faulty logic to true statements or by applying valid logic to false statements
- Understands that a reason may be sufficient to get a result but may not be the only way to get the result (i.e., may not be necessary), or a reason may be necessary to obtain a result but not sufficient (i.e., other things are also required; some reasons may be both necessary and sufficient)

Standard 4: Understands and applies basic principles of hypothesis testing and scientific inquiry

Grades K–2
- Asks "how do you know?" in appropriate situations and attempts to provide reasonable answers when others ask the same question
- Understands that changing one thing sometimes causes changes in something else, and that changing the same thing in the same way usually has the same result

Grades 3–5
- Distinguishes between actual observations and ideas or conclusions about what others have observed

Grades 6–8
- Understands that there are a variety of ways in which people can form hypotheses, including basing them on many observations, basing them on very few observations, and constructing them on only one or two observations
- Verifies results of experiments
- Understands that there may be more than one valid way to interpret a set of findings
- Reformulates a new hypothesis for study after an old hypothesis has been eliminated
- Makes and validates conjectures about outcomes of specific alternatives or events regarding an experiment

Grades 9–12
- Presents alternative explanations and conclusions to one's own experiments and those of others
- Critiques procedures, explanations and conclusions in one's own experiments and those of others

QUESTIONS TO ASK ROPES/CHALLENGE COURSE PROVIDERS

There are many providers of ropes/challenge course experiences. As more organizations build courses and market to a variety of audiences, the variety of programming grows as well. Can all ropes course providers be all things to all people? How do you know that your class is getting a quality experience?

Most providers are well trained, with state-of-the-art equipment and up-to-date methods. Staff are enthusiastic and willing to meet your needs. What makes the difference between a good experience and a great one? As with any experience, some providers are a better fit for your group than others. Here are some questions to ask that may help you find a provider who can meet your particular needs and ensure a safe experience, both physically and emotionally.

First, look for an organization that focuses on your population. If, for example, you take your class to a provider that works primarily with corporate groups, the facilitators may have difficulty relating to the developmental level of the students. On the other hand, if you take your class to a YMCA camp, where they are used to working with youth, they may be better prepared to deal with the dynamics and needs of your students.

Here are some questions to ask of a ropes/challenge course provider that may help you determine a good fit with your class's needs:

- **Who built your course?**
  These days, the Association for Challenge Course Technology (ACCT) is recognized as a leader in determining standards for ropes/challenge course construction. A course that is built by ACCT Professional Vendor Members means that a certain level of quality and safety standards has been met. Sometimes organizations build their own courses, and then have it inspected by an ACCT Professional Vendor Member to verify that the standards have been met.

- **When was the last time your course was inspected?**
  ACCT recommends a yearly inspection by an ACCT Professional Vendor Member, in addition to periodic inspections by the people who run the course. If the course has not been inspected by an outside source in a while, ask why. Also, if this organization has not had their course inspected, or does not feel it is important, consider taking your group elsewhere. An outside inspection is a small price to pay to ensure the physical safety of your class.

- **What kind of training do you require for your staff?**
  Typically, staff engage in an Adventure skills workshop from a reputable vendor that includes facilitation techniques, technical/safety skills and program philosophy. Some staff have this training when they are hired, while others go through the training after being hired. In addition, initial orientation for course protocols and periodic refreshers are given to staff so that they can maintain their skills. More training and staff development is a bonus.

  There should be at least one person with first aid and CPR certification working on the course while groups are there. If you are doing high elements, there should be at least one person on the course who is trained in rescue techniques.

- **Is your program accredited?**
  Much like AAA for hotels and dining, and American Camping Association for camps, the Association for Experiential Education (AEE) offers an accreditation program for ropes and challenge courses. Using industry standards, they have teams visit courses to look over entire programs. When a course is subsequently accredited, it is a sign that certain minimum standards have been met. Project Adventure also offers an accreditation program. **Accreditation is voluntary and is not required.** There are many ropes/challenge course programs out there that far exceed minimum industry standards yet are not accredited.

- **What is your plan in case of injury?**
  This should be a no-brainer. If they cannot rattle off what to do in case of an emergency, be wary.

- **Describe a typical day at your course.**
  Look for signs that they pay attention to the sequencing of activities, and that they are prepared to alter their plan based on the needs of the group.

- **What is your organization's philosophy on Challenge by Choice?**
  Ropes/challenge courses regularly put participants in vulnerable situations. Participants need to be allowed to choose their own level of challenge. This does not mean that facilitators take a hands-off approach, because there are times when students need an emotional nudge or encouragement to push themselves. It does mean that the staff have thought about this in advance and understand that individuals react differently to anxiety. A one-size-fits-all approach is problematic.

- **Do you have any ideas about how to help us transfer this experience back at school?**
  Although they are not responsible for connecting learning from this short experience back to the classroom, it is nice to know that they are thinking about it. Some organizations have strategies to help with this.

- **How do you deal with conflicts between group members?**
  Conflict is a natural part of the group process. Chances are that your students will be involved in it during the day at a ropes/challenge course. Have the staff thought about it? You know your students much better than a facilitator who has just met them, which can cause some awkward moments during a conflict situation. Are you ready to defer to them, and are they ready to enlist your help if necessary?

Although there are many more questions that could be listed here, these questions will give you the ability to "feel-out" the ropes/challenge course provider. If you can find the right provider to meet your needs, your students will have a more powerful experience.

Challenge Ropes Course Construction: Some Considerations

Building a ropes or challenge course entails more than getting a contractor to put the physical elements into the ground, up in the trees or into the rafters. Because we are dealing with a process, it is important to see the whole picture. It is also necessary to look into liability and risk management concerns.

Following is an annotated outline to help you develop not just a course, but a useful and meaningful program:

I. **Preplanning**
   A. **Goals**

   Your goals will drive the choices of elements for your program. For example, if your main goals center around teamwork, cooperation, collaboration and problem solving, then you are probably looking to build only low-challenge course elements. If, on the other hand, your goals encompass all of the above *and* an exploration of risk-taking, challenge and personal goal setting, then you may wish to consider adding some high elements.

   Training goals are important here, as well. The addition of a high course means that training is longer, more involved and specific.

   It is helpful to bring together stakeholders in the project. These are people who will be directly affected either by its use or by the fact that it physically exists. Find out the concerns, level of enthusiasm, hopes and fears for the project. Make sure you include custodians who will be responsible for cutting the grass around the poles, or might be worried about how they are going to work around the elements when trying to change a lightbulb. If possible, bring in potential participants (students, business community) as well.

   Set goals together to make sure people's concerns and agendas are being addressed.

   B. **Site selection—indoor and outdoor**
   Some factors to consider:
   - Purpose of course—will it only be used by this school? Will outside groups contract to use the course?
   - Population(s) to be served
   - Available land that can either handle the inclusion of poles or has mature and healthy trees
   - Accessibility for participants in wheelchairs or other physical issues
   - Accessibility when not in use. Can the doors be locked? Is it in a high-traffic area? (These issues can be remedied by making it possible to set up and take down the course.)
   - Scheduling—if indoor, is the gym used so much that the course is rarely available?
   - Weather considerations—indoor courses can be used more in extreme climate areas.
   - Aesthetics/Environment—being outside and getting out of the usual environment can have a positive effect on some groups/participants. It can also have a negative effect if people are not used to being in a more rugged environment.

C. **Choose possible elements**
Choose according to the goals, populations to be served, money and available time for training

D. **In-house risk management consultation**
1. Existing policies
2. Check with insurance provider about standards

Some school districts have risk-management departments, or at least a risk-management supervisor. It is important to bring these people into the process from the beginning.

Some insurance providers have installation standards that need to be met when building a course. Also, check with insurance providers about additional insurance needs, if necessary.

E. **Choose builder**
1. ACCT (Association for Challenge Course Technology) guidelines
2. Get initial estimates from prospective builders
3. Make a decision

ACCT is the organization that is setting installation, management and ethics standards for the ropes-course-building industry. Although not required, it is highly recommended that a builder be a Professional Vendor Member of ACCT. That way you know that they are building to the industry standards.

There are many qualified ropes course builders in every region. Take the time to get bids from at least three builders. This allows you to get ballpark cost estimates based on individual elements, travel, lodging, etc. You can then compare basic costs between builders. Contact ACCT for a list of Professional Vendor Members.

F. **Fundraising**
1. In-house funding
2. Grants
3. Foundation support
4. Fund raising events

G. **Site evaluation from builder**
1. Revisit elements based on site evaluation
2. Get revised estimate based on site evaluation and new element choices

Once a builder is chosen based on preliminary bids, they will usually want to visit your site to see what is actually possible to build. Indoor courses, for example, are unique because every building is different (the builder would appreciate blueprints if you can locate them). A tree course can only be built where the trees actually exist. A pole course, though, is more flexible because poles can be set according to the elements that are chosen.

At this time the revised estimate will more accurately reflect the total cost of the project.

H. Bring together all parties to discuss next steps
   1. Maintenance/custodial staff
   2. Administrators
   3. Representatives of possible users
   4. Purchasing department
   5. Risk management/insurance representatives
   6. Others
   Now that you have the course laid out, costs figured and fund raising started, bring together stakeholders again to revisit goals and tasks. Create new goals to address new information.

II. Building a Challenge/Ropes Course
   A. Set dates with builder

   B. Logistics
      1. Arrange for housing and transportation for builders
      2. Have someone available to take care of logistics for builders while there

   C. Assemble first aid kit for the ropes course

   D. Obtain rescue kit if high ropes

   E. Identify locked storage area for ropes course equipment

   F. Organize and store equipment/create "bag of tricks"

   G. Future facilitators obtain first aid and CPR certification

   H. Identify person to be course manager
   It is essential that someone be designated as course manager. This person makes sure that required maintenance and inspections are performed, equipment is logged and stored properly, and that only people who are trained are actually using the course. She or he will also maintain records for all facilitators to make sure they are current on training and refreshers.

III. Initial Preparation and Staff Training
   A. Learn standard operating procedures (SOPs) from a reputable vendor
      1. 5-day skills workshop (low/high elements)
      2. 3-day skills workshop (low elements only)
      3. Advanced skills workshop which includes rescue training (high elements)
   You can generally get training either through your builder or through other organizations that offer ropes course training. When looking for a ropes course facilitation provider, keep in mind that there is more to ropes course facilitation than physically doing the elements. Ask them for a curriculum outline and references. Make sure they are teaching more than technical skills and are addressing the needs of your client population.

If a high course is built, it is highly recommended that *at least* one person has been trained in advanced skills, and that a person with advanced skills training be on the course whenever it is in use.

    B. **Develop local operating procedures (LOPs)**
Every course needs a manual that articulates the protocols of that course. Your builder and training providers can help you establish the standard operating procedures. They can also offer insight into areas that are unique to your course that must be included in your local operating procedures.

    C. **Develop evacuation plan in case of injury at course/phone access**

    D. **Write initial ropes course manual with protocols and LOPs**

    E. **Develop equipment usage log**
        1. History of equipment usage
        2. Ropes course log for high elements

    F. **Develop curriculum to meet needs of user groups**

IV. **Maintenance**
    A. **Yearly inspections by ACCT Professional Vendor Member builder**
It is important that all ropes courses be inspected by an ACCT Professional Vendor Member builder every year. They will inspect the hardware, ropes, elements and logs. They will then write a report with suggestions and recommendations about your course so that it can remain in safe operating condition. This can be built into a yearly budget so that it is sure to happen.

    B. **Yearly facilitator refreshers**
Some facilitators use the course weekly or even daily. Others use it sporadically at best. There should be a yearly refresher course to update facilitators on both old and new protocols. You can also take the opportunity to answer questions, go over incidents and offer new techniques.

    C. **Plan for training new facilitators**
Some facilitators are there for life. Others move away, retire, have health problems or simply lose interest. How will you get new people trained? The continued use of an outside vendor for training helps assure that your program stays current with new information. Bringing new people into the mix can also jump-start the cycle of low energy that is bound to come.

    D. **Usage plan: who, why, how, when?**
Who is using your course, and how do they get to use it?

    E. **Equipment maintenance and replacement budget**
Make sure to include a yearly inspection in the budget!

NOTE: Every challenge/ropes course is unique, as are the needs of the organization installing a ropes course. Therefore, this is intended only as a guide for planning. Other questions, issues and considerations may arise according to the needs of the sponsoring agency.

Where Do the Activities Come From?

Adventure games and activities are similar to folk songs. Sometimes it is possible to trace their origin, but many times it is not. Every person who uses an activity presents it in her or his own way, adding a flair here and an adaptation there. In this way, the activities continue to evolve.

How one uses an activity has as much to do with sequencing as the activity itself. A simple game of tag can be turned into a trust activity by making the boundaries closer together, thus causing a greater likelihood of contact between participants.

Age and maturity level also play a part in where an activity fits in a sequence. Speed Rabbit, an activity where people are asked to act silly in front of each other, can be used on day one with a class of first graders, but is a sure-fire failure with students in grade 8 on the first day of school. They need much more time to get to know their classmates before pretending to be an elephant in front of them. Once they know that their classmates will not put them down though, a rousing game of Speed Rabbit is a sure-fire winner even in middle school.

Most of the activities in this book have been written about in previous books. Below is a list of these activities and where to find them.* By reading the descriptions in each book, you will find different perspectives on how to use an activity. Please use this only as a guide and remember to trust your judgment about the needs of your students and the issues that are important to your class. Each activity is assigned according to the part of the process where I might begin using the activity. In other words, an activity might require some problem solving, but it can be used as a cooperation activity (such as Line Ups or A What?). Other activities require a higher degree of trust or more complex problem solving, so they are put at the trust or problem solving level.

Undoubtedly you (and the authors of these books) will find activities on this grid and wonder, What was she thinking?! No two people will ever agree on the correct sequence. Consider these grids as a starting point, and when you start questioning my motives here it means that you are well on your way to creating your own sequencing instincts.

AECC: *Adventure Education for the Classroom Community* (Frank and Panico)
AIP: *Adventures in Peacemaking* (Kreidler and Furlong)
AP: *Affordable Portables* (Cavert)
DIA: *Diversity in Action* (Chappelle and Bigman)
FSI: *Funn Stuff I* (Rohnke)
FSII: *Funn Stuff II* (Rohnke)
FSIII: *Funn Stuff III* (Rohnke)
FSIV: *Funn Stuff IV* (Rohnke)
GFT: *Games (& Other Stuff) for Teachers* (Cavert and Frank)
GFG: *Games (& Other Stuff) for Group* (Cavert)
NGFWF: *New Games for the Whole Family* (LeFevre)
QS: *QuickSilver* (Rohnke and Butler)
SB: *Silver Bullets* (Rohnke)
TCC: *The Caring Classroom* (Frank)
TWTP: *Teamwork and Teamplay* (Cain and Jolliff)

---

* Please see the Bibliography for a greater description of each book.

Cooperation Activities (Ice Breakers and Deinhibitizers) and Just Plain Fun Games

Activity	AECC	AIP	AP	DIA	FS I, II, III, IV	GFG	GFT	NGFWF	QS	SB	TCC	TWTP
Bumpity Bump Bump												
1,2,3 Mississippi	p. 65							p. 107	p. 84		p. 46	
Community, Community, Commuity												
Cat and Mouse										p. 47		
Three's a Crowd								p. 76			p. 52	
Elbow Tag					IV: p. 72							
Pass Off Elbow Tag												
Commonalities												
Classroom Commonalities	p. 74	p. 202							p. 76		p. 42	
Differences and Commonalities												
Cross the Line				p. 242							p. 98	
Crossing the Feelings Line		p. 68		p. 340						p. 153	p. 58	
Everybody's It										p. 154		
Hospital Tag												
Face Falue												
Captain Video	p. 259				I: p. 6			p. 42			p. 43	
Interactive Video												
Find Your Place		p. 205										
The Line Forms Here		p. 65								p. 163		
Chronological Line-Up									p. 92		p. 41	p. 113
Where in the Circle Am I?									p. 126			
Name by Name												
Line Ups												
Line Up Like This -- No, Line Up Like That	p. 67											
Gotcha Lines	p. 54				II: p. 6						p. 50	
Get the Point							p. 114				p. 61	
Group Interview	p. 102										p. 59	
Growth Circles												
Have You Ever?	p. 256	p. 207		p. 67	I: p. 42				p. 224			
Switcheroo		p. 209			II: p. 6							
Celebration of Excellence					III: p. 90			p. 78	p. 209			
Pile Up												
Fruit Basket												
Neighbors	p. 188										p. 57	
Hoop Delight		p. 197										
Month by Month					III: p. 99				p. 85		p. 41	
Categories	p. 56				III: p.141							
On the Move												
Human Bingo		p. 214									p. 39	p. 39
Group Bingo												
Autographs												

Cooperation (cont.)

Activity	AECC	AIP	AP	DIA	FS I, II, III	GFG	GFT	NGFWF	QS	SB	TCC	TWTP
King Frog	p. 196	p. 165									p. 44	
King/Queen Frog											p. 99	
Emotion Motions												
Little Ernie								p. 61			p. 54	
Little Bert												
Look Up/Look Down					I: p. 13 III: p. 85							
Screaming Toes	p. 70										p. 49	
Making Connections						p. 15				p. 17	p. 32	
Memory Circle	p. 45											
Toss-A-Name Game					II: p. 12							
Name Game Circle												
Metamorphose											p. 48	
Morphing												
MeYouLisa		p. 52							p. 87			
Hustle Bustle											p. 34	
Name Tag			p. 9			p. 17 p. 37						
Name Ball												
Messages		p. 182		p. 169	I: p. 55 II: p. 59				p. 201		p. 124	p. 89
Group Anger Juggle												
Group Juggling												
Group Juggle Variations												
Group Juggle and Variations	p. 100											
Community Juggling	p. 128											
Emotional Gifts	p. 182											
Low Drop Juggle												
The "T" Juggle	p. 186				IV: 40						p. 55	p. 328
Night at the Improv. Theater Sports												
Story Circle	p. 60										p. 35	
Storyline												
Paired Activities												
Circulation Circles					IV: p. 21						p. 61	
Song Tag		p. 161										
Segue Sing Along								p. 132				
Speedy Threesome											p. 51	
Speed Rabbit					III: p. 87							
Speed Rabbit Roles												
Elephant, Rabbit, Palm Tree												
Feelings Speed Rabbit											p. 95	

ACTIVITY GRIDS 201

Trust Activities

Activity	AECC	AIP	AP	DIA	FS I, II, III	GFG	GFT	NGFWF	QS	SB	TCC	TWTP
60 Second Speeches	p. 105										p. 88	
All Together Now		p. 88								p. 156	p. 77	p. 91
Turnstile (The)												
Community Jump Rope											p. 103	
Anonymous Goals		p. 124										
Bumper Cars				p. 207			p. 137	p. 57			p. 80	
Driving in the Dark												
Car Car												
Drive My Car												
Circle Pass						p. 28						
Circle of Friends	p. 114										p. 93	
Willow in the Wind										p. 100	p. 84	
Everybody Up		p. 89		p. 137							p. 97	
Feelings Cards: Stories												
Find Your Partner		p. 134		p. 133					p. 202	p. 98	p. 82	
Hog Call			p. 82									
Friendship Walk				p. 347					p. 215		p. 105	
Field Wild Woosey					IV: p. 71							
Two Woosey Variations												
Wild Woosey												
Tension Traverse or Wild Woosey												
Team Switch			p. 52	p. 283			p. 143		p. 148	p. 24		
Minefield		p. 270							p. 205			
Challenge Field									p. 232			
Conflict Field (The)												
3-D Mine Field												
Minefield in a Circle												
Pitfall												
River of Life (The)	p. 123				III: p. 60						p. 100	
Miniature Yurt Circles									p. 258		p. 85	p. 151
Yurt Rope												
Dream Catcher												
Raccoon Circles												
Search and Rescue	p. 92										p. 80	
Evidence Rescue												
Sherpa Walk	p. 96									p. 89	p. 89	
Tension Traverse											p. 106	
Texas Big Foot				p. 172						p. 46		
Three Person Trust Lean											p. 92	
Pendulum Trust Lean												
Three Person Trust Walk											p. 102	

Trust (cont.)

Activity	AECC	AIP	AP	DIA	FS I, II, III	GFG	GFT	NGFWF	QS	SB	TCC	TWTP
Trust Pairs Walk				p. 344								
Pairs Walk									p. 229		p. 79	
Blindfold Trust Walk				p. 106								
Two Person Trust Lean											p. 90	
Trust Lean			p. 35									
Warning Bells						p. 31						
Shakers											p. 83	
Yurt Circle		p. 58									p. 87	
Hang Together to Hang Extreme	p. 62											

Problem Solving Activities

Activity	AECC	AIP	AP	DIA	FS I, II, III	GFG	GFT	NGFW F	QS	SB	TCC	TWTP
All Aboard Squared AKA Flip Side					III: p. 37					p. 106	p. 120	
Turn Over a New Leaf												p. 125
Magic Carpet												
Balloon Bash							p. 85					
Equally Frantic				p. 205						p. 19	p. 116	
Balloon Frantic											p. 145	
Batten Down the Hatches				p. 178							p. 128	
Blind Polygon	p. 165											
Blindfold Polygon Redux					II: p. 63							
Blindfold Polygon as Pairs					IV: p. 75							
Box Top			p. 73								p. 119	p. 70
All Aboard	p. 136											
Brainstorming		p. 269					p. 59				p. 142	
Enumerating		p. 281										
Brainstorming Our Brains	p. 233											
Butter Battle Escalator											p. 140	
Carpet Maze	p. 230		p. 77									
Pathfinder							p. 117				p. 118	p. 103
Gridlock												
Centerpiece		p. 274		p. 109					p. 156		p. 131	p. 189
Don't Touch Me												
Traffic Circle												
Channels	p. 88		p. 25		II: p. 19						p. 132	p. 128
Pipeline					IV: p. 73							
Half Pipe												
Marble Tubes												
Pipeline Unlimited												
Climbing the Wall				p. 353							p. 138	
Wall (The)											p. 147	
Compass Walk (The)											p. 143	
Conflicts—the Real...the Imagined		p. 171		p. 341								
Feelings Relay											p. 96	
Feelings Charades			p. 36								p. 133	
Islands		p. 86		p. 350					p. 186		p. 122	
Marshmallows												
Stepping Stones												
Stepping Stones with a Twist												
Graduation Trail	p. 82											
Moonball	p. 130		p. 16						p. 206	p. 31	p. 115	
Islands Moonball									p. 165			
Moonball -- Level II & Level III									p. 176			
Nitro Crossing				p. 281						p. 139	p. 133	

Problem Solving (cont.)

Activity	AECC	AIP	AP	DIA	FS I, II, III	GFG	GFT	NGFWF	QS	SB	TCC	TWTP
Number Game (The)							p. 29					
Group Number Game							p. 34					
Number Cruncher					III: p. 53						p. 129	
Numbers												
Puzzle Variation					I: p. 60							
Le Cav					II: p. 16						p. 127	
Puzzles												
Real Estate												p. 153
Roof Tops			p. 86									
Mohawk Walk					II: p. 62				p. 205	p. 140		
Virtual Mohawk					III: p.107							
Walk of Life											p. 106	
Roomination												
Rearrange the Classroom							p. 55				p. 144	
Setting the Table	p. 307										p. 121	
Spider Web				p. 245	II: p. 61				p. 209	p. 114	p. 136	
Hula Hoop Spider Web												
Surfing the Web I - IV												p. 169
Up Chuck or Barf Ball									p. 191		p. 123	
All Toss	p. 121											
All Catch	p. 126			p. 314							p. 114	
Warp Speed		p. 70							p. 159			
Eggspeediency												

Challenge Activities

Activity	AECC	AIP	AP	DIA	FS I, II, III	GFG	GFT	NGFWF	QS	SB	TCC	TWTP
Catwalk											p. 157	
Centipede											p. 157	
Community Exploration					II: p. 51						p. 163	
Portable Pamper Pole											p. 158	
Pamper Pole											p. 157	
Two Line Bridge											p. 160	
Urban Experience												
Zip Line											p. 159	

Processing Tools/Full Value Contract/Goal Setting

Activity	AECC	AIP	AP	DIA	FS I, II, III	GFG	GFT	NGFWF	QS	SB	TCC	TWTP
Anticipation/Result											p. 168	
Balloons											p. 167	
Bouncing Ball											p. 167	
Boxes											p. 168	
Creation											p. 167	
Feelings Marketplace Cards											p. 168	
Five Finger Contract											p. 63	
Hands All Around											p. 68	
Magic Circle											p. 168	
Partner Chats											p. 168	
Peaceable Being (The)		p. 14									p. 66	
PEEP											p. 64	
Play Hard, Play Fair, Play Safe, Have Fun											p. 66	
Postcards											p. 168	
Round Robin											p. 167	
Slam Dunk Suggestions									p. 268			
Crumpled Paper											p. 167	
Snapshot											p. 167	
Village (The)											p. 67	
What Do I need? What Can I Give?											p. 69	

REFERENCES

Archambault, Reginald D. (ed.). (1964). *John Dewey on Education: Selected Writings.* New York: Random House.

Conquest, Arthur Wellington. (1996, Summer). What (African-American) Children Need. *Ziplines, 29.* 44-45.

Dewey, John. (1938). *Experience and Education* (reprinted 1997, Touchstone). New York: Kappa Delta Pi.

Duckworth, Eleanor. (1987). *The Having of Wonderful Ideas and Other Essays on Teaching and Learning.* New York: Teachers College Press.

Falk, Beverly. (2000). *The Heart of the Matter: Using Standards and Assessment to Learn.* Portsmouth, NH: Heinemann.

Fluegelman, Andrew. (ed.). (1981). *The New Games Book.* Tiburon, CA: Doubleday.

Frank, Laurie and John Stanley. (1997). *Camp Manito-wish Leaders' Manual: Teacher Edition.* Milwaukee, WI: Hare Strigenz.

Gardner, Howard. (1993). *Multiple Intelligences: The Theory in Practice.* New York, Basic Books.

Goleman, Daniel. (1997). *Emotional Intelligence: Why it can Matter More than IQ.* New York: Bantam Books.

Gibbs, Jeanne. (1995). *TRIBES: A New Way of Learning and Being Together.* Sausalito, CA: CenterSource Systems.

Healthy Communities: 40 Developmental Assets. (1998). Minneapolis, MN: Search Institute.

Henton, Mary. (1996). *Adventure in the Classroom: Using Adventure to Create a Community of Lifelong Learners.* Hamilton, MA: Project Adventure, Inc.

Kendall, John S. and Robert J. Marzano. (1997). *Content Knowledge: A Compendium of Standards and Benchmarks for K-12 Education.* Aurora, CO: Mid-continental Regional Education Laboratory.

Knapp, Clifford E. (1992). *Lasting Lessons: A Teacher's Guide to Reflecting on Experience.* Charleston, WVA: ERIC Clearinghouse on Rural Education and Small Schools.

Kohn, Alfie. (1996). *Beyond Discipline: from Compliance to Community.* Alexandria, VA: Association for Curriculum and Supervision.

Kovalik, Susan. (1994). *ITI: The Model: Integrated Thematic Instruction.* Kent, WA: Susan Kovalik & Associates.

Kreidler, William J. and Lisa Furlong. (1996). *Adventures in Peacemaking: A Conflict Resolution Activity Guide.* Hamilton, MA: Project Adventure, Inc.

Leave No Trace: Seven Principles. (www.LNT.org).

Lewis, Barbara. (1995). *The Kids' Guide to Service Projects.* Minneapolis, MN: Free Spirit Press.

Luckner, John. L. and Reldan S. Nadler. (1997). *Processing the Experience: Strategies to Enhance and Generalize Learning.* (2nd ed.). Dubuque, IA: Kendall/Hunt.

Rohnke, Karl. (1984). *Silver Bullets: A Guide to Initiative Problems, Adventure, Games and Trust Activities.* Dubuque, IA: Kendall/Hunt.

Rohnke, Karl and Steve Butler. (1995). *QuickSilver.* Dubuque, IA: Kendall/Hunt.

Schoel, Jim, Dick Prouty and Paul Radcliffe. (1988). *Islands of Healing: A Guide to Adventure Based Counseling.* Hamilton, MA: Project Adventure, Inc.

Schoel, Jim and Michael Stratton. (1990). *Gold Nuggets: Readings for Experiential Education.* Hamilton, MA: Project Adventure, Inc.

Adventure/Experiential Education Resources

> **Code:** A = Activity book   T = Theory/Issues   O = Outdoor pursuits
> E = Environmental ed.   R = Readings   RC = Ropes course
> P = Processing tool

Publications and Teaching Materials

(T) Archambault, Reginald D. (ed.) (1994). *John Dewey on Education: Selected Writings.* New York: Random House.

(A) Barr, Linda and Harrington, Christine (1991). *Energize: Energizers and Other Great Cooperative Activities for All Ages.* Granville, OH: Quest International.

(T) Bigelow, Bill et al. (eds.) (1994). *Rethinking our Classrooms: Teaching for Equity and Justice.* Milwaukee, WI: Rethinking Schools.

(A) Bower, Nancy McPhee (1998). *Adventure Play: Adventure Activities for Preschool and Early Elemenatry Age Children.* Needham Heights, MA: Simon and Schuster Custom Publishing. (available through Project Adventure, Inc.: www.pa.org)

(A) Cain, Jim and Joliff, Barry (1998). *Teamwork and Teamplay: A Guide to Cooperative, Challenge Adventure Activities.* Dubuque, IA: Kendall/Hunt Publishing Company.

(T/A) Canfield, Jack and Wells, Harold C. (1976). *100 Ways to Enhance Self Concept in the Classroom.* Englewood Cliffs, NJ: Prentice-Hall Inc.

(A) Cavert, Chris (1996). *Affordable Portables: Working-Book of Initiative Activities & Problem Solving Elements.* Oklahoma City, OK: Wood 'N' Barnes Publishing.

(A) Cavert, Chris (1999). *Games (& Other Stuff) for Group.* Oklahoma City, OK: Wood 'N' Barnes Publishing.

(A) Cavert, Chris and Frank, Laurie (1999). *Games (& Other Stuff) for Teachers.* Oklahoma City, OK: Wood 'N' Barnes Publishing.

(T/A) Chappelle, Sharon and Bigman, Lisa (1998). *Diversity in Action: Using Adventure activities to explore issues of diversity with middle school and high school age youth.* Hamilton, MA: Project Adventure, Inc.

(P) Chiji Cards. Institute for Experiential Education (IEE), 115 Fifth Avenue South, Suite 430, La Crosse, WI 54601. 608/784-0789. www.chiji.com

(O) Colorado Outward Bound School (1981). *Backcountry Handbook for the Mountain, River and Desert Areas.* Colorado: Colorado Outward Bound School.

(T) Cousins, Emily and Rodgers, Melissa (1995). *Fieldwork: An Expeditionary Learning Outward Bound Reader, Volume I.* Dubuque, IA: Kendall/Hunt Publishing Company.

(T) John (1938). *Experience and Education.* New York, NY: Touchstone.

(T/A) Ellmo, Wendy and Graser, Jill (1995). *Adapted Adventure Activities: A Rehabilitation Model for Adventure Programming and Group Initiatives.* Dubuque, IA: Kendall/Hunt Publishing Company, and Project Adventure, Inc.

(P) Feelings Marketplace Cards (1995). Medway, MA : Effectiveness Resources International. (available through Project Adventure, Inc., www.pa.org)

(T) Falk, Beverly (2000). *The Heart of the Matter: Using Standards and Assessment to Learn.* Portsmouth, NH: Heinemann.

(A) Fluegelman, Andrew, and the New Games Foundation (1981). *The New Games Book.* Tiburon, CA: Dolphin Books/Doubleday and Company, Inc.

(A) Fluegelman, Andrew, and the New Games Foundation (1981). *More New Games.* Garden City, NY: Dolphin Books/Doubleday and Company, Inc.

(T/A) Frank, Laurie (1988). *Adventure in the Classroom: A Stress/Challenge Curriculum.* Madison, WI: Madison Metropolitan School District.

(T/A) Frank, Laurie and Stanley, John (1997). *Manito-wish Leaders Manual: Teacher Edition.* Waukesha, WI: The Manito-wish YMCA.

(T/A) Frank, Laurie and Panico, Ambrose (2000). *Adventure Education for the Classroom Community.* Bloomington, IL: National Education Service.

(T) Gaetano, Ronald J., Grout, Jim and Klassen-Landis, Marv (1991). *Please Talk With Me: A guide to teen-adult dialogue.* Dubuque, IA: Kendall/Hunt Publishing Company.

(T) Gardner, Howard (1993). *Multiple Intelligences: The Theory in Practice.* New York: BasicBooks.

(T) Gass, Michael A. (1995) *Book of Metaphors Volume II.* Boulder, CO: Association for Experiential Education.

(T/A) Gelatt, H.B., Varenhorst, Barbara and Carey, Richard (1972). Deciding. NY: College Entrance Exam Board.

(T) Georgia College and State University, Gillis, Lee and Hirsch, Jude (eds.). *Food For Thought: A workbook for developing metaphorical introductions to group activities.* Dubuque, IA: Kendall Hunt Publishing Company.

(T/A) Gibbs, Jeanne (2000). *TRIBES: A New Way of Learning and Being Together.* Sausalito, CA: CenterSource Systems.

(T) Goleman, Daniel (1997). *Emotional Intelligence: Why it can Matter More than IQ.* New York: Bantam Books.

(A) Gregson, Bob (1982). *The Incredible Indoor Games Book.* Belmont, CA: David S. Lake, Publishers.

(A) Gregson, Bob (1984). *The Outrageous Outdoor Games Book.* Belmont CA: David S. Lake, Publishers.

(A) Harrison, Martha, and the Nonviolence and Children Program (nd). *For the Fun of It! Selected Cooperative Games for Children and Adults.* Philadelphia, PA: Friends of Peace Committee.

(T) Hart, Leslie A. (1998). *Human Brain and Human Learning.* Kent, WA: Books for Educators, Inc.

(T) Havens, Mark D. (1991). *Bridges to Accessibility: A Primer for Including Persons with Disabilities in Adventure Curricula.* Hamilton, MA: Project Adventure, Inc.

(T) Henton, Mary. (1996). Adventure in the Classroom: *Using Adventure to Create a Community of Life-Long Learners.* Hamilton, MA: Project Adventure, Inc.

(T) Jennings, Wayne B., St. Germaine, Rick, and Begay, Gene, Jr. (1996). *Joining Hands A Resourcebook on Integrating Experiential Learning into the School Curriculum.* Dubuque, IA: Kendall/Hunt Publishing Company.

(T) Johnson, David W. and Johnson, Frank P. (1975). *Joining Together: Group Theory and Group Skills.* Englewood Cliffs, NJ: Prentice-Hall, Inc.

(A) Kamiya, Art (1985). *Elementary Teacher's Handbook of Indoor and Outdoor Games.* West Nyack, NY: Parker Publishing Company.

(T) Kohl, Herbert (1984). *Growing Minds: On Becoming a Teacher.* New York: Harper and Row, Publishers.

(T) Kohn, Alfie (1986). *No Contest: The Case Against Competition.* Boston: Houghton Mifflin.

(T) Kohn, Alfie (1990). *The Brighter Side of Human Nature.* New York: BasicBooks.

(T) Kohn, Alfie (1993). *Punished by Rewards: The Trouble with Gold Stars, Incentive Plans, A's, Praise, and Other Bribes.* Boston: Houghton Mifflin.

(T) Kohn, Alfie (1996). *Beyond Discipline: From Compliance to Community.* Alexandria, VA: ASCD.

(T) Kohn, Alfie (1999). *The Schools Our Children Deserve.* Alexandria, VA: ASCD.

(T) Kohn, Alfie (2000). *The Case Against Standardized Testing: Raising the Scores, Ruining the Schools.* Portsmouth, NH: Heinemann.

(T) Kovalkic, Susan (1994). *ITI: The Model: Integrated Thematic Instruction.* Kent, WA: Susan Kovalic & Associates.

(T) Kozol, Jonathan (1991). *Savage Inequalities: Children in America's Schools.* New York: Crown Publishers.

(T) Kozol, Jonathan (1995). *Amazing Grace.* New York: Crown Publishers.

(T/A) Kreidler, William J. (1984). *Creative Conflict Resolution.* Glenview, IL: Scott, Foresman and Company.

(T/A) Kreidler, William J. and Furlong, Lisa (1996). *Adventures in Peacemaking: A Conflict Resolution Activity Guide.* Cambridge, MA: Educators for Social Responsibility, and Project Adventure, Inc.

(T/A) Kreidler, William J. and Whittall, Sandy Tsubokawa (1999). *Adventures in Peace-making: Early Childhood,* (2nd ed). Cambridge, MA: Educators for Social Responsibility.

(T/A) Lewis, Barbara A. (1995). *The Kid's Guide to Service Projects.* Minneapolis, MN: Free Spirit Publishing.

(T/A) Lewis, Barbara A. (1998). *What Do You Stand For?: A Kid's Guide to Building Character.* Minneapolis, MN: Free Spirit Publishing.

(T) Lowe, Robert and Miner, Barbara Miner (eds.) (1996). *Selling Out our Schools.* Milwaukee, WI: Rethinking Schools.

(T) Luckner, John L. and Nadler, Reldan S. (1997). *Processing the Experience: Strategies to Enhance and Generalize Learning,* (2nd ed.). Dubuque, IA: Kendall/Hunt Publishing Company.

(T) Miles, John C. and Priest, Simon (eds.) (1999). *Adventure Programming.* State College, PA: Venture Publishing, Inc.

(E/A) Mitchell, John, and the Massachusetts Audobon Society (1980). *The Curious Naturalist.* Englewood Cliffs, NJ: Prentice-Hall, Inc.

(A) Orlick, Terry (1978). *The Cooperative Sports and Games Book.* New York: Pantheon Books.

(A)   Orlick, Terry (1982). *The Second Cooperative Sports and Games Book.* New York: Pantheon Books.

(T/A) Palmer, Libby et. al. (1999). *Adventures in Architecture: An Activity-Based Science Curriculum.* Needham Heights, MA: Simon and Schuster Custom Publishing, and Project Adventure, Inc.

(R)   Pritchard, Tracey and Severson, Jennifer (eds.) (nd). *Voyageur Outward Bound School Readings Book.* Minnesota: Voyageur Outward Bound School.

(T/A) Prutzman et al (1988). *The Friendly Classroom for a Small Planet.* Philadelphia, PA: New Society Publishers.

(T)   Ratliffe, Sharon, A. and Herman, Deidre M. (1982). *Self Awareness.* Skokie IL: National Textbook Co.

(A)   Rohnke, Karl (1993). *The Bottomless Bag, Again!* Dubuque, IA: Kendall/Hunt Publishing Company.

(A)   Rohnke, Karl. Challenge by Choice: *A Manual for the Construction of Low Elements on a Challenge Ropes Course.* Hamilton, MA: Project Adventure, Inc.

(RC) Rohnke, Karl (1989). *Cowstails and Cobras II.* Dubuque, IA: Kendall/Hunt Publishing Company, and Project Adventure, Inc.

(O)   Rohnke, Karl (1992). *Forget Me Knots.* Dubuque, IA: Kendall/Hunt Publishing Company, and Project Adventure, Inc.

(A)   Rohnke, Karl (1996). *Funn Stuff: Volume I.* Dubuque, IA: Kendall/Hunt Publishing Company.

(A)   Rohnke, Karl (1996). *Funn Stuff: Volume II.* Dubuque, IA: Kendall/Hunt Publishing Company.

(A)   Rohnke, Karl (1998). *Funn Stuff: Volume III.* Dubuque, IA: Kendall/Hunt Publishing Company.

(A)   Rohnke, Karl (2000). *Funn Stuff: Volume IV.* Dubuque, IA: Kendall/Hunt Publishing Company.

(A)   Rohnke, Karl (1984). *Silver Bullets: A Guide to Initiative Problems, Adventure, Games and Trust Activities.* Dubuque, IA: Kendall/Hunt Publishing Company, and Project Adventure, Inc.

(R)   Rohnke, Karl (1992). *Slightly Skewed Vignettes.* Dubuque, IA: Kendall/Hunt Publishing Company.

(A)   Rohnke, Karl (1996). *Top Tricks.* Dubuque, IA: Kendall/Hunt Publishing Company.

(A)   Rohnke, Karl and Butler, Steve (1995).*Quicksilver.* Dubuque, IA: Kendall/Hunt Publishing Company, and Project Adventure, Inc.

(RC) Rohnke, Karl, Tait, Catherine and Wall, Jim (1997). *The Complete Ropes Course Manual* (2nd ed.). Dubuque, IA: Kendall/Hunt Publishing Company.

(A)   Rohnke, Karl and Grout, Jim (1998). *Back Pocket Adventure.* Needham Heights, MA: Simon and Schuster Custom Publishing, and Project Adventure, Inc.

(T)   Schoel, Jim, Prouty, Dick and Radcliffe, Paul (1988). *Islands of Healing: A Guide to Adventure Based Counseling.* Hamilton, MA: Project Adventure, Inc.

(R)   Schoel, Jim and Stratton, Michael (1990). *Gold Nuggets: Readings for Experiential Education.* Hamilton, MA: Project Adventure, Inc.

(T) Search Institute (1998). *Healthy Communities: 40 Developmental Assets.* Minneapolis, MN: Search Institute.

(T) Starkman, Neal, Scales, Peter C. and Roberts, Clay (1999). *Great Places to Learn: How Asset Building Schools help Students Succeed.* Minneapolis, MN: Search Institute.

(T) Thomson, Barbara J. (1993). *Words Can Hurt You: Beginning a Program of Anti-Bias Education.* Menlo Park, CA: Addison-Wesley.

(RC) Webster, Steven E. (1989). *Project Adventure Ropes Course Safety Manual.* Dubuque, IA: Kendall/Hunt Publishing Company, and Project Adventure, Inc.

(E/A) Western Association of Fish and Wildlife Agencies, and Western Regional Environmental Education Council (1983). *Project Wild.* Boulder, CO: Project Wild.

(E/A) Western Regional Environmental Education Council, and American Forest Institute (1977). *Project Learning Tree.* Washington, DC: American Forest Institute.

Organizations

Association for Challenge Course Technology (ACCT)
PO Box 255, Martin, MI 49070-0255; (616) 685-0670, www.acctinfo.org.
Ropes course building and standards. Yearly conference. Memberships available.

Association for Experiential Education (AEE)
2305 Canyon Blvd. #100, Boulder, CO 80302; (303) 440-8844, www.aee.org.
Yearly international conference and regional conferences. Educational materials. Memberships available.

Project Adventure, Inc.
701 Cabot Street, beverly, MA 01915; (978) 524-4500, www.pa.org.
Workshops in adventure education, equipment catalog and challenge course services. Educational materials. Memberships available.

Teachers of Experiential and Adventure Methodology (TEAM)
Physical Education Program Northeastern Illinois University, 5500 N. St. Louis, Chicago, IL 60625; (773) 442-5564.
Yearly conference. Newsletter sent at no cost.

About the Author

Laurie Frank is available to facilitate workshops and inservices through:

GOAL Consulting
1337 Jenifer St.
Madison, WI 53703

(608) 251-2234   phone
(608) 251-5212   fax

LSFranken@AOL.com

ACTIVITY LIST

Activity Name	Activity Type	Page
1,2,3 Mississippi	Deinhibitizer	46
60-Second Speeches	Trust	88
All Aboard	Problem-solving initiative	119
All Toss	Problem-solving initiative	123
Anonymous Goals	Behavioral goal setting	103
Balloon Frantic	Problem-solving initiative	116
Batten Down the Hatches	Conflict resolution	145
Being, The	Full Value Contract	66
Blind Polygon	Problem-solving initiative	128
Books and Quilts	Academic content	148
Brainstorming	Conflict resolution	142
Butter Battle Escalator	Conflict resolution	140
Categories and Line Ups	Ice Breaker/Acquaintance	41
Catwalk, The	High ropes course	157
Centipede, The	High ropes course	157
Channels	Problem-solving initiative	132
City-County Building	Urban Experience	161
Community Exploration	Urban Experience	163
¿Como Estás?	Deinhibitizer	47
Compass Walk, The	Academic content	147
Conflicts—the Real...the Imagined	Conflict resolution	143
Crossing the Feelings Line	Feelings literacy	98
Differences and Commonalties	Ice Breaker/Acquaintance	42
Don't Touch Me	Problem-solving initiative	131
Dream Catcher	Trust	85
Elbow Tag	Deinhibitizer	52
Emotion Motions	Feelings literacy	99
Everybody Up	Trust	84
Everybody's It	Challenge by Choice	58
Feelings Cards: Charades	Feelings literacy	96
Feelings Cards: Stories	Feelings literacy	97
Feelings Speed Rabbit	Feelings literacy	95
Five Finger Contract	Full Value Contract	63
Get the Point	Deinhibitizer	50
Group Bingo	Ice Breaker/Acquaintance	39
Group Interview	Challenge by Choice	61
Group Juggle and Variations	Problem-solving initiative	124
Basic Juggle	Problem-solving initiative	124
You're In or You're Out	Problem-solving initiative	125
Low Drop Juggle	Problem-solving initiative	125
Juggling for Our Lives	Problem-solving initiative	126
Growth Circles	Challenge by Choice	59
Hands All Around	Full Value Contract	68
Hog Call	Trust	82
Interactive Video	Ice Breaker/Acquaintance	43
Islands	Low challenge ropes course: problem solving	133
King/Queen Frog	Ice Breaker/Acquaintance	44
Little Bert	Deinhibitizer	54

Activity Name	Activity Type	Page
Marshmallows	Problem-solving initiative	122
Memory Circle	Ice Breaker/Acquaintance	32
Moonball	Problem-solving initiative	115
Morphing	Deinhibitizer	48
Name Tag	Ice Breaker/Acquaintance	34
Neighbors	Challenge by Choice	57
Night at the Improv	Deinhibitizer	55
Nitro Crossing	Low challenge ropes course: problem solving	135
Numbers	Problem-solving initiative	129
Paired Activities	Ice Breaker/Acquaintance	35
Last Detail	Ice Breaker/Acquaintance	36
Tie Your Shoe	Ice Breaker/Acquaintance	36
Me Switch	Ice Breaker/Acquaintance	36
Macro Rock/Paper/Scissors	Ice Breaker/Acquaintance	37
High Fives	Ice Breaker/Acquaintance	37
1-1 Interview	Ice Breaker/Acquaintance	38
Celebration	Ice Breaker/Acquaintance	38
Paired Blindfold Trust Activities	Trust	79
Blindfold Trust Walk	Trust	79
Search and Rescue	Trust	80
Drive My Car	Trust	80
Pamper Pole	High ropes course	158
Pathfinder	Problem-solving initiative	118
PEEP	Full Value Contract	64
Pendulum Trust Lean	Trust	92
Play Hard, Safe, Fair, Have Fun	Full Value Contract	66
Puzzles	Problem-solving initiative	127
Rearrange the Classroom	Conflict resolution	144
River of Life, The	Behavioral goal setting	100
Screaming Toes	Deinhibitizer	49
Setting the Table	Problem-solving initiative	121
Shakers	Trust	83
Sherpa Walk	Trust	89
Song Tag	Challenge by Choice	61
Speed Rabbit	Deinhibitizer	51
Spider Web	Low challenge ropes course: problem solving	136
Tension Traverse	Low challenge ropes course: trust	106
Three-Person Trust Walk	Behavioral goal setting	102
Trust Lean	Trust	90
Turn Over a New Leaf	Problem-solving initiative	120
Turnstile	Trust	77
Two Line Bridge	High ropes course	157
Village, The	Full Value Contract	67
Walk of Life (Mohawk Walk)	Low challenge ropes course: trust	106
Wall, The	Low challenge ropes course: problem solving	138
Warp Speed	Problem-solving initiative	114
What Do I Need, What Can I Give?	Full Value Contract	69
Wild Woosey	Low challenge ropes course: trust	105
Willow in the Wind	Trust	93
Yurt Circle	Trust	87
Zip Line	High ropes course	159

INDEX

Academic/Academics: 103, 164; **content:** 22, 146, 176, 190; **content activities:** 109, 146–148; *goals* (see *Goals*); **standards:** (see *Standards*)
Accessible/Accessibility: 151; *Accessible Curriculum Supplement:* 33n
Accountability: 153
Acquaintance activities: (See *Ice Breakers*)
Action planning: viii, 25, 154
Active listening: 7, 22, 27, 30–31, 43–44, 55, 61, 72, 99, 172, 187; **activities:** 44, 55–56, 61–62, 99–100
Adventure: 146, 160, 162; **activities:** 14, 18, 107, 165; *Adventure in the Classroom:* 4, 9, 101, 190n; **approach:** 9, 113, 176, 178; **based counseling:** 176, 176; **education:** viii, 1, 3–4, 6, 16–17, 167, 180, 184; **in the classroom:** 176; **Integrated Model:** viii, 3–4, 9; **methodologies/techniques:** 1, 9; **philosophy:** 179, 193 **program:** 33n, 165, 179, 181; **programming:** 176; **skills workshop:** 193, 197 **Wave:** 167–173, 178
Adventures in Peacemaking: 52, 95, 113, 139
Affective Education: 1
Albert, Pete: 35, 76, 180
American Camping Association: 194
Anxiety: (see *Fear*)
Applying: (see also *Transfer*): 5, 167, 171, 179
Asking for help: 154, 162, 167; **activities:** 118–119
Asonwha, Floyd: 170n
Association for Challenge Course Technology (ACCT): 104, 157, 193, 196, 198; **professional vendor member (PVM) of ACCT:** 196, 198
Association for Experiential Education (AEE): 104n, 157, 194
Authentic: Assessment: 186; **learning:** vi
Behavior/Behavioral: 18, 23, 29, 75, 77, 127, 166, 174–175, 187, 189; **acting out behavior:** 29, 172; **appropriate behavior:** 7; **goals:** (See *Goals*)
Belay/belayer: 156–158, 167, 177
Berry, Wendell: 17
Bethel Horizons Adventure Center: 93
Binet, Alfred: 5
Bisson, Christian: 17n, 22n
Blanchard, Sharp and Cox: 101
Body size: 134, 137, 139; **image:** (see *Image*)
Borgwardt, Eric: 93
Borton, Terry: 168
Braby, Dave: 33n
Brain: 7; **based learning:** viii, 9; **compatible elements:** 7; **research:** 7, 11;
Brainstorm/Brainstorming: 30, 61–63, 68–70, 74, 97, 113, 141–142, 144, 161, 171
Briefing: 77, 167–168, 171
Brown, Christina: 169
Bully/Bullying: 72, 108, 174
Butler, Steve: 18–19, 177
Butter Battle Book (The): 140–141
Calling the Circle: 169
Camp Manito-wish YMCA: 112
Captain Kangaroo (Bob Keeshen): 183

Challenge/Challenges: viii, 3, 17, 22, 25, 34, 42, 46, 49, 60, 71, 78, 81–82, 89, 104, 107, 109–110, 113–114, 119, 121, 123–124, 128, 132, 136, 139, 153, 155–160, 163, 170, 172, 175, 179; **activities:** 156–164; **by choice:** 9, 14, 22–25, 27, 29, 56–57, 60, 62, 64, 73, 76, 88, 94, 139, 156, 178, 194; **by choice activities:** 56–62; **course:** (see *Ropes Course*); **group challenge:** (see *Group*); **individual/personal challenge:** 22, 149; **issues/skills:** 154; **when to move on to challenge:** 149–150

Children's Defense Fund: 183

Cliques: 21, 31, 72, 136

Collaborate/Collaboration/Collaborative: vi–viii, 7–8, 11, 15, 112, 124, 129–130, 149–150, 164, 180, 184, 195; **as lifelong guidelines:** 7; **leadership:** (see *Leadership*); **skills:** 9

Comfort zone: viii, 60, 76

Communicate/Communication: 11, 22, 29, 43–44, 61, 75, 77, 79, 81, 90, 92–94, 97–99, 104–105, 112, 124, 127, 133, 136, 154–155, 159, 166–167, 170, 187–188; **mis-communication:** 139

Community: vi–vii, 16, 19, 23, 25, 27, 30–31, 62–64, 73, 86, 110, 112–114, 149, 153–156, 160, 162, 164, 175–177, 181, 189–190; **agreements:** 8–9; **building:** 6, 8–9, 11, 17, 23–25, 27–28, 62, 71, 74, 163, 174, 176, 179–180, 186, 188–190; **building process/sequence:** ix, 21–22, 28, 30–31, 104, 113, 179–180; **circles:** 8–9; **classroom as community:** vii, 1, 6–7, 9, 164, 181; **compliance and community:** 7; **conditions for community:** viii, 11–12; **creating/creation of community:** 6, 8–9, 11, 76, 165; **exploration:** 163; **of learners:** viii–ix, 146; **school community:** 183; **service:** 3, 30, 153–154; **standards:** 16, 63, 71

Competition: vi–vii, 14, 21, 96, 136

Compromise: 111, 139, 146

Confidence: 23, 107, 159, 166

Conflict: vi, 12–15, 21–22, 25, 27, 72–73, 107–111, 117, 136, 139, 140–142, 144, 146, 161, 173, 183, 187–188, 194; **escalating/de-escalating conflict:** 113, 140–141, 150; **resolution:** vii–viii, 21–22, 29–30 109, 113, 131, 141, 150, 183; **resolution activities:** 139–146; **resolution skills/strategies:** 109, 113, 139, 144, 150, 164, 187

Consensus: 63, 110–111, 144–146

Cooperation: vii–viii, 11, 17, 22, 25, 27, 29, 31, 63, 72, 75, 107, 113, 139, 153, 175, 183, 195, 199; **activities:** 32–71, 111; **issues/skills:** 21, 28, 71

Cooperative Learning: vii, 8; **groups:** 134

Creely, Dan: 28n, 31, 169

Davids, Dorothy: 169n

Debrief, Debriefing: 81, 86, 133–34, 136, 139, 167–168, 171–173

Decision Making: 13–14, 21–22, 25, 29, 53, 77, 109–114, 127, 131, 150, 159, 172, 174, 179, 188, 190; **activities:** 114–117, 119–129, 131–139

Deinhibitizer: 22, 27–28, 32, 45; **activities:** 45–57, 73

Dependence/Dependent: 14, 27, 56, 164

Dewey, John: viii, ix, 1–4, 6, 8–9

Diversity: 41, 138, 151, 162, 186; **appreciate/appreciating diversity:** 28; **activities for appreciating diversity:** 41–42

Dr. Seuss: 138, 140

Duckworth, Eleanor: 146

Dunn, Jim: 38, 57n, 121n, 137

Edelman, Marian Wright: 183

Educators for Social Responsibility: 113, 139n

Emotional/Emotionally: 24, 27, 139, 176, 187–188; **growth:** 23; **illiteracy:** 6; **intelligence:** viii, 6, 9, 73; **learning:** 6; **literacy:** 6; **safe/safety:** (see *Safety: emotional*); self

awareness: 95, 113; **trust:** (see *Trust: physical/emotional*); **activities:** (see *Trust*)
Empathy: 8, 18, 22, 29, 31, 73-75, 107-108, 164, 188; **activities for empathy:** 79-81, 88-89, 90-94
Empower/Empowering: 24, 56, 76, 184
Encouragement/Encouraging: 4, 21, 24, 60, 71, 75-76, 100, 107-108, 153-155, 157-158, 161, 194; **and support:** 22, 76, 153-154
Exclude/Exclusion/Exclusive: 14, 29, 31, 38, 110, 113, 134, 136, 172, 174
Expeditionary Learning: vii, 3
Experience/Experiences: 2-5, 7, 13, 15, 18-19, 24, 29, 42, 56, 60, 62-63, 74, 101, 105, 109-111, 113, 116, 127, 137, 154-155, 158, 160-163, 165-68, 171, 189, 176-177; **classroom experience:** 4; **collective experience:** 15; **and education:** 1; **learning through experience:** 18, 76, 150, 171; **meaning from experience:** 6, **outdoor experience:** 160; **past experience:** 114; **processing the experience:** (see *Processing*); **reflecting upon experience:** (see *Reflect/Reflecting/Reflection*); **ropes course experience:** 159, 193; **urban experience:** 17, 22, 153, 160-162
Experiential: **education:** 1-4, 6, 8, 165, 179-80; **educator:** 17, 175n; **Learning Cycle:** viii, 4-5, 9, 165-167, 171, 178-179, 190; **learning methodology:** 9, 165
Exploring Islands of Healing: 168
Facilitate/Facilitating/Facilitation: 14, 17, 107, 173, 178; **communication:** 8, 119-122, 124; **the discussion:** 21; **group facilitation:** 16; **learning:** 177; **the process:** viii, 16, 30, 165, 171; **success:** 85-86; **techniques:** 193;
Facilitator: vii, 62, 104-05, 114, 133, 167-168, 172, 175-177, 193-194, 197-198; **role of the facilitator:** 168, 173
Falk, Beverly: 186n
Fear: 17, 29, 108, 158; **absence of fear:** 158; **and anxiety:** 22, 27, 153, 155-156, 158, 162, 194; **hopes and fears:** 193; **of failure:** 155-156; **of reprisal:** 15
Feelings: 17, 27, 30, 52, 65, 73-75, 77, 88, 95, 97, 99, 108, 111, 136, 166, 172-173; **literacy:** 22, 73, 95; **activities:** 95-100; **cards:** 96-97, 170; **vocabulary:** 73, 77, 95, 164
Flow: (see *Sequencing*)
Forming stage of group development: 13, 13n, 16-18
Frame/Framing: 167, 188
Frontload/Frontloading: 53, 167
Frustration: 6, 53, 99-101, 113, 117, 119, 123, 131, 164, 166, 171; **dealing with frustration:** 77-78, 113, 131-132, 155, 161; **symptoms of frustration:** 113
Full Value Contract: 3, 9, 22-23, 25, 27, 62-64, 71, 75, 105, 107, 110, 179; **activities:** 62-70
Funn Stuff: 85n
Furlong, Lisa: 95n, 113, 139
Games Not Names: 29
Gandhi: 28
Gardner, Howard: viii, 1, 5-6, 9, 179
Gass, Michael: 167
Gender: 72, 173, 188; **issues:** 173-174
Generalize/Generalization: **the experience:** 5, 166, 168, 171
Gibbs, Jeanne: viii, 1, 8-9, 12n, 16
Goal(s): 18, 35, 64, 67-69, 76, 86, 101-103, 105-106, 123-126, 128, 154-158, 165, 176, 186, 188-189, 191, 195, 197; **academic goals:** 6, 25, 146; **activities:** 67, 100-104, 121-133; **behavioral goals:** 6, 25, 73, 100, 154; **common goals:** vii, 11, 14, 31: **goal setting activities:** 85, 100-104, 114-117; **group/class goals:** 4, 14, 21-25, 30, 63, 109-111, 117, 126, 128, 131, 150, 154, 163, 176, 187; **individual/personal goals:** 6, 21-25, 67, 73, 76, 100, 103, 107, 150, 153-155, 157, 160, 163, 186, 195; **mutual**

goals: 112; **setting:** 3-4, 9, 22-23, 25, 73, 100, 104, 107-108, 111, 115-116, 127, 131, 155, 188; **SMART goals:** 100-02, 104; **task-oriented goals:** 25, 154

Goleman, Daniel: 1, 6, 9, 74, 179

GRABBS Modality Checklist: 18-19

Ground rules: (see *Rules*)

Group: **achievement:** 17, 22, 22n; **challenge/challenges:** 17, 21-22, 22n, 107, 109, 146, 174; **cohesion:** 17, 22n; **life cycle/stages of group:** 12-13, 16, 18-19, 21, 25, 105, 154, 168, 176, 178; **development:** viii, 4, 8-9, 12-13, 16-19, 172, 175, 177; **facilitation:** (see *Facilitation*); **formation:** 17, 21-22, 22n, 107; **goals:** (see *Goals*); **norms:** (see *Norms*); **process:** 3, 12, 14, 16-17, 23-24, 29, 105, 110, 175, 194; **purpose:** 176; **responsibility:** 73; **support:** 17, 22, 22n, 105; **-think:** 14

Hacker, Carla: 24, 125n

Hahn, Kurt: viii, 1-4, 9

Heffron, Ruth: 181

Hellenbrand, Kathy: 33n

Henton, Mary: 4, 9, 101, 190n

Hidden agendas: 21-23, 27, 29-30, 45, 53, 72, 110, 172; **activities:** 43, 52-53, 57-58

Huxley, Aldous: 5

Ice Breakers: 17, 21-22, 27-28, 32, 45, 48, 57, 165; **acquaintance activities:** 32-45

Image: **body image:** 84, 174; **self image:** 84, 174

Inclusion/Inclusive: 13, 16, 21, 24, 27-29, 31, 53, 75, 110, 170-171, 174; **by choice:** 24

Independence/Independent: 14, 56, 153-154, 156, 164

Influence: 13, 16, 21, 109, 111, 116, 172, 177

Initiatives: (see *Problem Solving*)

Integrated Adventure Model: (see *Adventure*)

Integrated: **curriculum:** viii, 148, 180; **Thematic Instruction:** 7

Interdependence/Interdependent: 1, 8, 10-11, 15-16, 110, 149-153-155, 164

Islands of Healing: 3-4, 9, 18, 167-168

James, Thomas: 2-3

Jensen, Dick: 37; **Mary Anne:** 13n, 16

Journals: 170, 173

Kebbekus, Leslie: 148n

Kendall, and Marzano: 186

Kid's Guide to Service Projects: 164n

King, Keith: 175n

Knapp, Clifford: 165, 168

Kohn, Alfie: viii, 1, 7-8, 31, 179, 186n

Kolb, David: 1, 4-5, 9, 165

Kovalik, Susan: viii, 1, 7, 179

Kreidler, William: 85n, 113, 139

Leader/Leaders/Leadership: 13-14, 16, 18, 21-22, 27, 32, 109-110, 112, 114, 127, 131, 135, 150, 167, 174, 184, 188; **activities:** 114-117, 119-123, 127-129, 131-139; **collaborative leadership:** 112

Learning styles: 5, 24

Leave No Trace: 159, 159n

Lewin, Kurt: 4

Lewis, Barbara A.: 164n

Life cycle of a group: (see *Group*)

Lincoln Elementary School: 164

Local Operating Procedures (LOPs): 198

Madison: Metropolitan School District (MMSD): 76, 137, 180-181; **City of Madison:** 161-162, 164, 181
Mann, Horace: 7
McRel: 186n
Mediation Center: 113n
Mentor/Mentoring: 14, 16, 22, 113-114, 175
Metaphor/Metaphors: 1, 13, 16, 68, 76, 81, 86, 105-106, 119, 127, 159, 167, 177; **frontloading a metaphor:** 167
Milwaukee Public Schools (MPS): 33n
Mistakes: learning from mistakes: viii, 18, 74-75, 78, 108, 112, 178; **making mistakes:** viii, 18, 21-22, 45, 72-74, 78, 99, 107-108, 117, 122-123, 178, 186-187: **activities for making mistakes:** 77-79
Mitten, Denise: 13n, 14
Mixing: 22, 27, 31, 48, 53, 72; **activities:** 35-42, 48-49, 51-53
Model/Modeling: 30-31, 38, 65, 70, 78, 90, 92-93, 105, 122, 137, 180
Multiple Intelligences: viii, 5-6, 24
Name Calling: 29
New Games Foundation: 23, 66n
Norms/Norming: 4, 12-14, 22, 25, 56, 74, 78, 109, 111, 153, 173, 183; **activities for establishing norms:** 63-65; **class/group norms:** 13, 62, 109, 153; **community standards and norms:** 16; **cultural norms:** 174; **developing norms:** 3, 14, 78; **process of norming:** 110; **stage of group development:** 13-14, 16-18; **uninvited norms:** 14;
Objectification/Objectifying: 21, 139, 174
Outdoor: experiences: 160; **education:** 4; **pursuits:** 6, 17, 22, 153, 159-160; **ropes course:** (see *Ropes Course*)
Outward Bound: viii, 2-3, 180
Pairing strategies: 15
Pausz, Gus: 116
Peck, M. Scott: vii
Peer: 29; **groups:** 175; **pressure:** 14, 23, 76; **teaching:** 147
Performing stage of group development: 13n, 16-18
Perspective Taking: 22, 27, 31, 72, 74; **activities:** 39-43, 57-62, 66
Peterson, Candace: 121n
Pfeffer: Joy: 181; **Patrick:** 181
Pie Chart: 63
Pieh, Jerry: 3
Plato: 3
Play for Peace: 116
PlayBoard: 29
Popowits, Michael: 55n
Presentations and Projects: 164
Problem Solving: viii, 17, 21-22, 25, 53, 107, 109, 111, 113, 131, 135, 150, 153, 155, 163, 166, 174, 179, 184, 189-190, 195, 199; **ABCD problem solving:** 143; **activities:** 113-148; **group problem solving:** 6; **initiatives:** 22, 111, 114, 122, 131, 134, 146, 166, 176; **issues and skills:** 110, 175; **when to move on to Problem Solving:** 107-108
Processing: 9, 21-22, 31-32, 48, 75, 77, 96, 100, 104, 111, 113, 132, 137, 167, 171, 174-179; **the experience:** 131, 178; **overprocessing:** 174, 177; **techniques/tools:** 5, 169-170
Progressive education: 2, 9
Project Adventure: vii-viii, 3-4, 9, 23, 86, 104n, 113, 137, 157, 179, 181, 190n, 194

Prouty, Dick: 3, 18
Put-Downs and Put-Ups: 21–22, 27–29, 31. 34, 45, 62–63, 65, 71–72, 75, 108, 155, 168–169, 171–172
Quicksilver: 18, 177
Raccoon Circles: 85n, 86
Radcliffe, Paul: 3, 18
Reflect/Reflecting/Reflection: 9, 17, 56, 154, 157, 159, 166–168, 171, 173, 175, 177, 179; **as a group:** 21; **methods of reflection:** 169; **on the experience:** 4, 6, 165, 169; **self-reflection:** 100, 155; **reflectors vs. doers:** 173–74
Respect/Respectful: vi–vii, 7, 11, 24–25, 29–31, 62, 64, 67, 69, 71, 75, 169, 173, 187
Risk Taking: viii, 11, 13–15, 21–23, 32, 45, 73–77, 88, 100, 104–105, 107–108, 121, 146, 149, 155–156, 166, 176, 179, 183, 195; **activities:** 79–94, 100–103, 105–107
Roark, Mark: 35
Roderick, Libby: 180
Rohnke, Karl: 3, 18–19, 85n, 137
Role of the teacher: 14–16, 32, 76–77, 113, 156, 173, 179
Ropes Course: 17, 76, 167, 172, 176, 179, 181, 194; **activities:** 104–107, 156–159; **construction:** 193, 195–98; **high ropes course:** 22, 30, 88, 104, 153–159, 177, 193; **log:** 198; **low challenge ropes course:** 22, 73, 104, 109, 133, 137; **proper training for ropes courses:** 104–107, 132, 136–137, 139, 157; **provider of ropes course services:** 104–105, 133, 156–157, 193–194; **universal ropes course elements:** 105, 133–139, 156–159; **standards:** 104, 196
Rule/Rules: **creating rules:** 69; **ground rules:** 23, 62, 70, 78; **of loud:** 110, 113, 137, 150; **play by the rules:** 29, 30, 66;
Sabotage: 23, 29, 110, 136, 150
Safety: ix, 4, 16, 22–23, 27–28, 32, 48, 59, 62–67, 69, 71, 73, 75, 77, 83, 91, 94, 103–104, 108, 131, 137, 156–157, 161, 168, 172–175, 183, 186, 193; **emotional safety:** 4, 23, 27–28, 62, 64–65, 74–75, 108, 193; **equipment:** 154; **guidelines:** 79; **inspection:** 156; **issues:** 27, 32, 75, 168; **personal safety:** 75; **physical safety:** 4, 23, 27, 62, 65, 74–75, 77, 92, 108, 193; **standards:** 193
Scapegoat/Scapegoating: 14, 31, 72, 172
Schoel, Jim: 3–4, 18
Scholastic Aptitude Test: 5
School Age Parent Program: 148n
Schools Our Children Deserve, The: 186n
Sectarianism: 29
Sequence/Sequencing: viii, 21, 25, 30, 76–78, 81, 86, 91, 94, 100, 156, 159, 176, 194, 199; **of activities:** 17–19; **art of sequencing:** 18; **community-building sequence:** 21, 30, 113, 153; **and flow:** 17–19, 175–178; **and group development:** 17; **hypothetically correct sequence:** 18–19; **science of sequencing:** 18–19
Service Learning: 4
Smith, Tom (Raccoon): 17, 85n, 175, 175n
Sorting: (see *Storming*)
Spiral of Renewal: 16
Spitzer, Dave: 164
Spotting/Spotter: 77, 83–84, 89–94, 104–108, 120, 136, 138–139, 174–175
Standard Operating Procedures (SOPs): 197
Standards: **educational standards:** 1, 6, 186–192; **industry (Ropes Course Construction) standards:** 104, 193–194, 196
Stating needs: 22, 153, 155–156

Stereotype/Stereotyping: 139, 174
Stewardship: 159-160
Stimac, Jane: 148n
Storming stage of group development: 13n, 13-14, 16-18, 109
Struggle: 12, 14, 78, 113, 119, 122, 129, 146, 149, 155, 157, 159, 164, 177; **power struggle:** 113, 172-173; **through conflict:** 107; **toward independence:** 154
Success/Successful: 57, 71, 128, 179, 189; **celebrating success:** 112; **and failure:** 2, 22, 153, 155-156
Support/Supportive: 17, 34, 60, 76, 105-108, 135, 139, 146, 149, 153, 155-156, 160, 187; **mutual support:** 22
Synergy: 112, 130
Taking Turns: 71, 78, 109, 111, 136, 150; **activities:** 115-116, 118-121, 123-129, 132-139
Talking Circle: 169
TEAM Conference: 137
Touching issues: 94
Transfer: theories of transfer: 167; (see also *Applying*)
Transforming stage of group development: 15-16, 18
TRIBES: vi, 8-9, 12n, 16
Trust: vii-ix, 4, 7, 11, 13, 25, 67, 71, 73-77, 81, 85, 87, 100, 104, 107, 113, 139, 153, 164. 174-175, 179, 199; **activities:** 77-105; **building trust:** 17, 22, 73, 81; **fall from height:** 107; **issues and skills:** 21, 45, 62, 71, 74, 82, 91, 172, 175-176; **physical/emotional trust:** 22, 73, 76-77, 108, 111, 176; **physical/emotional trust activities:** 79-94, 100-103, 105-107; **the process:** 12; **when to move on to Trust:** 71-72
Trustworthy/Trustworthiness: 7, 21-22, 73, 75, 77, 88, 100, 108, 175; **activities:** 79-82, 84-94, 100-103, 105-107
Tuckman, Bruce: 13n, 16-17
Tull, Dee: 181
United Mine Workers: 183
Urban Experience: (see *Experience*)
Verona, Wisconsin: 181
Wellington Conquest, III, Arthur: 184
Wilderness: 17, 158
Win-Win solutions: 111, 144-146, 150